# ANGUS WILSON

A Bibliography

1947–1987

*Angus Wilson, 1980.*
*Photograph by and courtesy of Tony Garrett.*

# ANGUS WILSON

## A Bibliography

### 1947–1987

J.H. Stape and Anne N. Thomas

*With a Foreword by Angus Wilson*

MANSELL PUBLISHING LIMITED

London and New York

First published 1988 in Great Britain by Mansell Publishing Limited
6 All Saints Street, London N1 9RL, England

British Library Cataloguing in Publication Data

Stape, J.H.
    Angus Wilson : bibliography, 1947–1987.
    1.  Wilson, Angus, *1913-* ——Bibliography
    I. Title   II. Thomas, Anne N.
    016.823'914        Z8976.485

    ISBN 0–7201–1872–7


Library of Congress Cataloging-in-Publication Data

Stape, J. H. (John Henry)
    Angus Wilson : a bibliography, 1947–1987 / J. H. Stape and
Anne N. Thomas; with a foreword by Angus Wilson.
        p.    cm.
    Includes index.
    ISBN 0–7201–1872–7
    1.  Wilson, Angus——Bibliography.   I.  Thomas, Anne N.
(Anne Nieuwehuis)  II. Title.
Z8976.485.S7   1988
[PR6045.N577]
016.823'914——dc19          87–31246 CIP

This book has been printed and bound in
Great Britain: typeset in Compugraphic Plantin
by Colset (Private) Ltd., Singapore, and printed and
bound by Anchor Brendon Ltd., Tiptree on Windrush
Antique Book Wove Cream.

# CONTENTS

CONTENTS

# ILLUSTRATIONS

# FOREWORD

Not to have written anything until 1946 when I was already over thirty has been, perhaps, the most treasured fact in my professional life. First, of course, because it is not usual; secondly, because it has meant that to become a professional writer has had a separate and strongly marked place in my life. I was a highly placed librarian in one of the world's great libraries — the British Museum Reading Room — and I do not think that I ever saw my relation to books as anything more central to the English social system of my time. And yet I have held two principal roles in the world of books. What one of my aunts called "Angus's perpetual fiddling 'round with books" has been the centre of my life, my social philosophy and my concern with beauty and ideas. In my philosophy these are the very centre of existence. And now here is a book — a detailed account of my literary contributions, whether academic or popular, written or spoken — that I believe, relying as I do on the creative powers of Anne Thomas and John Stape, will give a total picture to readers of the meaning of an active literary life. Their fine, detailed listing brings alive, it seems to me, the very meaning of the life of a man of letters, however unmodish that expression may be.

Perhaps most exciting to me throughout my literary career has been the international quality of my publications, and what could better express this diversity than a book edited by two scholars of different nationality to myself and to each other. Anything that vaunts the international spread of literature in our day seems to me of the highest civilised worth, and the career that is outlined here makes much of all the literary diversity that it is my pride to record as my contribution to life. For the form it takes here I am wholly grateful for the hard work, the literary concern and the scholarly accuracy of Anne Thomas and John Stape.

Angus Wilson

# PREFACE

This bibliography of the work of Angus Wilson is addressed primarily to
the student of contemporary literature rather than to the bibliophile or
collector. Hence Sections A. and B. are summary descriptions of the works
listed therein. None the less, it is hoped that a variety of audiences will find
this compilation useful, and to that end Section A. includes information,
where available, about publication date, original list price of a volume and
size of print-run. Martin Secker & Warburg, Ltd, Wilson's English publisher, have generously made their archives available to us, but access to
publishers' records in the United States has been limited. As a result,
Section A. is less detailed than it might have been; lack of access to American
records has also dissuaded us from attempting an analytical bibliography.
We must regretfully note that extant records of publication are generally
incomplete.

Section H. Manuscripts is also of necessity preliminary, since during the
final stages of our project, the University of Iowa Libraries acquired the
bulk of Wilson's papers related to works published after 1970. This addi-
tion to an already extensive collection means that most of Wilson's manuscripts are available at a single location, although a number of institutions,
both public and private, hold letters. We have made no attempt, however,
to list individual owners of correspondence, as one of our guiding principles has been accessibility.

Despite our efforts, certain items have proved elusive. We have been
unable to identify or confirm the following possible translations or foreign
anthology uses: a translation into Afrikaans published by Kinder Kultuur
Vereniging/Kindervoorligtingsdiens van Suid-Afrika, Johannesburg
(1956); Czechoslovak translations of 'A Bit off the Map,' 'A Sad Fall' and
'Mother's Sense of Fun' in *Svetova Literatura*, Prague (1958 and 1973); a
Danish use of 'Realpolitik' by Stig Vendelgkaers Forlag, Copenhagen
(1968); a German anthology use of 'Higher Standards' by F.A. Herbig

Verlag, Munich (1969/1970); German translations of 'Realpolitik' published by Mosaik Verlag, Berlin (1967) and of 'The Wrong Set' published by Blick in die Welt, Frankfurt (1949); an Italian translation of 'What Do Hippos Eat?' published by Aldo Martello Editore, Milan (1957); a Hungarian use of 'Crazy Crowd' by Európa Könykiadó, Budapest (1970/1971); a Japanese anthology use of 'Raspberry Jam' by Gakuseisha, Tokyo (1966); a Polish translation of a Wilson short story in *Panorama Pólnocy*, Olsztyn (1962); and a Norwegian translation of 'The Men with Bowler Hats' in *Aftonposten*, Oslo (1957). All dates are approximate. The reader may wish to know that as we go to press translations into Mandarin are being undertaken.

Since the publication of Robert J. Stanton's preliminary list of Wilson's work as well as of critical articles and reviews in *A Bibliography of Modern British Novelists* (Troy, NY: Whitston, 1978), scholarly investigation of Wilson's writing has not abated, and his later novels and books have been widely reviewed. As Stanton included reviews, we decided early in our collaboration to do likewise, taking account, as Stanton did not, of English Sunday reviewing practice. Although reviews have no doubt escaped our notice, the reader and scholar now have available the means of assessing Wilson's position among contemporary writers.

With very rare exception, justified by the stature of the reviewer or by a special claim to new critical insight, we have excluded from our listing reviews of translations and broadcast reviews. Only reviews offering evaluative comment are included, and thus blurbs and simple summaries have not been collected. The number of reviews in languages other than English testifies to an early interest in Wilson's writings on the Continent, particularly in Scandinavia and The Netherlands.

The first comprehensive bibliography of a contemporary writer will inevitably contain errors and lacunae, and we should appreciate having these brought to our attention. The state of indexing in humanities fields determines the effective terminal date of compilation for items in sections J. through N. as 1982, although items published later have been included. Throughout, the absence of a page number in an entry indicates that the item has not been verified. The place of publication of periodicals and newspapers, except those published in London or identified by title, is provided in Part I; where not specified in Part II, the reader should refer to the second index. Abbreviations have been kept to a minimum: the standard postal abbreviations for American state names and ns for new series (or nf in the case of German periodicals).

We are grateful for the generous cooperation extended to us by Sir Angus Wilson and Mr Tony Garrett. J.H. Stape wishes to acknowledge research grants from the University of Toronto during 1981-82 and from the Social Sciences and Humanities Research Council of Canada in 1983 and 1986-87. Anne N. Thomas acknowledges that some of her work originally appeared, in a different form, in a doctoral dissertation for Drew University.

We should like to thank the following individuals and institutions for answering enquiries and otherwise offering assistance: Altea, Taurus, Alfaguara, S.A.; Albert Bonniers Förlag, and Barbro Ek, Archivist; the British Broadcasting Corporation Play Library, Sound Archives, Television Script Unit and Written Archives Centre, and especially Messrs Neil Sommerville and John Jordan (Written Archives); the British Library and British Newspaper Library; the British Library, National Sound Archive, and Mr Jonathan Vickers, Curator, Recorded Literature; the Library of Congress; the British Talking Book Service for the Blind, Aylesbury; Mr James Brockway, The Hague; Curtis Brown (London), and Miss Anne C. Duffin and Ms Jane Greenwood; Mr James Oliver Brown, New York; Butler Library, Columbia University; Cambridge University Library; the Canadian Gay Archives, Toronto, and Mr Alan V. Miller, Archivist; the Dickens House Museum, and Dr David Parker; Drew University Library, Interlibrary Loan and Reference Divisions; Eton College, School Library, and Mr M.C. Meredith; Professor Jay L. Halio, Newark, Delaware; Dr Jaidev, Simla; Ms Inge-Lise Jensen, Herning Public Library, Jutland; the Johns Hopkins University Ferdinand Hamburger, Jr Archives, and Mr James Stimpert, Assistant Archivist; Dr Joseph M. Kissane, New York; the Independent Broadcasting Authority, and Mrs Kathleen M. Turtle, Deputy Librarian; Kodansha Ltd, Tokyo, and Messrs Michio Komatsu and Tokuya Matsumoto, Editor; Dr Claire Larrière; Mr Mark Limacher, Sydney; the Location Register of Twentieth-Century English Literary Manuscripts and Letters, and Dr David C. Sutton; Dr Jakob Lothe, Oslo; Professor Frederick P.W. McDowell, Iowa City; Professor Kerry McSweeney, Montreal; Mr C.L. van Minnen, Leiden; Professor Sylvère Monod, Paris; the National Diet Library, Tokyo, and Mr Konosuke Hayashi; the National Library for the Blind and Physically Handicapped, and Mr Thomas J. Martin, Network Services Section; Penguin Books, and Mrs Sue Jones, Archivist; Mr B.A. Pike, London; *Publishers Weekly* and Miss Miriam E. Phelps, Research Librarian; Recording for the Blind; Ms Patricia Rice, *St Louis Post-Dispatch*; Martin Secker & Warburg Ltd, and Mr Peter Grose, former Managing Director; Dr Vivian B. Smith, Sydney; Ms Toos Streng, Amsterdam; Ms Cynthia Sugars, Vancouver; Ms Lucilla Teoh, Singapore; Thames Television, and Mr Bill Parker, Archivist; the Theatre Royal, Bury St Edmunds, and Mr Stephen Walton, Administrator; Times Newspapers Limited (London), and Mrs Anne C.D. Pigott, Archivist and Records Manager; the University of Arizona, and Professor L.D. Clark; the University of British Columbia Library, Interlibrary Loan and Reference Divisions, and especially Ms Rita Penco, Ms Pia Andersen and Mr Patrick Dunn; the University of Durham and Mr David Burnett, Assistant Librarian; the University of Iowa Libraries, and Messrs Frank Paluka and Robert A. McCown, Special Collections; the University of Missouri—St Louis, and Professor Marcia A. Dalbey and Ms Margaret E. Patterson, Producer-Director, Creative Aging series; the University of Pittsburgh and Dr W. Austin Flanders; the University of Reading Special Collections Division and Dr J.A. Edwards, Keeper of Archives and Manuscripts; Mr Hans van Marle, Amsterdam; and Viking Penguin Inc. We should like especially to thank Mr John W. Thomas, Jr for technical assistance in the preparation of the Index and to acknowledge the useful advice and assistance of our editor Miss Veronica Higgs.

# CHRONOLOGY

| | |
|---|---|
| 1913 | Born 11 August, Bexhill-on-Sea, Sussex, the youngest of six sons of William Thomas Francis and Maude Ellen (*née* Caney) Johnstone Wilson |
| 1922-23 | In Durban, South Africa with his mother's family |
| 1924-27 | Ashampstead Preparatory School, Seaford, Sussex, under the headmastership of an elder brother, W.W. Johnstone Wilson |
| 1927-31 | Westminster School, London, day boy living with his parents in various private hotels |
| 1929 | Maude Johnstone Wilson dies |
| 1932-36 | Reads medieval and modern history at Merton College, Oxford; B.A.(honours), 1936 |
| 1937 | Joins Department of Printed Books, the British Museum |
| 1938 | William Johnstone Wilson dies |
| 1942-46 | In the Foreign Office Intelligence Section, Bletchley Park, Buckinghamshire |
| 1946 | Returns to the British Museum; begins to write short stories over week-ends |
| 1949 | Deputy Superintendent of the British Museum Reading Room; *The Wrong Set*, March; meets Tony Garrett |
| 1950 | *Such Darling Dodos*, July |
| 1952 | *Emile Zola*, February; *Hemlock and After*, July; *Skeletons and Assegais* broadcast |
| 1953 | Executive, International P.E.N. English Centre until 1957; *For Whom the Cloche Tolls*, July |
| 1955 | Resigns from the British Museum to write full time; moves to Bradfield St George, Suffolk, where he lives until late 1985, while retaining a London flat and travelling extensively; *The Mulberry Bush* performed by the Bristol Old Vic Company, Theatre Royal, 27 September |

1956    *The Mulberry Bush*, published in February, mounted as the English Stage Company's first production, Royal Court Theatre, London, 2 April; *Anglo-Saxon Attitudes*, Book Society Fiction Choice, May

1957    Attends Congress of the International P.E.N. Clubs, Tokyo, September; *A Bit off the Map*, October; *The Mulberry Bush* televised

1958    *The Middle Age of Mrs Eliot*, November; awarded James Tait Black Memorial Prize in England (1959) and Prix du Meilleur Roman Etranger in France (1960); Fellow, Royal Society of Literature

1959    Lecture, International Association of Professors of English, Lausanne; *After the Show* televised

1960    *The Stranger* televised; Ewing lectures, University of California at Los Angeles; Bergen Lecturer, Yale University; William Vaughan Moody Lecturer, University of Chicago

1961    Northcliffe Lecturer, University College, London; *The Old Men at the Zoo*, September; revisits South Africa

1962    Opens East/West Dialogue, University of British Columbia; reading in Berlin; Vice-chairman, Formentor Literary Prize, Majorca

1963    Leslie Stephen Lecture, Cambridge University; *The Invasion* televised; *The Wild Garden*, based on the Ewing Lectures, published in England, November and in California, December; part-time lecturer, School of English and American Studies, University of East Anglia, 1963-66; Professor of English Literature, 1966-78

1964    Attends International Writers' Conference, Moscow—Leningrad; Member, Homosexual Law Reform Committee until 1967; *Late Call* and *Tempo: The Impact of Television on the Arts*, November

1966    Guest of honour, Adelaide Festival of the Arts; Committee member, Royal Literary Fund; Deputy Chairman, Arts Council Literature Panel until 1968

1967    Beckman Professor, University of California at Berkeley; *No Laughing Matter*, October

1968    Commander, Order of the British Empire; Honorary Fellow, Cowell College, University of California, Santa Cruz; Chairman, Arts Council Literature Panel until 1969

1969    *Death Dance*, collected stories, May; Arts Council tour of North Wales; Public Orator of the University of East Anglia until 1975; visits Tokyo for British Week, September

1970    *The World of Charles Dickens*, May (*Yorkshire Post* Book of the Year, non-fiction); President, Powys Society until 1980

1971    Chairman, National Book League until 1974

1972    Member, Council of the Society of Authors; Chevalier de l'Ordre des Arts et des Lettres; Companion of Literature and Vice-president, Royal Society of Literature; Vice-president, Eastern Arts Association; Vice-president, Dickens Fellowship until 1973

1973    *As If By Magic*, May

1974    John Hinkley Visiting Professor, Johns Hopkins University; *Late Call* televised; President, Dickens Fellowship until 1975

1975    Chairman, Booker Prize committee

1976    *The Naughty Nineties*

1977    Honorary DLitt., Leicester; *The Strange Ride of Rudyard Kipling*, November; Visiting Distinguished Professor, University of Delaware, returns 1980 and 1983; editor, *Writers of East Anglia*

1978    Visiting professor, University of Iowa, returns 1986; Professor emeritus, University of East Anglia

1979    Visiting Professor, Georgia State University, spring; University of Michigan, autumn; Honorary DLitt., East Anglia and Liverpool

1980    Hill Professor, University of Minnesota, spring; knighted for contributions to English literature; *Setting the World on Fire*, July; honorary member, American Academy and Institute of Arts and Letters

1981    Honorary DLitt., Sussex; Andrew Mellon Visiting Professor, University of Pittsburgh, autumn; President, Kipling Society

1982    Visiting Professor, University of Missouri—St Louis, autumn; President, Royal Society of Literature; editor, *East Anglia in Verse and Prose*

1983    British Council lecture tour of India, January-February; British Council reading in Paris; honorary doctorate, Sorbonne; editor, *The Portable Dickens*; *Diversity and Depth in Fiction*, August; *The Old Men at the Zoo* televised

1984    Distinguished Visiting Professor, Creative Writing Program, University of Arizona, autumn

1985    Moves to St-Rémy-de-Provence, autumn

1986    *Reflections in a Writer's Eye*, January

# PART I: WORKS BY ANGUS WILSON

# A. BOOKS

A1        THE WRONG SET AND OTHER        1949
STORIES

*a. First edition*:

London: Secker & Warburg, 24 March 1949. 2000 copies printed. 9s. 6d.

There were further printings in April 1949 (1500 copies), June 1949 (1500 copies), December 1950, 1957, 1961, March 1969 (1500 copies) and November 1971 (2000 copies).

*b. First American edition. 1950*:

New York: William Morrow, 15 March 1950. $3.00.

There were further printings in March, April and May 1950.

*c. Second English edition (Penguin Books). [1959]*:

Harmondsworth: Penguin Books, 23 April 1959. Vol. 1355. 2s. 6d.

There were further printings in 1960, 1966 and 1976 and a reissue by Granada Publishing—Panther Books (London) in March 1982.

Contents: Fresh Air Fiend — Union Reunion — Saturnalia — Realpolitik — A Story of Historical Interest — The Wrong Set — Crazy Crowd — A Visit in Bad Taste — Raspberry Jam — Significant Experience — Mother's Sense of Fun — Et Dona Ferentes

## A2      SUCH DARLING DODOS AND OTHER     1950 STORIES

*a. First edition*:

London: Secker & Warburg, 20 July 1950. 9s. 6d.

There were further printings in 1950, 1954, 1959 and November 1970 (2000 copies).

*b. First American edition. 1951*:

New York: William Morrow, 10 January 1951. $2.50.

*c. Second English edition (Penguin Books). [1960]*:

Harmondsworth: Penguin Books, 27 October 1960. Vol. 1508. 2s. 6d.

There was a further printing in 1968 and a reissue by Granada Publishing —Panther Books (London) in January 1980.

Contents: Rex Imperator — A Little Companion — Learning's Little Tribute — Sister Superior — Such Darling Dodos — Necessity's Child — Christmas Day in the Workhouse — Totentanz — Mummy to the Rescue — Heart of Elm — What Do Hippo's Eat?

*Note*: Totentanz was not included in the first American edition. What Do Hippos Eat? replaces the title of the first English edition in subsequent editions.

## A3            EMILE ZOLA          1952 AN INTRODUCTORY STUDY OF HIS NOVELS

*a. First edition*:

London: Secker & Warburg, 14 February 1952. 10s. 6d.

*b. First English edition—American issue. 1953*:

New York: William Morrow, 4 September 1952. $3.00.

Further printings were issued by Apollo Editions (New York) in 1961, by Paul Smith (Gloucester, MA) in 1962 and by Folcroft Library Editions (Folcroft, PA) in 1972.

*c. First English edition revised. [1964]*:

London: Secker & Warburg, 31 December 1964. 3847 copies printed plus 1040 U.S. copies.

A further printing was issued as Mercury Book No. 57 on 22 February 1965 (2500 copies).

## A4          HEMLOCK AND AFTER         1952

*a. First edition*:

London: Secker & Warburg, 17 July 1952. 12s. 6d.

There were further printings in August and October 1952, February 1953, February 1960, 1966, 1971 (1500 copies) and 1980 (Uniform edition, 2000 copies).

*b. First American edition. 1952*:

New York: Viking Press, 29 September 1952. $3.00.

*c. Second English edition (Penguin Books). [1956]*:

Harmondsworth: Penguin Books, 26 April 1956. Vol. 1086. 2s. 6d.

There was a further printing issued by Granada Publishing—Panther Books (London) in October 1979.

## A5      FOR WHOM THE CLOCHE TOLLS     1953
        A SCRAPBOOK OF THE TWENTIES

Illustrated by Philippe Jullian.

*a. First edition*:

London: Methuen, 18 June 1953. 10s. 6d.

This edition was reprinted by Secker & Warburg (London) on 30 July 1973 (3000 copies). £1.95.

There was a printing by Penguin Books (Harmondsworth) in July 1976 (12,000 copies) and a further printing issued by Granada Publishing—Panther Books (London) in February 1982.

*b. First edition—American issue. 1973*:

New York: Viking Press, 12 March 1973. $6.95.

There was a further printing issued by Curtis Books (New York) in 1973.

*Note*: An extract was published in *Harper's Bazaar* (London), May 1953, pp. 70-71, 94, 96 (C65).

## A6      THE MULBERRY BUSH      1956
## A PLAY IN THREE ACTS

*a. First edition*:

London: Secker & Warburg, 13 February 1956. 3000 copies. 10s. 6d.

*b. Second English edition. 1957*:

London: Evans Brothers, March 1957. 6s.

Foreword by Wilson, pp. [5-6].

*c. Third English edition (Penguin Books). [1966]*:

*Novelists' Theatre*. Harmondsworth: Penguin Books, September 1966, pp. 21-104. Penguin Plays No. PL 65. Introduction by Eric Rhode. 6s.

## A7      ANGLO-SAXON ATTITUDES      1956

*a. First edition*:

London: Secker & Warburg, 14 May 1956. 13,750 English Book Society Choice copies. 15s.

There were further printings in 1961, 1967 (1500 copies), May 1971 (2000 copies) and 1979 (Uniform edition, 1500 copies).

*b. First edition—American issue. 1956*:

New York: Viking Press, 4 October 1956. $4.50.

There was a further printing issued by Viking—Compass Books, 1960.

*c. Second English edition (Penguin Books). [1958]*:

Harmondsworth: Penguin Books, 25 September 1958. Vol. 1311. 3s. 6d.

There were further printings in 1961, 1968, 1972, 1974, 1976 and 1978 and printings issued by Granada Publishing—Panther Books (London) in 1983 and Grafton Books (London) in 1985.

*d. First American edition (Signet Books). 1963*:

New York: New American Library—Signet Books, 6 February 1963. Signet Classic CT151. Foreword by Frank Kermode.

An extract was published in *Vogue* (London), March 1956, pp. 140-141, 223 (C143).

*Note*: The first edition—American issue does not include J.R. Green "History of the English People" 1877 in the Appendix.

## A8 A BIT OFF THE MAP AND OTHER STORIES 1957

*a. First edition*:

London: Secker & Warburg, 14 October 1957. 13,000 copies printed. 13s. 6d.

*b. First American edition. 1957*:

New York: Viking Press, 24 October 1957. $3.50.

*c. Second English edition (Penguin Books). [1968]*:

Harmondsworth: Penguin Books, April 1968. Vol. 2375. 4s. 6d.

There were further printings in 1976 and 1978 and a printing issued by Granada Publishing—Panther Books (London) in January 1982.

Contents: A Bit off the Map — A Flat Country Christmas — More Friend than Lodger — Once a Lady — After the Show — Higher Standards — A Sad Fall—Ten Minutes to Twelve

## A9 THE MIDDLE AGE OF MRS ELIOT 1958

*a. First edition*:

London: Secker & Warburg, 5 November 1958. 20,575 copies printed. 18s.

There was a further printing in March 1980 (Uniform edition, 2000 copies).

*b. First American edition. 1959*:

New York: Viking Press, 20 March 1959. $4.95.

A further printing was issued by Meridian Books (New York) in 1960.

*c. Second English edition (Penguin Books). [1961]*:

Harmondsworth: Penguin Books, 23 February 1961. Vol. 1502. 4s.

There were further printings in March 1969 and 1982 and a printing issued by Granada Publishing—Panther Books (London) in November 1979.

*d. First edition—American issue.* [*1982*]:

New York: Penguin Books, 1982. $6.95.

## A10                    THE OLD MEN AT THE ZOO                    1961

*a. First edition*:

London: Secker & Warburg, 25 September 1961. 20,000 copies printed.
18s.

A cheap edition was issued 15 February 1965.

*b. First edition—American issue. 1961*:

New York: Viking Press, 27 October 1961. $5.00.

*c. Second English edition* (*Penguin Books*). [*1964*]:

Harmondsworth: Penguin Books, 24 June 1964. Vol. 2079. 5s.

There were further printings issued by Granada Publishing—Panther
Books (London) in December 1979 and December 1983.

## A11                    THE WILD GARDEN                    1963
##                    OR SPEAKING OF WRITING

*a. First edition*:

London: Secker & Warburg, 11 November 1963. 4000 copies printed (and
2506 copies for the U.S. publisher). 16s.

*b. First edition—American issue. 1963*:

Berkeley and Los Angeles: University of California Press, December 1963.
2506 copies. $3.75.

There was a further printing (paperbound) in 1965.

*Note*: An extract was published in *The Sunday Telegraph*, 8 September 1963,
pp. 4-5 (C369).

## A12                         LATE CALL                         1964

*a. First edition*:

London: Secker & Warburg, 9 November 1964. 15,400 copies printed. 25s.

There was a further printing in February 1965.

*b. First American edition. 1965*:

New York: Viking Press, 11 January 1965. $4.95.

*c. Second English edition.*

London: The Book Club, 196?

*d. Third English edition (Penguin Books). [1968]*:

Harmondsworth: Penguin Books, April 1968. Vol. 2791. 6s.

There was a further printing in 1976 and a printing issued by Granada Publishing—Panther Books (London) in April 1982.

A13          TEMPO: THE IMPACT OF          1964
                TELEVISION ON THE ARTS

*a. First edition*:

London: Studio Vista Books, 16 November 1964. 25s.

*b. First edition—American issue. [1966]*:

Chester Springs, PA: Dufour Editions, 1966.

A14                NO LAUGHING MATTER                1967

*a. First edition*:

London: Secker & Warburg, 4 October 1967. 20,020 copies printed including 2965 copies issued by Heron Books and 3400 copies by the Book Club Association. 42s.

There were further printings in January 1968 (1500 copies), February 1968 (1500 copies), March 1969 and March 1980 (Uniform edition, 2000 copies).

*b. First American edition. 1967*:

New York: Viking Press, 14 November 1967. $6.95.

*c. Second English edition (Penguin Books). [1969]*:

Harmondsworth: Penguin Books, May 1969. Vol. 2971. 8s.

There was a further printing issued by Granada Publishing—Panther Books (London) in 1979.

# A15          DEATH DANCE          1969
## TWENTY-FIVE STORIES

*First edition. 1969*:

New York: Viking Press, 12 May 1969. $6.95.

Contents: The Wrong Set — Saturnalia — Realpolitik — Union Reunion — A Story of Historical Interest — Crazy Crowd — A Visit in Bad Taste — Raspberry Jam — Mother's Sense of Fun — Et Dona Ferentes — Such Darling Dodos — A Little Companion — Learning's Little Tribute — Necessity's Child — Christmas Day in the Workhouse — Mummy to the Rescue — What Do Hippos Eat? — Totentanz — A Bit Off the Map — A Flat Country Christmas — More Friend than Lodger — Once a Lady — Higher Standards — A Sad Fall — After the Show


# A16          THE WORLD OF CHARLES DICKENS          1970

*a. First edition*:

London: Secker & Warburg, 26 May 1970. 17,500 copies printed (and 5000 copies issued by the Book-of-the-Month Club). £4.00.

There was a further printing in November 1970 and a printing issued by Studio Vista Books (London) in 1970.

*b. First edition—American issue. 1970*:

New York: Viking Press, 31 August 1970. $12.95.

*c. Second English edition (Penguin Books). [1972]*:

Harmondsworth: Penguin Books, September 1972. £1.50.

There was a further printing issued by Granada Publishing—Panther Books (London) in 1983.

*Note*: Extracts were published in *Observer Magazine*, 17 May 1970, pp. 24-25 (C455) and 24 May 1970, pp. 37-38, 41-43 (C456).


# A17          AS IF BY MAGIC          1973

*a. First edition*:

London: Secker & Warburg, 29 May 1973. 12,000 copies printed. £2.50.

There was a further printing issued by the New Fiction Society, September 1974 (500 copies).

*b. First edition—American issue. 1973*:

New York: Viking Press, October 1973. $8.95.

*c. Second English edition (Penguin Books). [1976]*:

Harmondsworth: Penguin Books, February 1976. 12,000 copies printed. 90 p.

There was a further printing in April 1976 (10,000 copies) and 1978 and a printing issued by Granada Publishing—Panther Books (London) in January 1982.

*Note*: A section deleted from the final version was published in *Iowa Review*, 3 no. 4 (1972), 106-108 (C485). An extract was published in *Vogue* (New York), 1 September 1973, pp. 290-291, 338, 340-341 (C497).

## A18    THE NAUGHTY NINETIES    1976

*First edition*:

London: Eyre Methuen, 1976. £3.95.

## A19    THE STRANGE RIDE OF RUDYARD KIPLING    1977
## HIS LIFE AND WORKS

*a. First edition*:

London: Secker & Warburg, 7 November 1977. 7000 copies printed. £6.90.

There was a further printing in February 1978.

*b. Second English edition (Panther Books). [1977]*:

London: Granada Publishing—Panther Books, 1977.

There was a further printing in October 1979 and a printing issued by Penguin Books (Harmondsworth) in August 1979 (12,500 copies).

*c. First edition—American issue. 1978*:

New York: Viking Press, 14 March 1978. $17.50

## A20    SETTING THE WORLD ON FIRE    1980

*a. First edition*:

London: Secker & Warburg, 7 July 1980. 8000 copies printed. £6.50.

*b. First edition—American issue. 1980*:

New York: Viking Press, 30 October 1980. 7500 copies printed. $12.95.

*c. Second English edition (Panther Books). [1981]*:

London: Granada Publishing—Panther Books, December 1981.

*Note*: An extract was published in *The Times*, 5 July 1980, p. 6 (C594).


A21     DIVERSITY AND DEPTH IN FICTION     1983
        SELECTED CRITICAL WRITINGS OF
        ANGUS WILSON

Edited by Kerry McSweeney.

*a. First edition*:

London: Secker & Warburg, 30 August 1983. 3000 copies printed (2000 copies for the U.S. publisher). £15.00.

*b. First edition—American issue. 1984*:

New York: Viking Press, August 1984. 2000 copies. $27.50.

Contents: Foreword — Editor's Introduction — Evil in the English Novel — Richardson's *Clarissa* — William Godwin's Novels — Conflicts in Jane Austen's Novels — Charles Dickens: A Haunting — Dickens and Dostoevsky — Meredith's *The Egoist* — Zola's *L'Assommoir* — Gissing's *New Grub Street* — Kipling's *Kim* — The View from the 1950s: i Virginia Woolf (I), ii The Future of the English Novel, iii Lawrence and Leavis, iv Diversity and Depth, v Letter from London — Arnold Bennett — Galsworthy's *Forsyte Saga* — The English Novel 1912-1922 — Marcel Proust — Dorothy Richardson's *Pilgrimage* — Virginia Woolf (II) — John Cowper Powys — Ivy Compton-Burnett — Aldous Huxley — Evelyn Waugh — Henry Green — Christopher Isherwood — Claude Simon — Albert Camus — Günther Grass — The Dilemma of the Contemporary Novelist — The Novelist and the Narrator — *Iowa Review* Interview

*Note*: Claude Simon, noted as published for the first time, previously appeared in *UEA Bulletin* (University of East Anglia, Norwich), December 1973 (C502).

A22          REFLECTIONS IN A WRITER'S EYE          1986
             TRAVEL PIECES BY ANGUS WILSON

*a.* First edition:

London: Secker & Warburg, 21 January 1986. 1600 copies printed. £10.95.

*b.* First edition—American issue. 1986:

New York: Viking Press, 30 September 1986. $15.95.

Contents: Introduction — Some Japanese Observations — Night and Day in Tokyo — The Jolliest Resort in the World — South Africa — A visit to my Mother's Land — On a Black Sea Holiday with Mr K — Russia — What Khrushchev told the Writers — Confessions of a Zoo Lover — The Channel Islands — New and Old on the Grand Trunk Road — Martinique — America — A Celebration — Sri Lankan Journal — Arizona

*Note*: The Channel Islands, Martinique and Arizona are published for the first time. The acknowledgements misdates the original publication of New and Old on the Grand Trunk Road (C547).

# B. Contributions to Books and Books Edited by Angus Wilson. Stories in Anthologies

B1    WHO FOR SUCH DAINTIES? *The Pick of Today's Short Stories*. 3rd ser. Selected by John Sleigh Pudney. London: Odhams, 1952, pp. 232-236. Story.

B2    INTRODUCTION. Emile Zola, *Restless House*. Trans. Percy Pinkerton. London: Weidenfeld & Nicolson, 1953; New York: Farrar, Straus & Young, 1953, pp. vii-xii.

    Reprinted: New York: Bantam, 1953; London: Elek Books, 1957; London: Granada—Panther Books, 1985, pp. 5-10.

B3    EDITOR'S NOTE. F. Dubrez Fawcett, *Hole in Heaven*. British Science Fiction Library No. 1. London: Sidgwick and Jackson, 1954, p. 5.

B4    PREFACE. Emile Zola, *Earth*. Trans. Ann Lindsay. London: Elek Books, 1954, pp. 5-8.

    Reprinted: New York: Grove Press, 1955, pp. 5-8.

B5    INTRODUCTION. Emile Zola, *The Kill*. Trans. A. Teixeira de Mattos. London: Weidenfeld & Nicolson, 1954; New York: Farrar, Straus & Young, 1954, pp. v-x.

Reprinted: London: Elek Books, 1957; London: Granada — Panther Books, 1986, pp. 5-9.

B6 ANIMALS OR HUMAN BEINGS. *The Third Ghost Book*. Ed. Cynthia, Lady Asquith. London: Barrie, 1955, pp. 265-270. Story.

Reprinted: London: Pan Books, 1957, pp. 224-228.

B7 INTRODUCTION. *A.D. 2500: "Observer" Prize Stories, 1954*. London: Heinemann, 1955, pp. vii-xi.

B8 PREFACE. Emile Zola, *Zest for Life*. Trans. Jean Stewart. London: Elek Books, 1955; Bloomington, IN: Indiana University Press, 1956, pp. 5-7.

Reprinted: London: Elek — Bestseller Library, 1959, pp. 5-7.

B9 *Twentieth Century Authors: A Biographical Dictionary of Modern Literature*. Ed. Stanley J. Kunitz. New York: Wilson, 1955. First supplement, pp. 1093- 1094. Autobiographical comments.

B10 INTRODUCTION. Germaine Brée, *Marcel Proust and Deliverance from Time*. London: Chatto & Windus, 1956, pp. vii-xi.

B11 INTRODUCTION. Villy Sørensen, *Strange Stories*. Trans. Maureen Neiiendam. London: Secker & Warburg, 1956, pp. vii-xi; *Tiger in the Kitchen and Other Strange Stories*. New York: Abelard-Schuman, 1957, pp. vii-xi.

Reprinted: Freeport, NY: Books for Libraries Press, 1969, pp. vii-xi.

B12 PREFACE. John Petty, *Five Fags a Day: The Last Year of a Scrap-Picker*. London: Secker & Warburg, 1956, pp. 5-6.

B13 *The Author and the Public: Problems of Communication*. London: Hutchinson, 1957, pp. 28-31. Proceedings of the Congress of the International P.E.N. Clubs, London, July 1956. *See also* G25.

B14 *P.E.N. Report/Compte-rendu*. Proceedings of the 29th Congress of the International P.E.N. Clubs, Tokyo, 1-9 September 1957. Tokyo: Japanese P.E.N. Centre, [1957], pp. 50-54, 204-205, 253-255, 263-265.

B15 IN MODERATION. *The Compleat Imbiber: An Entertainment* [Vol. 2]. Ed. Cyril Ray. London: Putnam, 1958, pp. 121-129. Story.

B16    THE NOVELIST AND THE NARRATOR. *English Studies Today*, 2nd ser. Lectures and papers read at the Fourth Conference of the International Association of University Professors of English, Lausanne and Bern, August 1959. Ed. G.A. Bonnard. Bern: Francke Verlag, 1961, pp. 43-50.

Reprinted: *Diversity and Depth in Fiction*, 1983.

B17    CHARLES DICKENS: A HAUNTING. *The Dickens Critics*. Ed. George H. Ford and Lauriat Lane. Ithaca: Cornell University Press, 1961; London: Oxford University Press, 1962, pp. 374-385. Reprint of C259.

Reprinted: *Dickens: Modern Judgments*. Ed. A.E. Dyson. London: Macmillan, 1968, pp. 30-39.

Reprinted: *Diversity and Depth in Fiction*, 1983.

B18    AFTERWORD. Emile Zola, *L'Assommoir*. Trans. Atwood H. Townsend. New York: New American Library—Signet Books, 1962, pp. 488-497.

Reprinted: *Diversity and Depth in Fiction*, 1983.

B19    ANGUS WILSON ON EMILE ZOLA. *Novelists on Novelists: An Anthology*. Ed. Louis Kronenberger. Garden City, NY: Doubleday, 1962, pp. 137-157. Extract from *Emile Zola: An Introductory Study of His Novels*, Chapter II (A3).

B20    ENVY. *The Seven Deadly Sins*. Angus Wilson et al. London: Sunday Times Publications, 1962, pp. 2-11; London and New York: Morrow, 1962, pp. 2-11. Reprint of C288.

Reprinted: Freeport, NY: Books for Libraries Press, 1970, pp. 2-11.

B21    FOREWORD. Finn Carling, *And Yet We Are Human*. London: Chatto & Windus, 1962, pp. 9-13.

B22    THE HEROES AND HEROINES OF DICKENS. *Dickens and the Twentieth Century*. Ed. John Gross and Gabriel Pearson. London: Routledge & Kegan Paul, 1962, pp. 3-11. Reprint of C275.

Reprinted: Toronto: University of Toronto Press, 1962; London: Routledge & Kegan Paul, 1963; London: Routledge Paperback No. 60, 1966, pp. 3-11.

Reprinted: *British Victorian Literature: Recent Revaluations*. Ed.

Shiv K. Kumar. London: University of London Press, 1969; New York: New York University Press, 1969, pp. 243-252.

Reprinted: *Charles Dickens: A Critical Anthology*. Ed. Stephen Wall. Penguin Critical Anthologies series. Harmondsworth: Penguin Books, 1970, pp. 433-442.

B23 AFTERWORD. Charles Dickens, *Great Expectations*. New York: New American Library—Signet Books, 1963, pp. 523-531.

B24 AFTERWORD. Charles Dickens, *Little Dorrit*. New York: New American Library—Signet Books, 1963.

B25 AFTERWORD. George Meredith, *The Egoist*. New York: New American Library—Signet Books, 1963, pp. 501-508.

Reprinted: *Diversity and Depth in Fiction*, 1983.

B26 THERE'S A TYRANT IN THE CRITIC'S CORNER. *Opinions and Perspectives from "The New York Times Book Review"*. Ed. Francis Brown. Boston: Houghton Mifflin — Riverside Press, 1964, pp. 222-229. Reprint of C276.

B27 PREFACE. Margaret K. Black, *No Room for Tourists*. London: Secker & Warburg, 1965, pp. 9-13.

B28 INTRODUCTION. Charles Dickens, *Oliver Twist*. Ed. Peter Fairclough. Harmondsworth: Penguin Books, 1966, pp. 11-27.

B29 ANGUS WILSON: EXTRACT FROM *Anglo-Saxon Attitudes* (1956). *Novels of Today: Extracts from Contemporary English Novels*. Ed. Penelope J. Manners. London: University of London Press, 1967, pp. 85-89. Extract from *Anglo-Saxon Attitudes*, pp. 46-49. *See also* J133.

B30 INTRODUCTION. Rex Warner, *The Aerodrome: A Love Story*. London: Bodley Head, 1966; Boston: Little, Brown, 1966, pp. 9-11.

Reprinted: London: Sphere Books, 1968, pp. 9-10.

B31 INTRODUCTION. W. Somerset Maugham, *A Maugham Twelve*. Ed. Angus Wilson. London: Heinemann, 1966, pp. vii-x; *"Cakes and Ale" and Twelve Short Stories*. Garden City, NY: Doubleday, 1967, pp. 5-8.

B32 *Authors Take Sides on Vietnam: Two Questions on the War in*

*Vietnam Answered by the Authors of Several Nations.* Ed. Cecil Woolf and John Bagguley. London: Peter Owen, 1967, pp. 133-134; New York: Simon & Schuster, 1967, p. 76.

B33   THE DILEMMA OF THE CONTEMPORARY NOVELIST. *Approaches to the Novel.* Ed. John Colmer. Edinburgh and London: Oliver & Boyd, 1967, pp. 115-132.

Reprinted: *Diversity and Depth in Fiction*, 1983.

B34   THE NEIGHBOURHOOD OF TOMBUCTOO: CONFLICTS IN JANE AUSTEN'S NOVELS. *Critical Essays on Jane Austen.* Ed. B.C. Southam. London: Routledge & Kegan Paul, 1968, pp. 182-199.

Reprinted: London: Routledge & Kegan Paul, 1970, 1979, 1983.

Reprinted: *Diversity and Depth in Fiction*, 1983.

B35   DICKENS AND DOSTOEVSKY. *Dickens Memorial Lectures 1970.* London: Dickens Fellowship. 1970, pp. 41-61. Supplement to *The Dickensian* (C462).

Reprinted: *Diversity and Depth in Fiction*, 1983.

B36   DICKENS ON CHILDREN AND CHILDHOOD. *Dickens 1970: Centenary Essays.* Ed. Michael Slater. London: Chapman & Hall, 1970; New York: Stein & Day, 1970, pp. 195-227.

B37   INTRODUCTION. Charles Dickens, *David Copperfield.* 2 vols. London: Watts, 1971, vol. 1, pp. vii-xvii. Extract with minor alterations from *The World of Charles Dickens*, pp. 211-216.

B38   INTRODUCTION. *England.* Photographs by Edwin Smith. London: Thames & Hudson, 1971; New York: Viking Press, 1971, pp. 7-8, 11-18, 21-28, 31-34, 37-43. *See also* C472.

B39   ANGUS WILSON COMMENTS. *Contemporary Novelists.* Ed. James Vinson. London and Chicago: St James Press, 1972, pp. 1374-1375; 2nd edn. London: St James Press, pp. 1374-1375; New York: St Martin's Press, 1976, pp. 1514-1515; 3rd edn. London: Macmillan, 1982, pp. 703-705.

B40   IVY COMPTON-BURNETT. *The Art of I. Compton-Burnett: A Collection of Critical Essays.* Ed. Charles Burkhart. London: Gollancz, 1972, pp. 129-136, 192-194. Reprint of C116 and C446.

B41    INTRODUCTION. John Cowper Powys, *Weymouth Sands: A Novel.* Cambridge: Rivers Press, 1973, pp. 7-13.

Reprinted as: John Cowper Powys: *Weymouth Sands. Diversity and Depth in Fiction,* 1983.

B42    INTRODUCTION. Charles Dickens, *The Mystery of Edwin Drood.* Ed. Arthur J. Cox. Harmondsworth: Penguin Books, 1974, pp. 11-28.

B43    INTRODUCTION. Sir Arthur Conan Doyle, *The Return of Sherlock Holmes* [*The Sherlock Holmes Collected Edition,* Vol. 6]. London: Murray/Cape, 1974, pp. 7-17.

Reprinted: London: Pan Books, 1976, 1979, pp. 7-17.

B44    *An Anthology: Green River Review 1968-1973.* Selected by Angus Wilson. University Center, MI: Green River Press, 1975.

B45    INTRODUCTION. Charles Dickens, *American Notes for General Circulation.* Avon, CT: Cardavon Press, Limited Editions Club, 1975, pp. ix-xv.

B46    CHARLES DICKENS. A.E. Dyson and Angus Wilson. *The English Novel: Questions in Literature.* Ed. Cedric Watts. London: Sussex Books, 1976, pp. 53-75. *See also* F11.

B47    *Writers of East Anglia.* Ed. Angus Wilson. London: Secker & Warburg, 1977. Introduction by Wilson, pp. ix-xiii.

B48    *My Oxford.* Ed. Ann Thwaite. London: Robson Books, 1977, pp. 91-108. Reprint of C558.

B49    EDMUND WILSON. *An Edmund Wilson Celebration.* Ed. John Wain. Oxford: Phaidon Press, 1978; *Edmund Wilson: The Man and His Work,* New York: New York University Press, 1978, pp. 28-34.

B50    FOREWORD. Iain Mackintosh, *Pit, Boxes & Gallery: The Story of the Theatre Royal, Bury St Edmunds 1819 to 1976.* London: National Trust, 1979, p. 4.

B51    INTRODUCTION. Elizabeth Bowen, *The Collected Stories of Elizabeth Bowen.* London: Cape, 1980; New York: Knopf, 1980, pp. 7-11.

Reprinted: Harmondsworth: Penguin Books, 1983, 1985, pp. 7-11.

B52 JOHN COWPER POWYS. *Recollections of the Powys Brothers: Llewelyn, Theodore and John Cowper.* Ed. Belinda Humfrey. London: Peter Owen, 1980, pp. 262-265.

B53 INTRODUCTION. Rudyard Kipling, *Kim.* London: Macmillan, 1981, pp. v-xxii.

Reprinted: *Diversity and Depth in Fiction,* 1983.

Reprinted: London: Macmillan, 1984, 1985.

B54 LOWER DEPTHS OF LITERATURE. *George Gissing: Critical Essays.* Ed. Jean-Pierre Michaux. London: Vision Press, 1981; New York: Barnes & Noble, 1981, pp. 123-125. Reprint of C424.

Reprinted: *Diversity and Depth in Fiction,* 1983.

B55 *East Anglia in Verse and Prose.* Ed. Angus Wilson. Research by Tony Garrett. London: Secker & Warburg, 1982. Introduction by Wilson, pp. 1-3.

Reprinted: Harmondsworth: Penguin Books, 1984, pp. 1-3.

B56 FOREWORD. *Diversity and Depth in Fiction: Selected Critical Writings of Angus Wilson.* Ed. Kerry McSweeney. London: Secker & Warburg, 1983, pp. ix-x.

B57 *The Portable Dickens.* Ed. Angus Wilson. New York: Viking Press, 1983; Harmondsworth: Penguin Books, 1983. Introduction by Wilson, pp. xi-xliii.

B58 SRI LANKAN JOURNAL. *Firebird 2: Writing Today.* Ed. T.J. Binding. Harmondsworth: Penguin Books, 1983, pp. 267-284.

Reprinted: *Reflections in a Writer's Eye,* 1986.

B59 *As If By Magic:* ANGUS WILSON ON HIS OWN NOVEL. *The Best of DQR.* Ed. F. G. A. Maarts et al. Amsterdam: Rodopi, 1984, pp. 259-277. Reprint of C538.

B60 *Essays by Divers Hands, Being the Transactions of the Royal Society of Literature.* Ed. Sir Angus Wilson. Woodbridge, Suffolk: Boydell Press, 1984. Introduction by Wilson, pp. ix-xiii.

B61 *Evelyn Waugh: The Critical Heritage.* Ed. Martin Stannard. London: Routledge & Kegan Paul, 1984, pp. 405-408, 482-489. Reprint of C242 and C530.

B62 THE NEW AND THE OLD ISHERWOOD. *The Chelsea House Library of Literary Criticism, Twentieth Century British Literature, Volume III.* New York: Chelsea House, 1986, pp. 1400-1403. Reprint of C91.

B63 FOREWORD. *Angus Wilson: A Bibliography, 1947-1987.* J.H. Stape and Anne N. Thomas. London: Mansell, 1988, p. ix.

## STORIES IN ANTHOLOGIES

B64 MUMMY TO THE RESCUE. *Stories, British and American.* Ed. Jack Barry Ludwig and W. Richard Poirier. Cambridge, MA: Houghton Mifflin — Riverside Press, 1953, pp. 457-463.

B65 HER SHIP CAME HOME. *Did It Happen? Stories.* London: Oldbourne, 1956, pp. 211-216. Reprint of C109. Story.

B66 ET DONA FERENTES. *The Short Story.* Ed. James B. Hall and Joseph Langland. New York: Macmillan, 1956, pp. 300-314. *See also* J88.

B67 RASPBERRY JAM. *Best Horror Stories.* Ed. John Keir Cross. London: Faber & Faber, 1957, 1962, pp. 49-68.

B68 REALPOLITIK. *English Short Stories of Today.* 2nd ser. Ed. Dan Davin. London: Oxford University Press for the English Association, 1958, pp. 236-243.

B69 REALPOLITIK. *Understanding Fiction.* Ed. Cleanth Brooks and Robert Penn Warren. 2nd edn. New York: Appleton-Century-Crofts, 1959, pp. 446-451.

B70 MORE FRIEND THAN LODGER. *Stories from The New Yorker 1950-1960.* New York: Simon & Schuster, 1960, pp. 641-665.

B71 TOTENTANZ. *31 Stories.* Ed. Michael R. Booth and Clinton S. Burhans, Jr. Englewood Cliffs, NJ: Prentice-Hall, 1960, pp. 328-341.

B72 MUMMY TO THE RESCUE. *Best Fantasy Stories.* Ed. Brian W. Aldiss. London: Faber & Faber, 1962, pp. 96-102.

B73 MUMMY TO THE RESCUE. *A Chamber of Horrors: An*

*Anthology of the Macabre in Words and Pictures.* John Hadfield, comp. London: Studio Vista Books, 1965; Boston: Little, Brown, 1965, pp. 198-200, 203-204.

B74   TEN MINUTES TO TWELVE. *English Short Stories of Today.* T.S. Dorsch, comp. 3rd ser. London: Oxford University Press for the English Association, 1965, pp. 204-218.

B75   REALPOLITIK. *The Sense of Fiction.* Ed. Robert L. Welker and Herschel Gower. Englewood Cliffs, NJ: Prentice-Hall, 1966, pp. 414-420.

B76   TOTENTANZ. *The World of Modern Fiction: Vol. 2 European.* Ed. Steven Marcus. New York: Simon & Schuster, 1966, pp. 246-261.

B77   RASPBERRY JAM. *The Penguin Book of English Short Stories.* Ed. Christopher Dolley. Harmondsworth: Penguin Books, 1967, pp. 313-329.

Reprinted annually: Harmondsworth: Penguin Books, 1968-1981; 1983-1985.

B78   REALPOLITIK. *British Short Stories: Classics and Criticism.* Ed. Leonard R.N. Ashley and Stuart L. Astor. Englewood Cliffs, NJ: Prentice-Hall, 1968, pp. 323-329.

B79   REALPOLITIK. *Adventures in Modern Literature.* Ed. Robert Freier and Arnold Lazarus. New York: Harcourt, Brace & World, 6th edn., 1970, pp. 80-89.

B80   TOTENTANZ. *Modern Satiric Stories: The Impropriety Principle.* Ed. Gregory Fitzgerald. Glenview, IL: Scott, Foresman, 1971, pp. 253-274.

B81   AFTER THE SHOW. *The Second Penguin Book of English Short Stories.* Ed. Christopher Dolley. Harmondsworth: Penguin Books, 1972, pp. 271-300.

Reprinted annually: Harmondsworth: Penguin Books, 1973-1986.

B82   ANIMALS OR HUMAN BEINGS. *The Lucifer Society: Macabre Tales by Great Modern Writers.* Ed. Peter Haining. New York: Taplinger, 1972, pp. 96-100.

B83   RASPBERRY JAM. *The Norton Introduction to Literature: Com-*

*bined Shorter Edition*. Ed. Carl E. Bain, Jerome Beaty and J. Paul Hunter. New York: Norton, 1st edn., 1973, pp. 175-186.

B84  RASPBERRY JAM. *The Norton Introduction to Literature: Fiction*. Ed. Jerome Beaty. New York: Norton, lst edn., 1973, pp. 216-227.

B85  A LITTLE COMPANION. *The Haunted and the Haunters: Tales of Ghosts and Other Apparitions*. Kathleen Lines, comp. New York: Farrar, Straus, Giroux, 1975, pp. 113-128.

B86  MUMMY TO THE RESCUE. *Demons Within & Other Disturbing Tales*. Ed. Helen Hoke. New York: Taplinger, 1977, pp. 42-48.

B87  A LITTLE COMPANION. *Twice-Told Tales: An Anthology of Short Fiction*. Ed. Gerard A. Barker. Boston: Houghton Mifflin, 1979, pp. 341-352.

# C. Contributions to Periodicals and Newspapers

Place of publication is London unless otherwise indicated.

## 1947

C1    MOTHER'S SENSE OF FUN. *Horizon*, no. 95 (November 1947), 255-268. Story.

Reprinted: *The Wrong Set*, 1949; *Death Dance*, 1969.

## 1948

C2    CRAZY CROWD. *Horizon*, no. 99 (April 1948), 246-263. Story.

Reprinted: *The Wrong Set*, 1949; *Death Dance*, 1969.

C3    REALPOLITIK. *Listener*, 40 (16 September 1948), 423-424. Story.

Reprinted: *The Wrong Set*, 1949; *Death Dance*, 1969.

## 1949

C4    WHAT DO HIPPOS EAT? *Listener*, 41 (21 April 1949), 673, 675-676. Story.

Reprinted: *Such Darling Dodos*, 1950; *Death Dance*, 1969.

C5     TOTENTANZ. *Horizon,* no. 113 (May 1949), 337-354. Story.

Reprinted: *The Wrong Set,* 1950 (New York); *Such Darling Dodos,* 1950; *Death Dance,* 1969.

C6     *Horizon,* no. 115 (July 1949), 73-75. Review of *The Circus of Dr Lao* by Charles G. Finney.

C7     NEW NOVELS. *New Statesman and Nation,* ns 38 (27 August 1949), 226-227. Review of *The Poor Girl* by Max van der Meersch, *Fontagré* by Jean Orieux, *The Uniform* by Anthony Rhodes and *The Huntsman in His Career* by Erik de Mauny.

C8     REX IMPERATOR. *Arena,* 1 no. 2 (September 1949), 37-49. Story.

Reprinted: *Such Darling Dodos,* 1950.

C9     NEW NOVELS. *New Statesman and Nation,* ns 38 (24 September 1949), 336, 338. Review of *Focus* by Arthur Miller and *The Dark Peninsula* by Ernest Frost [John Lehmann].

C10    TWO STORIES: LIFE AND LETTERS/ET DONA FERENTES. *Partisan Review* (New York), 16 no. 10 (October 1949), 982-994/995-1010.

Reprinted: Life and Letters as: Fresh Air Fiend, *The Wrong Set,* 1949/Et Dona Ferentes, *The Wrong Set,* 1949; *Death Dance,* 1969.

C11    RAW MATERIAL. *Listener,* 42 (13 October 1949), 639-640. Review of *A Writer's Notebook* by W. Somerset Maugham.

C12    SHORT STORIES. *New Statesman and Nation,* ns 38 (15 October 1949), 435-436. Review of *Tea with Mr Rochester* by Frances Towers, *Character and Situation* by Christopher Sykes and *The Pick of Today's Short Stories,* edited by John Sleigh Pudney.

C13    SUCH DARLING DODOS. *Botteghe Oscure* (Rome), no. 4 (1949), 400-419. Story.

Reprinted: *Harper's Bazaar,* July 1950, pp. 67, 78, 80-82.

Reprinted: *Such Darling Dodos,* 1950.

C14    SHORT STORIES. *New Statesman and Nation,* ns 38 (3 December 1949), 656, 658. Review of *Encounters* by Elizabeth Bowen, *Intimacy* by Jean-Paul Sartre, *The World Is a Wedding* by Delmore

Schwartz, *Boy with a Trumpet* by Rhys Davies and *Tomato Cain* by Nigel Kneale.

C15 PROUST AS A SET BOOK. *New Statesman and Nation*, ns 38 (24 December 1949), 760. Review of *The Mind of Proust* by F.C. Green.

## 1950

C16 NEW NOVELS. *Listener*, 43 (9 February 1950), 261. Review of *The Dreams* by Anna Sebastian, *The Sure Thing* by Merle Miller, *The Big Wheel* by John Brook and *The Ruthless Innocent* by Patrick Balfour.

C17 NEW NOVELS. *Listener*, 43 (23 February 1950), 357. Review of *The Factory* by Vera Panova, *Be Clean, Be Tidy* by Elizabeth Berridge, *All Thy Conquests* by Alfred Hayes and *Tender Mercy* by Leonard Kaufman.

C18 NEW NOVELS. *Listener*, 43 (9 March 1950), 444. Review of *A Voice Through a Cloud* by Denton Welch, *Dear Life* by H.E. Bates, *The Miraculous Barber* by Marcel Aymé and *Abide with Me* by Cedric Belfrage.

C19 LETTERS FROM PROUST. *New Statesman and Nation*, ns 39 (18 March 1950), 312. Review of *Letters to a Friend* by Marcel Proust, translated by A. and E. Henderson.

C20 NEW NOVELS. *Listener*, 43 (30 March 1950), 577. Review of *Prince Isidore* by Harold Acton, *The Man Who Carved Women from Wood* by Max White, *Faster! Faster!* by Patrick Bair and *Scenes from Provincial Life* by William Cooper.

C21 DICKENS FOR TODAY. *Circus: The Pocket Review of Our Time*, 1 no. 1 (April 1950), 44-47. Review of *Charles Dickens* by Jack Lindsay.

C22 NEW NOVELS. *Listener*, 43 (6 April 1950), 621. Review of *Clouds in the Wind* by F.L. Green, *No Man Pursues* by Hugh Sykes Davies, *The Outer Edges* by Charles Jackson and *A Stranger on the Stair* by Chapman Mortimer.

C23 NEW SHORT STORIES. *Listener*, 43 (27 April 1950), 758. Review of *A Tree of Night* by Truman Capote, *Mascarade* by

Gabriel Chevallier, *The Man from the Tunnel* by Theodora Benson and *Truth Lies Sleeping* by Bryan Forbes.

C24    DICKENS AND THE DIVIDED CONSCIENCE. *Month*, 189 no. 3 (May 1950), 349-360.

C25    ZOLA AND THE ENGLISH READER. *Circus: The Pocket Review of Our Time*, 1 no. 2 (May 1950), 42-46. Review of *The Masterpiece* by Emile Zola, translated by Thomas Walton.

C26    NEW NOVELS. *Listener*, 43 (4 May 1950), 801. Review of *The Image of a Drawn Sword* by Jocelyn Brooke, *The Lost Traveller* by Antonia White, *Nothing* by Henry Green and *The Leaden Cupid* by Basil Creighton.

C27    AUNT CORA. *Contact*, 1 no. 1 (May-June 1950), 31. Story.

C28    AN UNMEMORABLE WRITER. *Circus: The Pocket Review of Our Time*, 1 no. 3 (June 1950), 48-50. Review of *Maupassant* by Francis Steegmuller.

C29    PARIS TOURISTS: AN ANATOMY. *Contact*, 1 no. 2 (July-August 1950), 5-6, 45.

C30    SENSE AND SENSIBILITY IN RECENT WRITING. *Listener*, 44 (24 August 1950), 279-280. Broadcast talk on Virginia Woolf (*see* G3).

Reprinted as: Virginia Woolf (I). *Diversity and Depth in Fiction*, 1983.

C31    MARCEL PROUST. *Observer*, 10 September 1950, p. 7. Review of the Scott-Moncrieff translation of *Remembrance of Things Past* by Marcel Proust.

C32    ZOLA AND THE TRANSLATORS. *Times Literary Supplement*, 3 November 1950, p. 692. Review of *The Masterpiece* by Emile Zola, translated by Thomas Walton. Unsigned.

C33    PROUST ALONE. *New Statesman and Nation*, ns 40 (11 November 1950), 434, 436. Review of *The Letters of Marcel Proust*, translated and edited by Mina Curtiss.

C34    THE OLD, OLD MESSAGE. *New Statesman and Nation*, ns 40 (23 December 1950), 648, 650. Story.

Reprinted as: A Flat Country Christmas. *A Bit Off The Map*, 1957; *Death Dance*, 1969.

## 1951

C35    THE DAY BEFORE YESTERDAY. *New Statesman and Nation*, ns 41 (24 February 1951), 222, 224. Review of *English Stories from "New Writing"*, edited by John Lehmann.

C36    BROKEN PROMISE: ANGUS WILSON ON THE ENGLISH NOVEL, 1912-1922. *Listener*, 45 (12 April 1951), 575-576. Broadcast talk (*see* G6).

Reprinted as: The English Novel 1912-1922. *Diversity and Depth in Fiction*, 1983.

C37    A LETTER FROM LONDON. *American Mercury* (New York), 72 (May 1951), 571-577.

C38    STUDIES ON D.H. LAWRENCE. *Times Literary Supplement*, 4 May 1951, p. 278. Review of *D.H. Lawrence* by Anthony West and *D.H. Lawrence and Human Existence* by William Tiverton. Unsigned.

C39    AN ELEPHANT NEVER FORGETS. *Panorama and Harlequin*, no. 5 (Spring/Summer 1951), 30-35. Story.

C40    THE NOVELS OF WILLIAM GODWIN. *World Review*, ns 28 (June 1951), 37-40.

Reprinted as: William Godwin's Novels. *Diversity and Depth in Fiction*, 1983.

C41    THE SOLITARY CHILDREN. *New Republic* (New York), 125 (13 August 1951), 20-21. Review of *The Man Who Was Loved* by James Stern.

C42    THE NOSTALGIC BACKWARD GLANCE. *Harper's Bazaar*, November 1951, pp. 67, 103-104.

C43    LETTER FROM LONDON: THE REVOLUTION IN BRITISH READING. *American Mercury* (New York), 73 (December 1951), 47-54.

## 1952

C44    AUNT MATHILDE'S DRAWINGS. *Evening Standard,* 5 March 1952, p. 8. Story.

C45    THE PRINCE OF MIDDLEBROWS. *New Statesman and Nation,* ns 43 (15 March 1952), 312, 314. Review of *Hugh Walpole* by Rupert Hart-Davis.

C46    A CRITIC'S FAILURE. *Observer,* 16 March 1952, p. 7. Review of *I Thought of Daisy* by Edmund Wilson.

C47    A PERSONAL ODYSSEY. *Observer,* 11 May 1952, p. 7. Review of *Pigeon Pie* by Nancy Mitford.

C48    NEW SHORT STORIES. *New Statesman and Nation,* ns 43 (21 June 1952), 738. Review of *The Circus in the Attic* by Robert Penn Warren, *The Women on the Wall* by Wallace Stegner, *Mixed Company* by Irwin Shaw, *The Smoking Mountain* by Kay Boyle and *A Breathless Child* by Frances Bellerby.

C49    WORLD OF DREAMS. *Observer,* 29 June 1952, p. 7. Review of *The Illustrated Man* by Ray Bradbury.

C50    SILENT PIANIST. *Evening Standard,* 11 September 1952, p. 8. Story.

C51    SCIENCE FICTION: FANTASY FREE. *Observer,* 28 September 1952, p. 8. Review of *The Weapon Shops of Isher* by A.E. van Vogt; *Possible Worlds of Science Fiction,* edited by Geoff Conklin; *New Tales of Space and Time,* with a preface by Gerald Heard; *I, Robot* by Isaac Asimov and *Islands in the Sky* by Arthur C. Clarke.

C52    A TATTERED IDYLL. *New Statesman and Nation,* ns 44 (4 October 1952), 382, 384. Review of *Mary Wollstonecraft* by Ralph M. Wardle.

C53    MR HUXLEY'S SPLIT MIND. *New Statesman and Nation,* ns 44 (1 November 1952), 516, 518. Review of *The Devils of Loudun* by Aldous Huxley.

C54    INFLUENCE GRANDISSANTE DE ZOLA EN ANGLE-TERRE. *Ici Londres: Bulletin hebdomadaire des services européens de la BBC,* no. 249 (6 novembre 1952), 3. Broadcast talk (*see* G9). [Translated into French.]

C55 THE CONSUMING FIRE. *Listener*, 48 (4 December 1952), 941, 943. Review of *The Denton Welch Journals*, edited by Jocelyn Brooke.

C56 PRIZEWINNERS. *Observer*, 7 December 1952, p. 9. Review of *"The Observer" Prize Stories*.

C57 THE TROUBLEMAKER. *Woman's Own*, 18 December 1952, pp. 8-9, 16. Reprint of Sister Superior.

## 1953

C58 HIGHER STANDARDS. *Listener*, 49 (15 January 1953), 107-108. Story. *See also* G11.

Reprinted: *A Bit Off The Map*, 1957; *Death Dance*, 1969.

C59 GOTHIC TALES. *Observer*, 22 February 1953, p. 8. Review of *Satan in the Suburbs* by Bertrand Russell.

C60 HORTENSE CALISHER. *Manchester Guardian Weekly*, 19 March 1953, p. 10. Review of *In the Absence of Angels* by Hortense Calisher.

C61 THE DIFFIDENT HERO. *New Statesman and Nation*, ns 45 (21 March 1953), 347. Review of *Francis Younghusband* by George Seaver.

C62 NUNC DIMITTIS. *Partisan Review* (New York), 20 (March-April 1953), 236-239. Review of *The Correspondence between Paul Claudel and André Gide* and *Madeleine, Et Nunc Manet in Te* by André Gide.

C63 PARTIES: BEING A HOST. *Punch*, 22 April 1953, p. 482.

C64 VICTORIAN LIONESS. *Observer*, 26 April 1953, p. 8. Review of *Marie Corelli* by Eileen Bigland.

C65 FOR WHOM THE CLOCHE TOLLS. *Harper's Bazaar*, May 1953, pp. 70-71, 94, 96. Pre-publication extracts.

C66 THE MEN WITH BOWLER HATS. *Evening News*, 5 May 1953, p. 9. Story.

Reprinted as: Men with Bowler Hats. *Argosy*, November 1957, pp. 105-109.

C67    NEW NOVELS: FUN AND GAMES. *Observer*, 17 May 1953, p. 13. Review of *Patience* by John Coates, *Rebecca Redfern* by R.P. Lister, *A Ball in Venice* by Anthony Rhodes and *A Change of Sky* by Frank Singleton.

C68    ON PARTIES—BEING A GUEST. *Punch*, 20 May 1953, p. 602.

C69    NEW FICTION: A BRAZILIAN CLASSIC. *Observer*, 31 May 1953, p. 15. Review of *Epitaph of a Small Winner* by Machado de Assis, *A Long View of Nothing* by H.A. Manhood and *The Wounded* by Tom Clarkson.

C70    THROUGHOUT THE COUNTRY. *New Statesman and Nation*, ns 45 (13 June 1953), 696, 698. On the coronation festivities.

C71    THE BICENTENARY OF THE BRITISH MUSEUM—II. *Listener*, 49 (18 June 1953), 1005-1006, 1014. Broadcast talk (*see* G12).

C72    THE UNDEFEATED. *Observer*, 21 June 1953, p. 11. Review of *J.P. Marquand, Esquire: A Portrait in the Form of a Novel* by Philip Hamburger.

C73    THE PROPHET OF A NEW AGE. *Listener*, 49 (25 June 1953), 1065. Review of *Emile Zola* by F.W.J. Hemmings.

C74    SO COMPLETELY UNSPOILED. *Punch*, 6 July 1953, p. 14.

C75    ARE THE GAY 'TWENTIES COMING IN AGAIN? *Sunday Express*, 2 August 1953, p. 4.

C76    NEW SHORT STORIES. *New Statesman and Nation*, ns 46 (15 August 1953), 187. Review of *For Esmé—With Love and Squalor* by J.D. Salinger, *Shepherd's Hey* by Gwyn Jones and *The Other Place* by J.B. Priestley.

C77    VIRGINIA WOOLF. *Observer*, 1 November 1953, p. 9. Review of *A Writer's Diary* by Virginia Woolf.

C78    THE TWELVE BEST AND MOST REPRESENTATIVE

ENGLISH NOVELS BY AUTHORS WHO ARE NOT ALIVE: *WIADOMOŚCI'S* QUESTIONNAIRE. *Wiadomości,* 15 November 1953, pp. 1-2 (2).

C79      TRUCULENT HERO. *Observer,* 22 November 1953, p. 8. Review of *Along My Line* by Gilbert Harding.

## 1954

C80      ORWELL AND THE INTELLECTUALS. *Observer,* 24 January 1954, p. 8. Review of *England, Your England and Other Essays* by George Orwell.

C81      NEW NOVELS. *Observer,* 28 February 1954, p. 9. Review of *The Flaw in the Crystal* by Godfrey Smith, *A Passage in the Night* by Sholem Asch and *Fiesta* by Prudencio de Pereda.

C82      NEW NOVELS. *Observer,* 14 March 1954, p. 9. Review of *Invitation from Minerva* by March Cost, *An Impossible Marriage* by Pamela Hansford Johnson and *Those in Peril* by Russell Braddon.

C83      UNWANTED HEROINE. *Homes and Gardens,* 35 no. 9 ([15] March 1954), 38-40, 124, 127, 129. Story.

C84      NEW NOVELS. *Observer,* 28 March 1954, p. 9. Review of *The End of an Old Song* by J.D. Scott, *Fahrenheit 451* by Ray Bradbury and *The Woman with No Past* by Serge Groussard.

C85      NEW NOVELS. *Observer,* 11 April 1954, p. 11. Review of *African Diversions* by Ernst Juenger, *A Flame for Doubting Thomas* by Richard Llewellyn and *Soldier Adrift* by L. Steni.

C86      THE FUTURE OF THE ENGLISH NOVEL. *Listener,* 51 (29 April 1954), 746. Broadcast talk (*see* G13).

Reprinted: *Diversity and Depth in Fiction,* 1983.

C87      OUT OF THE ORDINARY. *Observer,* 9 May 1954, p. 9. Review of *The Adventures of Augie March* by Saul Bellow, *A Handful of Blackberries* by Ignazio Silone and *One* by David Karp.

C88      NEW NOVELS. *Observer,* 23 May 1954, p. 9. Review of *Bhowani Junction* by John Masters, *The Affable Hangman* by Ramón

J. Sender, *The Love Eaters* by Mary Lee Settle and *The Deserters* by Honor Tracy.

C89     NEW NOVELS. *Observer*, 6 June 1954, p. 7. Review of *Under the Net* by Iris Murdoch, *The Charm of Hours* by Peter Skelton, *The Other Side of the Square* by Neil Macmillan, *A Villa in Summer* by Penelope Mortimer and *Old Men Have Grey Beards* by Leopold Louth.

C90     OTHER NEW NOVELS. *Observer*, 20 June 1954, p. 9. Review of *The Primitives* by S.B. Hough, *The Ampersand* by Jack Common, *The Night of the Hunter* by Davis Grubb and *Yield to the Night* by Joan Henry.

C91     THE NEW AND THE OLD ISHERWOOD. *Encounter*, 3 no. 2 (August 1954), 62-68. Review of *The World in the Evening* by Christopher Isherwood.

        Reprinted as: Christopher Isherwood. *Diversity and Depth in Fiction*, 1983.

        Reprinted: *The Chelsea House Library of Literary Criticism, Twentieth Century British Literature, Volume III*. New York: Chelsea House, 1986, pp. 1400-1403 (B62).

C92     NEW FICTION. *Observer*, 1 August 1954, p. 7. Review of *The Course of Love* by Rachel Trickett, *Jumping Joan* by C.H.B. Kitchin, *The Golden Waterwheel* by Leo Walmsley and *The Butterfly Net* by John Lodwick.

C93     NEW NOVELS. *Observer*, 15 August 1954, p. 7. Review of *Swamp Angel* by Ethel Wilson, *Ash on a Young Man's Sleeve* by Dannie Abse, *Photo Finish* by Howard Mason and *Waybent* by J.C. Badcock.

C94     NEW NOVELS. *Observer*, 29 August 1954, p. 7. Review of *A Pride of Lions* by John Brooks, *The Creedy Case* by Edward Crankshaw, *Bella North* by Diana Marr-Johnson and *The White Wand* by L.P. Hartley.

C95     ARNOLD BENNETT'S NOVELS. *London Magazine*, 1 no. 9 (October 1954), 59-67.

        Reprinted as: Arnold Bennett. *Diversity and Depth in Fiction*, 1983.

C96     THE SHORT STORY CHANGES. *Spectator*, 193 (1 October

1954), 401-402. Review of *A Crown of Convolvulus* by Margaret
Lane, *Children Are Bored on Sunday* by Jean Stafford, *The Night-
mare* by Antonia White and *The Romantic Egoists* by Louis
Auchincloss.

C97      NEW LIGHT ON GEORGE ELIOT. *Observer*, 21 November
1954, p. 8. Review of *The George Eliot Letters*, Vols. I-III, edited
by Gordon S. Haight.

C98      DISHONOURABLE PLEASURE. *Spectator*, 193 (3 December
1954), 726, 728. Review of *O Rare Amanda!* by Jack Loudan.

C99      THE SHORT STORY. *P.E.N. News*, no. 185 (Winter 1954),
6-7.


## 1955

C100     OSCAR WILDE. *London Magazine*, 2 no. 2 (February 1955),
71-78. Review of *Son of Oscar Wilde* by Vyvyan Holland.

C101     THE HIGHER S.F. *Spectator*, 194 (11 February 1955), 160, 162.
Review of *Best S.F.: Science Fiction Stories*, edited by Edmund
Crispin.

C102     O POWIÉSCI ANGIELSKIEJ [ON THE ENGLISH
NOVEL]. *Wiadomości*, 13 February 1955, p. 4. Review of *The
English Novel: A Short Critical History* by Walter Allen. [Trans-
lated into Polish.]

C103     IMAGES OF HORROR: THE UNKNOWN AND FAMILIAR.
*Times Literary Supplement*, 25 February 1955, Special Section,
"Detective Fiction," pp. iii-iv. Unsigned.

C104     GREAT CATHERINE. *Spectator*, 194 (4 March 1955), 261-262.
Review of *The Memoirs of Catherine the Great*, edited by
Dominique Maroger.

C105     THE COCKNEY AND THE JEW. *Observer*, 20 March 1955,
p. 8. Review of *Working-Class Anti-Semite: A Psychological Study
in a London Borough* by James H. Robb.

C106     LADIES OF DEVONSHIRE HOUSE. *Spectator*, 194 (1 April
1955), 410, 412. Review of *Dearest Bess* by D.M. Stuart and *Three
Howard Sisters*, edited by Maud, Lady Leconfield.

C107    THE LADDER OF CLASS. *Observer*, 24 April 1955, p. 15.
Review of *English Social Differences* by T.H. Pear.

C108    THE FIRES OF VIOLENCE. *Encounter*, 4 no.5 (May 1955),
75-78. Review of *Night Rider* by Robert Penn Warren.

C109    HER SHIP CAME HOME. *Evening Standard*, 9 May 1955,
p. 19. Story.

Reprinted: *Did It Happen? Stories*. London: Oldbourne, 1956,
pp. 211-216 (*see* B65).

C110    FULL-BLOODED HERO. *Observer*, 15 May 1955, p. 17.
Review of *Alexandre Dumas* by André Maurois.

C111    HUMANIST. *Observer*, 22 May 1955, p. 16. Review of *The Crisis
of Our Time* by H. Idris Bell.

C112    FLIGHT TO NOWHERE. *Encounter*, 4 no. 6 (June 1955),
73-74, 76. Review of *Utopian Fantasy* by Richard Gerber.

C113    CLARITY OF VISION. *Spectator*, 194 (3 June 1955), 711.
Review of *A Train of Powder* by Rebecca West.

C114    ITALIAN SHORT STORIES. *Spectator*, 194 (10 June 1955),
748. Review of *Modern Italian Short Stories*, selected and edited by
W.J. Strachan.

C115    GIANT AND MYSTIC. *Observer*, 26 June 1955, p. 21. On *A
Glastonbury Romance* by John Cowper Powys.

C116    IVY COMPTON-BURNETT. *London Magazine*, 2 no. 7 (July
1955), 64-70.

Reprinted: *The Art of I. Compton-Burnett: A Collection of Critical Essays*. Ed. Charles Burkhart. London: Gollancz, 1972,
pp. 129-136 (B40).

Reprinted: *Diversity and Depth in Fiction*, 1983.

C117    THE NAIVE EMANCIPATOR. *Encounter*, 5 no. 1 (July 1955),
73-76. Review of *The Genius and the Goddess* by Aldous Huxley.

Reprinted as: Aldous Huxley. *Diversity and Depth in Fiction*, 1983.

C118    SCIENCE FICTION. *Spectator*, 195 (8 July 1955), 64-65.
Review of *The Currents of Space* by Isaac Asimov, *Hellflower* by

George O. Smith, *Angelo's Moon* by Alec Brown, *Utopia 239* by Rex Gordon, *White August* by John Boland and *Mrs Seaward's Secret Weapon* by Leonard Wibberley.

C119    THE SOVIET STYLE. *Observer*, 17 July 1955, p. 8. Review of *The Ninth Wave* by Ilya Ehrenburg.

C120    HOGARTH. *Spectator*, 195 (22 July 1955), 129-130. Review of *Hogarth's Progress* by Peter Quennell.

C121    THE HOUSE PARTY NOVELS. *London Magazine*, 2 no. 8 (August 1955), 53-56. On *Crome Yellow* and *Those Barren Leaves* by Aldous Huxley.

C122    TO KNOW AND YET NOT TO FEAR REALITY. *Encounter*, 5 no. 2 (August 1955), 79-82. Review of *The Opposing Self* by Lionel Trilling.

C123    LABOUR IN VAIN. *Observer*, 7 August 1955, p. 8. Review of *The Life of J.-K. Huysmans* by Robert Baldick.

C124    "ONE OF US." *Spectator*, 195 (26 August 1955), 284-285. Review of *Elinor Glyn* by Anthony Glyn.

C125    THIS GENTL'D ISLE. *Encounter*, 5 no. 3 (September 1955), 84-87. Review of *Exploring English Character* by Geoffrey Gorer.

C126    WORLD'S GREATEST MUSEUM. *Holiday* (New York), September 1955, pp. 48, 50-52, 54-55, 93. On the British Museum.

C127    STUDIES IN CIVILITY. *Observer*, 4 September 1955, p. 11. Review of *Good Behaviour* by Harold Nicolson.

C128    JAZZMAN. *Spectator*, 195 (9 September 1955), 342. Review of *The Trouble with Cinderella* by Artie Shaw.

C129    EXPERIMENTAL. *Observer*, 23 October 1955, p. 13. Review of *The Psychological Novel, 1900-1950* by Leon Edel.

C130    KING OF BEASTS. *Observer*, 6 November 1955, p. 10. Review of *Zola* by Armand Lanoux.

C131    A RETICENT BIOGRAPHY. *Observer*, 13 November 1955, p. 10. Review of *Rudyard Kipling* by Charles Carrington.

C132    THE CAPEL LETTERS. *Spectator*, 195 (18 November 1955), 679-680. Review of *The Capel Letters*, edited by the Marquess of Anglesey.

C133    NEW SHORT STORIES. *New Statesman and Nation*, ns 50 (19 November 1955), 679-680. Review of *A Beginning* by Walter de la Mare, *The Bride of the Innisfallen* by Eudora Welty and *The Daffodil Sky* by H.E. Bates.

C134    AT THE HEART OF LAWRENCE. *Encounter*, 5 no. 6 (December 1955), 81-83. Review of *D.H. Lawrence* by F.R. Leavis.

   Reprinted as: Lawrence and Leavis. *Diversity and Depth in Fiction*, 1983.

C135    TWO LADIES. *Spectator*, 195 (2 December 1955), 772-773. Review of *Alicella* by Averil Stewart.

C136    MRS PECKOVER'S SKY. *Evening Standard*, 13 December 1955, p. 19. Story.

C137    SCHOLAR-CRITIC. *Observer*, 18 December 1955, p. 10. Review of *All in Due Time* by Humphry House.


### 1956

C138    EXORCISING THE PAST. *Encounter*, 6 no. 1 (January 1956), 86-88. Review of *The Expansion of Elizabethan England* by A.L. Rowse.

C139    BEAVERBROOK. *Encounter*, 6 no. 2 (February 1956), 88-90. Review of *Beaverbrook: A Study in Power and Frustration* by Tom Driberg.

C140    THE ANGLO-SAXON WORLD. *New Statesman and Nation*, ns 51 (11 February 1956), 159-160. Review of *An Introduction to Anglo-Saxon England* by Peter Hunter Blair.

C141    THE OTHER BROWNING. *Observer*, 12 February 1956, p. 11. Review of *Victorian Eton and Cambridge* by H.E. Wortham.

C142    SUFFERING. *Observer*, 26 February 1956, p. 11. Review of *I Am Fifteen and I Do Not Want To Die* by Christine Arnothy.

C143    A LADY OF THE THEATRE. *Vogue*, March 1956, pp. 140-141, 223. Extract from *Anglo-Saxon Attitudes*, pp. 46-49.

C144    THE SCHOLAR IN THE PANTRY. *Encounter*, 6 no. 3 (March 1956), 76-78. Review of *The Domestic Servant Class in Eighteenth Century England* by J. Jean Hecht.

C145    REASSESSMENTS: GALSWORTHY'S *Forsyte Saga*. *New Statesman and Nation*, ns 51 (3 March 1956), 187.

Reprinted as: Galsworthy's *Forsyte Saga*. *Diversity and Depth in Fiction*, 1983.

C146    THE NOVELIST AND THE THEATRE. *Observer*, 18 March 1956, p. 16. On the divorce between English novelists and the theatre.

C147    NOVELS AND HIGHBROWS. *Encounter*, 6 no. 4 (April 1956), 75-77. Review of *Dickens and His Readers* by George H. Ford.

C148    A PASTORAL POET. *Observer*, 8 April 1956, p. 13. Review of *John Clare: His Life and Poetry* by John and Anne Tibble.

C149    TOO WIDE A NET. *New Statesman and Nation*, ns 51 (21 April 1956), 426-427. Review of *The Hero in Eclipse in Victorian Fiction* by Mario Praz.

C150    MR PRIESTLEY AS ESSAYIST. *Observer*, 22 April 1956, p. 12. Review of *All About Ourselves* by J.B. Priestley.

C151    *London Magazine*, 3 no. 5 (May 1956), 69-71. On *Confessions of Felix Krull* by Thomas Mann.

C152    SOUND MAN'S SCRAPBOOK. *Observer*, 27 May 1956, p. 13. Review of *Life Since 1900* by Charles Furth.

C153    WHEN EUROPE TREMBLED. *Encounter*, 6 no. 6 (June 1956), 91-93. Review of *The Lisbon Earthquake* by T.D. Kendrick.

C154    A GENERATION OF POUJADISTS? *Observer*, 1 July 1956, p. 11. Review of *Time and Place* by George Scott.

C155    SUCCESS STORY. *Observer*, 15 July 1956, p. 9. Review of *The George Eliot Letters*, Vols. IV-VII, edited by Gordon S. Haight.

C156    NEW NOVELS. *Encounter*, 7 no. 2 (August 1956), 83-88. Review of *Disquiet and Peace* by William Cooper, *Lucy Crown* by Irwin Shaw, *The Self-Educated* by David Stacton, *The Pillar of Salt* by Albert Memmi and *Turn to the Dark* by A.S. Mopeli-Paulus.

C157    FACETIAE. *Observer*, 12 August 1956, p. 9. Review of *The Funny Bone* by J. Maclaren-Ross.

C158    WHERE DO WE GO FROM HERE? *Observer*, 26 August 1956, p. 9. Review of *The New Outline of Modern Knowledge*, edited by Alan Pryce-Jones.

C159    BURIED TREASURE. *Observer*, 30 September 1956, p. 12. Review of *Recent Archaeological Excavations in Britain*, edited by R.L.S. Bruce-Mitford.

C160    A. D. 1956. *Encounter*, 7 no. 4 (October 1956), 80-83. Review of *An Historian's Approach to Religion* by Arnold Toynbee.

C161    HER EXCELLENCY. *Observer*, 14 October 1956, p. 17. Review of *Clare Booth Luce: Ambassador Extraordinary* by Alden Hatch.

C162    OFF THE RAILS. *Observer*, 25 November 1956, p. 12. Review of *Lady Mary Wortley Montagu* by Robert Halsband.

C163    THE LIVING DEAD—IV. BERNARD SHAW. *London Magazine*, 3 no. 12 (December 1956), 53-58. Review of *Bernard Shaw: His Life, Work and Friends* by St John Ervine.

C164    SUICIDES IN LONDON. *Encounter*, 7 no. 6 (December 1956), 82, 84-85. Review of *Suicide in London* by Peter Sainsbury.

C165    LIGHT ON LAWRENCE. *Observer*, 16 December 1956, p. 10. Review of *The Dark Sun* by Graham Hough.

C166    THE DRINK PROBLEM. *The Compleat Imbiber* (Gilbey Vintners Ltd), Christmas 1956, pp. 4, 6.

## 1957

C167    AN ODDITY OFF STAGE. *New Statesman and Nation*, ns 53 (26 January 1957), 109-110. Review of *Margaret the First* by Douglas Grant.

C168   PASSION & IRONY. *Observer*, 27 January 1957, p. 13. Review of *The Collected Stories of Isaac Babel*.

C169   A CHURCH OF COMPROMISE. *Encounter*, 8 no. 2 (February 1957), 81-83. Review of *Past Finding Out* by G.K. Balleine.

C170   A MEDIEVAL MATERIALIST. *Observer*, 10 February 1957, p. 12. Review of *The Merchant of Prato* by Iris Origo.

C171   TOIL AND TROUBLE. *New Statesman and Nation*, ns 53 (2 March 1957), 282. Review of *A Mirror of Witchcraft* by Christina Hole.

C172   PRIVATE PASSIONS. *Observer*, 3 March 1957, p. 14. Review of translations of Emile Zola's *The Abbé Mouret's Sin*, *A Love Affair*, *The Beast in Man* and *Doctor Pascal*.

C173   A CENTURY OF JAPANESE WRITING. *Encounter*, 8 no. 4 (April 1957), 83-85. Review of *Modern Japanese Literature*, edited by Donald Keene.

C174   SKETCH OF A SUPERMAN. *Observer*, 7 April 1957, p. 16. Review of *Honoré de Balzac* by Herbert J. Hunt.

C175   PICKINGS. *New Statesman and Nation*, ns 53 (13 April 1957), 491-492. Review of *The Twenties* by John Montgomery.

C176   SCHOLAR AND KING. *Observer*, 12 May 1957, p. 17. Review of *Alfred the Great and His England* by Eleanor Duckett.

C177   THE INSECT HUNTER. *Observer*, 26 May 1957, p. 16. Review of *Things Worth While* by Evelyn Cheesman.

C178   CIGARS & BRANDY. *Observer*, 9 June 1957, p. 12. Review of *The Prince of Storytellers* by Robert Standish.

C179   THE SEX WAR. *Encounter*, 9 no. 1 (July 1957), 84-86. Review of *Votes for Women* by Roger Fulford.

C180   UNKNOWN DICKENS. *Observer*, 21 July 1957, p. 13. Review of *Dickens at Work* by John Butt and Kathleen Tillotson.

C181   MORE FRIEND THAN LODGER. *New Yorker*, 10 August 1957, pp. 28-34, 36, 38, 43-46, 48, 50-55. Story.

Reprinted: *A Bit Off The Map*, 1957; *Death Dance*, 1969.

C182    ONCE A LADY. *New Yorker*, 31 August 1957, pp. 23-29. Story.

Reprinted: *A Bit Off The Map*, 1957; *Death Dance*, 1969.

C183    MEDIEVAL TAPESTRY. *Observer*, 1 September 1957, p. 12.
Review of *The Devil's Brood* by Alfred Duggan.

C184    BEST SELLERS OF THE CENTURY—1: SEX AND SNOB-
BERY. *Observer*, 6 October 1957, p. 13. Review of *The Green Hat*
by Michael Arlen.

C185    PROTEST MEETING. *Observer*, 13 October 1957, p. 18.
Review of *Declaration*, edited by Tom Maschler.

C186    A CONVERSATION WITH E.M. FORSTER. *Encounter*, 9 no.
5 (November 1957), 52-57.

C187    THE REVOLT OF SAMUEL BUTLER. *Atlantic* (Boston),
November 1957, pp. 190, 192, 194, 196, 198.

C188    DUMAS: FATHER AND SON. *Observer*, 3 November 1957,
p. 17. Review of *Three Musketeers: A Study of the Dumas Family* by
André Maurois.

C189    SOUND AND FURY. *Observer*, 24 November 1957, p. 18.
Review of *Warwick the Kingmaker* by Paul Murray Kendall.

C190    SOME JAPANESE OBSERVATIONS—II. *Encounter*, 9 no.
6 (December 1957), 51-55.

Reprinted as: Some Japanese Observations. *Reflections in a Writer's Eye*, 1986.

C191    TEN MINUTES TO TWELVE. *Esquire* (New York), December
1957, pp. 162, 164-166, 168, 169, 171. Story.

Reprinted from: *A Bit Off The Map*, 1957.

C192    CRITICAL ANGLES. *Observer*, 8 December 1957, p. 17.
Review of *Joseph Conrad* by Thomas Moser and *Joseph Conrad
and His Characters* by Richard Curle.

C193    L'ECRIVAIN DANS L'ANGLETERRE D'AUJOURD'HUI.
*Les Nouvelles littéraires* (Paris), 12 décembre 1957, pp. 1, 7.
[Translated into French by Christine Lalou.]

## 1958

C194    NEW NOVELS. *Observer*, 26 January 1958, p. 16. Review of *A Letter to Elizabeth* by Bettina Linn, *The Man on the Rock* by Francis King, *Leave Me Alone* by David Karp and *On the Last Day* by Mervyn Jones.

C195    JUNGLE WORLD. *Observer*, 9 February 1958, p. 15. Review of *My Face for the World To See* by Alfred Hayes, *The Enemy in the Blanket* by Anthony Burgess, *The Feast of Lupercal* by Brian Moore and *The Assize of Dying* by Edith Pargeter.

C196    DEATH IN LIFE. *Observer*, 23 February 1958, p. 17. Review of *The Dark Tower* by Ernst Pawel, *In Deep* by Bernard Wolfe, *The Miscreant* by Jean Cocteau and *A Love Affair in Rome* by Ercole Patti.

C197    NEW NOVELS. *Observer*, 9 March 1958, p. 16. Review of *Spinster* by Sylvia Ashton-Warner, *The Malefactor* by Humphrey Slater, *Orders of Chivalry* by Peter Vansittart and *The Actress* by Bessie Breuer.

C198    NEW NOVELS: EGOIST-IDEALIST. *Observer*, 23 March 1958, p. 16. Review of *The Changeling* by Robin Jenkins, *The Birth of a Grandfather* by May Sarton and *The Untrodden Snow* by Denise Robins.

C199    MOOD OF THE MONTH—III. *London Magazine*, 5 no. 4 (April 1958), 40-44. On status and the writer in contemporary England.

C200    NEW NOVELS: A JEW AMONG GENTILES. *Observer*, 6 April 1958, p. 14. Review of *The Intruder* by Adriaan van der Veen, *The Hard Man* by W.J. White, *Teddy Boy* by Ernest Ryman and *The Blockhouse* by Jean-Paul Clébert.

C201    BACK TO GALSWORTHY. *Observer*, 13 April 1958, p. 17. Review of *By Love Possessed* by James Gould Cozzens.

C202    NEW NOVELS: JANE AUSTEN IN JAPAN. *Observer*, 27 April 1958, p. 17. Review of *The Makioka Sisters* by Junichiro Tanizaki, *The Setting Sun* by Osamu Dazai and *Victors and Vanquished* by Francis Stuart.

C203    BEXHILL AND AFTER. *Spectator*, 200 (9 May 1958), 583-584.
On Wilson's school days.

C204    NEW NOVELS: TWO KINDS OF WITCH-HUNT. *Observer*,
11 May 1958, p. 17. Review of *Ten Years After* by Herbert
Steinhouse and *The Director* by Alan Thomas.

C205    NEW NOVELS: A SCHOOL FOR SCANDAL. *Observer*, 25
May 1958, p. 16. Review of *Special Friendships* by Roger
Peyrefitte, *The Monkey Puzzle* by Veronica Hull, *The Mountain Is
Young* by Han Suyin and *Papa, You're Crazy* by William Saroyan.

C206    NEW NOVELS: THE APPRENTICE EMPEROR. *Observer*, 8
June 1958, p. 17. Review of *The Young Caesar* by Rex Warner,
*Things Fall Apart* by Chinua Achebe, *Bonfire* by Nicolette Devas
and *Water Music* by Bianca Van Orden.

C207    NEW NOVELS: THROUGH CHILDHOOD'S EYES. *Observer*, 22 June 1958, p. 17. Review of *No Bedtime Story* by Mary
Crawford, *An End and a Beginning* by James Hanley, *The Visitors*
by Mary McMinnies and *Close Quarters* by Angela Thirkell.

C208    NIGHT AND DAY IN TOKYO. *Lilliput*, 43 no. 1 (July 1958),
36, 38-39, 76-77.

Reprinted: *Reflections in a Writer's Eye*, 1986.

C209    NEW NOVELS: MORAVIA: HEIR TO ZOLA. *Observer*, 6 July
1958, p. 17. Review of *Two Women* by Alberto Moravia, *The
Happy Warriors* by Halldor Laxness, *Gather No Moss* by Sean
O'Hanlon and *Sheldrake* by Michael Wharton.

C210    NEW NOVELS: ANCIENT & MODERN. *Observer*, 20 July
1958, p. 15. Review of *Son of Dust* by H.F.M. Prescott, *Flight to
Afar* by Alfred Andersch, *Clerks in Lowly Orders* by Stuart
Mitchel, *The Wilderness* by R.H. Ward and *Life at Happy Knoll* by
J.P. Marquand.

C211    THE JOLLIEST RESORT IN THE WORLD. *Holiday* (New
York), August 1958, pp. 46, 48-49, 116-117, 119.

Reprinted: *Reflections in a Writer's Eye*, 1986.

C212    NEW NOVELS. *Observer*, 3 August 1958, p. 10. Review of *The
Law* by Roger Vailland, *Mackerel Plaza* by Peter De Vries, *Mary*

*Ann* by Alex Karmel, *Two Lakes* by Winston Brebner and *Matters of Concern* by Stanley Wade Baron.

C213    DIVERSITY AND DEPTH. *Times Literary Supplement*, 15 August 1958, Special Section, "Books in a Changing World," p. viii.

Reprinted: *Diversity and Depth in Fiction*, 1983.

C214    A TOTAL VIEW OF CULTURE. *Observer*, 19 October 1958, p. 21. Review of *Culture and Society, 1780-1950* by Raymond Williams.

C215    THE ENGLISH CHURCH. *Observer*, 23 November 1958, p. 15. Review of *Collins Guide to English Parish Churches*, edited by John Betjeman.

C216    PLAYBOYS OF THE WESTERN WORLD. *Observer*, 14 December 1958, p. 15. Review of performances of *West Side Story* and *The Bright One*.

C217    AT THE THEATRE: PANTO PLEASURES. *Observer*, 21 December 1958, p. 11. Review of performances of the Christmas pantomime *Cinderella*, *Who's Your Father* by Denis Cannan and Douglas Seale's productions of *Macbeth* and *Two For the See-Saw*.

C218    AT THE THEATRE: CHILDREN'S HOURS. *Observer*, 28 December 1958, p. 7. Review of performances of three Christmas pantomimes: *The Sleeping Beauty*, *Peter Pan* and *Babes in the Wood*.

## 1959

C219    AT THE THEATRE: BEATING THE BOOM. *Observer*, 4 January 1959, p. 13. Review of performances of *Billy Bunter's Mystery Christmas*, *The Christmas Carol*, *King Charming*, *The Silver King* and *Radio Rescue*.

C220    AT THE THEATRE: RELUCTANT KILLERS. *Observer*, 11 January 1959, p. 17. Review of performances of *The Long and the Short and the Tall* by Willis Hall and *Eighty in the Shade* by Clemence Dane.

C221    MIDDLE-CLASS MORALITY. *Observer*, 25 January 1959, p. 17. Review of performance of *The Woman on the Stair* by James Parish.

C222    AT THE THEATRE: CHARADES AND REVOLUTION. *Observer*, 1 February 1959, p. 17. Review of performances of *Valmouth*, adapted by Sandy Wilson, *Madame de . . .* and *Traveller Without Luggage* by Jean Anouilh and *Danton's Death* by Anton Buchner.

C223    AT THE THEATRE: THE LITERARY VIEW. *Observer*, 8 February 1959, p. 19. Review of performance of *Prince Genji* by William Cooper.

C224    AT THE THEATRE: FROM LANCASHIRE TO THE WEST END. *Observer*, 15 February 1959, p. 19. Review of performances of *A Taste of Honey* by Shelagh Delaney, *Sganarelle* and *Tartuffe* by Molière and Ibsen's *An Enemy of the People*, adapted by Arthur Miller.

C225    NABOKOV'S BASEMENT. *Spectator*, 202 (20 March 1959), 412. Review of *Nabokov's Dozen* by Vladimir Nabokov.

C226    STRINDBERG IN A COMIC VEIN. *Observer*, 22 March 1959, p. 25. Review of *The People of Hemso* by August Strindberg.

C227    REALIST OR ROMANTIC? *Observer*, 26 April 1959, p. 23. Review of *Balzac's "Comédie Humaine"* by Herbert J. Hunt.

C228    FREEDOM OF THOUGHT. *Observer*, 31 May 1959, p. 25. Review of *The Broken Mirror*, edited by Pawel Mayewski.

C229    THE INTELLECTUAL ON THE AISLE. *Encounter*, 12 no. 6 (June 1959), 68-70. Review of *Sights and Spectacles* by Mary McCarthy.

C230    MAN OF LETTERS. *Spectator*, 202 (12 June 1959), 861. Review of *Edward Marsh* by Christopher Hassall.

C231    THE TWO FACES OF JAPAN. *Observer*, 28 June 1959, p. 21. Review of *Thousand Cranes* by Yasunari Kawabata and *No Longer Human* by Osamu Dazai.

C232    AT SCHOOL TOGETHER, AS YOU MIGHT SAY. *Trifler* (Westminster School), July 1959, pp. 13-15.

C233 WEST END REBIRTH. *New York Times*, 2 August 1959, Sect. 2, p. 1. On the British theatre scene.

C234 THE MAN BEHIND THE MASK. *Observer*, 9 August 1959, p. 10. Review of *The Psychology of the Actor* by Yoti Lane and *I Know the Face but . . .* by Peter Bull.

C235 FULFILMENT IN TIME. *Observer*, 20 September 1959, p. 22. Review of *Marcel Proust: A Biography* by George D. Painter.

C236 NEW PLAYWRIGHTS. *Partisan Review* (New York), 26 (Fall 1959), 631-634. Review of *A Taste of Honey* by Shelagh Delaney, *New English Dramatists: Each His Own Wilderness* by Doris Lessing, *The Hamlet of Stepney Green* by Bernard Kops and *Chicken Soup with Barley* by Arnold Wesker.

C237 ROOM AT THE TOP-ISM. *Spectator*, 203 (2 October 1959), 435. Contribution to a symposium entitled "X Marks the Spot: Election Comments by Kingsley Amis, E.M. Forster, Lord Beveridge, Christopher Hollis, Wolf Mankowitz, Angus Wilson, Evelyn Waugh, Trog."

C238 HARROD AND HERO-WORSHIP. *Spectator*, 203 (9 October 1959), 479-480. Review of *The Prof* by R.F. Harrod.

C239 MERELY A NOVELIST. *Observer*, 25 October 1959, p. 23. Review of *Marcel Proust* by Richard H. Barker.

C240 THE FLAUBERT-JAMES PARTY LINE. *Guardian*, 27 November 1959, p. 12. Review of *Novelists on the Novel*, edited by Miriam Allott.

Reprinted as: The Flaubert-James Line. *Manchester Guardian Weekly*, 3 December 1959, p. 11.

C241 THE TERNAN AFFAIR. *Observer*, 29 November 1959, Christmas Books section, pp. 1-2. Review of *Dickens Incognito* by Felix Aylmer.

## 1960

C242 WAUGH'S KNOX. *Encounter*, 14 no. 1 (January 1960), 78-80. Review of *Ronald Knox* by Evelyn Waugh.

Reprinted: *Evelyn Waugh: The Critical Heritage*. Ed. Martin

Stannard. London: Routledge & Kegan Paul, 1984, pp. 405-408 (B61).

C243    AESTHETE IN JAPAN. *Observer*, 3 January 1960, p. 16. Review of *Bridge of the Brocade Sash* by Sacheverell Sitwell.

C244    LAYABOUT. *Spectator*, 204 (8 January 1960), 46. Review of *Stand on Me* by Frank Norman.

C245    BOVARY IN ITALY. *Observer*, 17 January 1960, p. 21. Review of *The Wayward Wife* by Alberto Moravia.

C246    RESCUING THE WORKERS. *Spectator*, 204 (29 January 1960), 140-141. Review of *Weekend in Dinlock* by Clancy Sigal.

C247    HORROR BELOW THE QUARTERDECK. *Observer*, 31 January 1960, p. 20. Review of *Joseph Conrad* by Jocelyn Baines.

C248    ALBERT CAMUS, HUMANIST. *Spectator*, 204 (26 February 1960), 293.

Reprinted as: Albert Camus. *Diversity and Depth in Fiction*, 1983.

C249    AMERICANS IN BRITAIN. *Esquire* (New York), March 1960, pp. 24, 26, 28, 32.

C250    GOOD COMPANION. *Listener*, 63 (3 March 1960), 405-406. Review of *Literature and Western Man* by J.B. Priestley.

C251    GOING TO GROUND. *Observer*, 13 March 1960, p. 20. Review of *A Hermit Disclosed* by Raleigh Trevelyan.

C252    *London Magazine*, 7 no. 4 (April 1960), 71-73. Review of *The Picaresque Saint* by R.W.B. Lewis and *Camus* by Germaine Brée.

C253    DIVINE IDIOT. *Observer*, 10 April 1960, p. 21. Review of *A Voice from the Cell* by Saverio Montalto.

C254    FOR GENTILES. *Spectator*, 204 (22 April 1960), 586-587. Review of *The Jews in Our Time* by Norman Bentwich.

C255    ANTI-BOURGEOIS LEGEND. *Encounter*, 14 no. 5 (May 1960), 74-75. Review of *The Dandy* by Ellen Moers.

C256 NEW WOMAN. *Spectator*, 204 (6 May 1960), 668-669. Review of *Nancy Astor* by Maurice Collis.

C257 MAN IN THE MIRROR. *Observer*, 5 June 1960, p. 19. Review of *Journal of a Man of Letters* by Paul Léautaud.

C258 FALLING BETWEEN TWO STOOLS. *Observer*, 12 June 1960, p. 27. Review of *Mr Love and Justice* by Colin MacInnes.

C259 CHARLES DICKENS: A HAUNTING. *Critical Quarterly* (Hull), 2 (Summer 1960), 101-108.

Reprinted: *The Dickens Critics*. Ed. George H. Ford and Lauriat Lane. Ithaca: Cornell University Press, 1961; London: Oxford University Press, 1962, pp. 374-385 (B17).

Reprinted: *Diversity and Depth in Fiction*, 1983.

C260 ANGLO-AFRICAN ATTITUDES. *Trifler* (Westminster School), July 1960, pp. 9-10.

C261 THE PULPIT AND THE COLUMN. *Observer*, 3 July 1960, p. 26. Review of *Dean Inge* by Adam Fox.

C262 NO ONE THERE. *Spectator*, 205 (22 July 1960), 138. Review of *A Bundle of Sensations* by Goronwy Rees.

C263 PAPERBACK CHOICE: BEFORE THE CRACK-UP. *Observer*, 31 July 1960, p. 21. Review of *Memoirs of a Fox-Hunting Man* by Siegfried Sassoon.

C264 PALESKIN'S REDFACE. *Encounter*, 15 no. 2 (August 1960), 82-83. Review of *Apologies to the Iroquois* by Edmund Wilson.

C265 PICTURES OF HEALTH. *Observer*, 14 August 1960, p. 20. Review of *For Love or Money* by Richard Rees.

C266 CHORUS OF LOVE-HATE. *Observer*, 28 August 1960, p. 26. Review of *Alienation*, edited by Timothy O'Keefe and *The Pleasures of Exile* by George Lamming.

C267 VISION, VISION! MR WOODCOCK! *New Statesman*, 60 (3 September 1960), 298, 300. On how trade unions could help the arts in Britain.

## 1961

C268    NEW CATALOGUE FOR BRITISH MUSEUM LIBRARY. *Canadian Library* (Ottawa), 17 (January 1961), 182-183. Broadcast talk (*see* G31).

C269    SOUTH AFRICA THROUGH THE WHITE MAN'S EYES. *Sunday Telegraph*, 19 February 1961, p. 4.

Reprinted with C270 as: South Africa—A Visit to My Mother's Land. *Reflections in a Writer's Eye*, 1986.

C270    SOUTH AFRICA THROUGH THE WHITE MAN'S EYES— II. AFRIKANER BACKS TO THE WALL. *Sunday Telegraph*, 5 March 1961, p. 5.

C271    THE STATUS OF S.F. *Observer*, 12 March 1961, p. 28. Review of *New Maps of Hell* by Kingsley Amis.

C272    COUNTY COMPANIONS. *Observer*, 23 April 1961, p. 31. Review of *Suffolk: A Shell Guide* by Norman Scarfe and *Suffolk* by Nikolaus Pevsner.

C273    NOVELIST'S CHOICE. *Times*, 15 June 1961, p. 17. On Wilson's reading habits.

C274    A CRITIC IN UTOPIA. *Observer*, 25 June 1961, p. 25. Review of *A Clean, Well-Lighted Place* by Kathleen Nott.

C275    THE HEROES AND HEROINES OF DICKENS. *Review of English Literature*, 2 (July 1961), 9-18.

Reprinted: *Dickens and the Twentieth Century*. Ed. John Gross and Gabriel Pearson. London: Routledge & Kegan Paul, 1962, pp. 3-11 (B22).

C276    IF IT'S NEW AND MODISH IS IT GOOD? *New York Times Book Review*, 2 July 1961, pp. 1, 12.

Reprinted as: A Plea Against Fashion in Writing. *Moderna Sprak* (Stockholm), 55 (1961), 345-350.

Reprinted as: Against New Orthodoxies. *Books and Bookmen*, 7 no. 6 (March 1962), pp. 10-11, 13.

Reprinted as: There's a Tyrant in the Critic's Corner. *Opinions and Perspectives from "The New York Times Book Review"*. Ed.

Francis Brown. Boston: Houghton Mifflin—Riverside Press, 1964, pp. 222-229 (B26).

Reprinted as: Letter from London. *Diversity and Depth in Fiction*, 1983.

C277    THE BROTHER'S STORY. *Observer*, 23 July 1961, p. 20. Review of *Branwell Brontë* by Winifred Gérin.

C278    IDEALOGY AND THE NOVEL. *Guardian*, 28 July 1961, p. 7. Review of *Politics and the Novel* by Irving Howe.

Reprinted: *Manchester Guardian Weekly*, 3 August 1961, p. 10.

C279    THE LAST AMATEURS. *Listener*, 66 (3 August 1961), 181. Review of *The Garnett Family* by Carolyn Heilbrun.

C280    OUTSIDER ON OLYMPUS. *Observer*, 22 August 1961, p. 18. Review of *The Imagination of Charles Dickens* by A.O.J. Cockshut.

C281    MY HUSBAND IS RIGHT. *Texas Quarterly* (Austin), 4 no. 3 (Autumn 1961), 139-145. Fragment from *Goat and Compasses*, an unfinished novel.

C282    THE WHITES IN SOUTH AFRICA. *Partisan Review* (New York), 28 (September 1961), 612-632.

C283    CHAMPAGNE WITH ROSE. *New Statesman*, 62 (15 September 1961), 351. Review of *Saying Life: The Memoirs of Sir Francis Rose*.

C284    RICHNESS IN A NARROW PLACE. *Observer*, 17 September 1961, p. 30. Review of *The Mighty and Their Fall* by Ivy Compton-Burnett.

C285    THE LIVES OF THE SAINTS OF SARSAPARILLA. *Observer*, 29 October 1961, p. 30. Review of *Riders in the Chariot* by Patrick White.

C286    *London Magazine*, ns 1 no. 9 (December 1961), 89, 91-92. Review of *The Last Hours of Sandra Lee* by William Sansom.

C287    VICTORIANS AT SCHOOL. *Observer*, 3 December 1961, p. 29. Review of *Godliness and Good Learning: Four Studies on a Victorian Ideal* by David Newsome.

C288    THE SEVEN DEADLY SINS: I—ANGUS WILSON ON ENVY. *Sunday Times*, 10 December 1961, p. 25.

Reprinted: *The Seven Deadly Sins*. Angus Wilson et al. London: Sunday Times Publications, 1962, pp. 2-11; London and New York: Morrow, 1962, pp. 2-11 (B20).

Reprinted: Freeport, NY: Books for Libraries Press, 1970, pp. 2-11.

1962

C289    FOURTEEN POINTS. *Encounter*, 18 no. 1 (January 1962), 10-12. Things that have angered Wilson.

C290    SOUTH AFRICAN EXILES. *Observer*, 21 January 1962, p. 31. Review of *Guilty Land* by Patrick van Rensburg and *White Madam* by Myrna Blumberg.

C291    KEEPING IN TOUCH. TELEVISION. *Queen*, 30 January 1962, p. 11.

C292    ACADEMIC CROSSFIRE ON THE NOVEL. *Observer*, 4 February 1962, p. 31. Review of *The Moral and the Story* by Ian Gregor and Brian Nicholas.

C293    KEEPING IN TOUCH. TELEVISION. *Queen*, 6 February 1962, p. 11.

C294    KEEPING IN TOUCH. TELEVISION. *Queen*, 13 February 1962, p. 13.

C295    KEEPING IN TOUCH. TELEVISION. *Queen*, 20 February 1962, p. 11.

C296    KEEPING IN TOUCH. TELEVISION. *Queen*. 27 February 1962, p. 17.

C297    VIEWS OF THE DAMNED. *Observer*, 4 March 1962, p. 30. Review of *Down There on a Visit* by Christopher Isherwood.

C298    KEEPING IN TOUCH. TELEVISION. *Queen*, 6 March 1962, p. 11.

C299    KEEPING IN TOUCH. TELEVISION. *Queen*, 13 March 1962, p. 17.

C300    BEAVERBROOK'S ENGLAND. *New Statesman*, 63 (16 March 1962), 374. Review of *Courage* by Lord Beaverbrook.

C301    SKELETONS AND ASSEGAIS: FAMILY REMINIS-CENCES. *Transatlantic Review* (London—New York), 9 (Spring 1962), 19-43. Radio drama. *See also* G10.

C302    UTOPIES. *Cahier des Saisons* (Paris), no. 29 (printemps 1962), 415-416. Contribution to "Portrait de Jean-Louis Curtis." On *Un Saint au néon*. [Translated into French by Gabriel Vascaux.]

C303    MARY, QUITE CONTRARY. *Encounter*, 18 no. 6 (June 1962), 71-72. Review of *On the Contrary* by Mary McCarthy.

C304    WHO CARES? *Guardian*, 8 June 1962, p. 6. Review of *An Unofficial Rose* by Iris Murdoch.

Reprinted as: Love Among the Old Roses. *Manchester Guardian Weekly*, 14 June 1963, p. 11.

C305    KEEPING IN TOUCH. TELEVISION. *Queen*, 12 June 1962, p. 13.

C306    A POSITIVE ANSWER TO COMMUNISM. *Observer*, 17 June 1962, p. 25. Review of *The Strangled Cry* by John Strachey.

C307    KEEPING IN TOUCH. TELEVISION. *Queen*, 19 June 1962, p. 11.

C308    KEEPING IN TOUCH. TELEVISION. *Queen*, 26 June 1962, p. 11.

C309    KEEPING IN TOUCH. TELEVISION. *Queen*, 3 July 1962, p. 17.

C310    GENIUS FROM THE LOWER DEPTHS. *Observer*, 8 July 1962, p. 24. On *A Daughter of the Snows* and *The People of the Abyss* by Jack London.

C311    KEEPING IN TOUCH. TELEVISION. *Queen*, 10 July 1962, p. 11.

C312   NOT FOR BANNING. *New Statesman*, 64 (13 July 1962), 50-51. Review of *To Deprave and Corrupt*, edited by John Chandos.

C313   KEEPING IN TOUCH. TELEVISION. *Queen*, 17 July 1962, p. 9.

C314   SOCIAL REFORM AND MR SCROOGE. *Observer*, 5 August 1962, p. 14. Review of *Dickens and Crime* by Philip Collins.

C315   KEEPING IN TOUCH. TELEVISION. *Queen*, 7 August 1962, p. 10.

C316   KEEPING IN TOUCH. TELEVISION. *Queen*, 15 August 1962, p. 14.

C317   RICHES OF THE SPHINX. *Observer*, 19 August 1962, p. 17. Review of *The Little Ottleys* by Ada Leverson.

C318   KEEPING IN TOUCH. TELEVISION. *Queen*, 21 August 1962, p. 9.

C319   KEEPING IN TOUCH. TELEVISION. *Queen*, 28 August 1962, p. 11.

C320   THE THEATRE OF THREE OR FOUR. *Listener*, 68 (30 August 1962), 327. Review of *The Essay Prize* by John Bowen.

C321   THE TRAGIC VIEW OF LIFE. *Observer*, 16 September 1962, p. 22. Review of *Sprightly Running* by John Wain. *See also* C383.

C322   PRIESTLEY LOOKS BACK. *Observer*, 23 September 1962, p. 28. Review of *Margin Released* by J.B. Priestley.

C323   KEEPING IN TOUCH. TELEVISION. *Queen*, 25 September 1962, p. 21.

C324   KEEPING IN TOUCH. TELEVISION. *Queen*, 2 October 1962, p. 21.

C325   KEEPING IN TOUCH. TELEVISION. *Queen*, 9 October 1962, p. 33.

C326   KEEPING IN TOUCH. TELEVISION. *Queen*, 16 October 1962, p. 29.

C327    KEEPING IN TOUCH. TELEVISION. *Queen*, 23 October 1962, pp. 25-26.

C328    JOHN COWPER POWYS. *New Statesman*, 64 (26 October 1962), 588.

C329    THE MIDDLE-CLASS PASSENGER. *Observer*, 28 October 1962, p. 27. Review of *Ship of Fools* by Katherine Anne Porter.

C330    KEEPING IN TOUCH. TELEVISION. *Queen*, 30 October 1962, p. 17.

C331    KEEPING IN TOUCH. TELEVISION. *Queen*, 6 November 1962, p. 21.

C332    INSIDE YOUNG ENGLAND. *Observer*, 11 November 1962, p. 25. Review of *Sum Total* by Ray Gosling.

C333    KEEPING IN TOUCH. TELEVISION. *Queen*, 13 November 1962, p. 18.

C334    JUDGMENTS ON GENIUS. *Observer*, 25 November 1962, p. 29. Review of *Dostoevsky: A Life* by David Magarshack, *The Undiscovered Dostoevsky* by Ronald Hingley and *Dostoevsky: A Self-Portrait* by Jessie Coulson.

C335    KEEPING IN TOUCH. TELEVISION. *Queen*, 27 November 1962, p. 14.

C336    KEEPING IN TOUCH. TELEVISION. *Queen*, 4 December 1962, pp. 21-22.

C337    KEEPING IN TOUCH. TELEVISION. *Queen*, 11 December 1962, pp. 17-18.

C338    EVIL IN THE ENGLISH NOVEL: ANGUS WILSON ON RICHARDSON AND JANE AUSTEN. *Listener*, 68 (27 December 1962), 1079-1080. The first in a series of four broadcast talks based on Wilson's Northcliffe Lectures at University College, London, 1961. *See also* G56.

Reprinted (with minor revisions) with C342, C344 and C346 as: Evil in the English Novel. *Kenyon Review* (Gambier, OH), 29 (March 1967), 167-194.

Reprinted: *Diversity and Depth in Fiction*, 1983 (reprint from *Kenyon Review*).

## 1963

C339    GOING INTO EUROPE: SYMPOSIUM (II). *Encounter*, 20 no. 1 (January 1963), 53-64 (63). On the Common Market.

C340    "MYTHOLOGY" IN JOHN COWPER POWYS'S NOVELS. *Review of English Literature*, 4 (January 1963), 9-20.

Reprinted as: John Cowper Powys: "Mythology." *Diversity and Depth in Fiction*, 1983.

C341    QUICK CUES. TV. *Queen*, 2 January 1963, pp. 12-14.

C342    EVIL IN THE ENGLISH NOVEL: FROM GEORGE ELIOT TO VIRGINIA WOOLF. *Listener*, 69 (3 January 1963), 15-16. Second in a series of four broadcast talks. *See also* G57.

C343    THE BRITISH MUSEUM: DILEMMA OF A 19TH CENTURY TREASURE HOUSE. *Sunday Times Colour Section*, 6 January 1963, pp. 1-3, 6, 8, 10, 14.

C344    EVIL IN THE ENGLISH NOVEL: OUTSIDE THE CENTRAL TRADITION. *Listener*, 69 (10 January 1963), 63-65. Third in a series of four broadcast talks. *See also* G58.

C345    QUICK CUES. TV. *Queen*, 16 January 1963, pp. 14-15.

C346    EVIL IN THE ENGLISH NOVEL: EVIL AND THE NOVELIST TODAY. *Listener*, 69 (17 January 1963), 115-117. Last in a series of four broadcast talks. *See also* G60.

C347    LOOKING BACK IN PLEASURE. *Observer*, 20 January 1963, p. 23. Review of *My Life and Times* by Compton Mackenzie.

C348    QUICK CUES. TV. *Queen*, 30 January 1963, pp. 14-15.

C349    QUICK CUES. TV. *Queen*, 13 February 1963, pp. 14-15.

C350    QUICK CUES. TV. *Queen*, 27 February 1963, pp. 21-22.

C351    IMPRESSIONS OF AN EXILE. *Observer*, 31 March 1963, p. 27. Review of *Time of Arrival* by Dan Jacobson.

C352 A NOVELIST'S WORKING NOTEBOOKS. *Guardian*, 5 April 1963, p. 12. Review of *Carnets, 1935-1942* by Albert Camus.

C353 QUICK CUES. TV. *Queen*, 10 April 1963, pp. 38-39.

C354 QUICK CUES. TV. *Queen*, 24 April 1963, pp. 23-24.

C355 FALLACIES ABOUT HOMOSEXUALITY. *Man and Society*, 1 no. 5 (Spring 1963), 16-18.

C356 QUICK CUES. TV. *Queen*, 8 May 1963, pp. 33-34.

C357 QUICK CUES. TV. *Queen*, 22 May 1963, pp. 20-22.

C358 FRIENDS, FOES AND FIDGETS. *Observer*, 26 May 1963, p. 27. Review of *The Sphinx and Her Circle: A Memoir of Ada Leverson* by Violet Wyndham, *Bosie: The Story of Lord Alfred Douglas* by Rupert Croft-Cooke and *Oscar Wilde: The Aftermath* by H. Montgomery Hyde.

C359 TASTE AND SYMPATHY. *Commentary* (New York), 35 (June 1963), 542-544. Review of *Puzzles and Epiphanies* by Frank Kermode.

C360 TW TO THE THIRD POWER. *Show* (New York), June 1963, pp. 18-19. On the BBC programme "That Was The Week That Was."

C361 QUICK CUES. TV. *Queen*, 5 June 1963, pp. 13-15.

C362 THE WORLD OF J.C. POWYS. *Observer*, 23 June 1963, p. 23. Eulogy.

C363 A MOMENT OF CRYSTAL. *Spectator*, 211 (5 July 1963), 22-23. On contemporary Japanese fiction.

C364 THE KNOWING CHILD. *Observer*, 7 July 1963, p. 22 Review of *Selected Writings of Truman Capote* with an introduction by Mark Schorer.

C365 ON A BLACK SEA HOLIDAY WITH MR K. *Daily Express*, 16 August 1963, p. 6.

Reprinted: *Reflections in a Writer's Eye*, 1986.

C366    BLACK SEA NOTEBOOK: WHAT KHRUSHCHEV TOLD THE WRITERS. *Observer*, 18 August 1963, p. 11.

Reprinted as: Russia—What Khrushchev Told the Writers. *Reflections in a Writer's Eye*, 1986.

C367    MYTH-LOVER AND LIFE-LOVER. *Observer*, 11 August 1963, p. 17. Review of *No! In Thunder* by Leslie Fiedler and *Re-Appraisals* by Martin Green.

C368    NEW NOVELS: REBIRTH AND REVIVAL. *Observer*, 25 August 1963, p. 18. Review of *Cat and Mouse* by Günter Grass and *After the Banquet* by Yukio Mishima.

C369    HOW TO LIVE ON YOUR LUCK. *Sunday Telegraph*, 8 September 1963, pp. 4-5. Extract (with additions) from *The Wild Garden*.

C370    FROM WELFARE TO AFFLUENCE. *Observer*, 22 September 1963, p. 24. Review of *The New Look* by Harry Hopkins.

C371    LOOKING FORWARD TO LIFE WITH THE YOUNG ONES. *Daily Express*, 30 September 1963, p. 12.

C372    STATE OF GRACE. *New Statesman*, 66 (11 October 1963), 492-493. Review of *Instead of a Letter* by Diana Athill.

C373    OTHER PEOPLE'S LIVES: A NINETIES BOYHOOD. *Observer*, 13 October 1963, p. 25. Review of *My Life and Times: Octave Two 1891-1900* by Compton Mackenzie.

C374    RECONSTRUCTING OUR YESTERDAYS. *Observer*, 17 November 1963, p. 24. Review of *The Age of Illusion: England in the Twenties and Thirties* by Ronald Blythe.

C375    IL ANNONCE LE NOUVEAU ROMAN. *Le Figaro littéraire* (Paris), 21 novembre 1963, p. 26. Contribution to a symposium entitled "Swann, l'éternel, a cinquante ans" marking the fiftieth anniversary of the publication of Proust's *A la recherche du temps perdu*.

C376    SQUEERS AND CO. *Observer*, 22 December 1963, p. 16. Review of *Dickens and Education* by Philip Collins.

## 1964

C377   KAM PO LENINGRADU [WHERE TO AFTER LENIN-
GRAD]? *Plamen* (Prague), no. 1 (1964), 146-151 (150-151). On
the International Writers' Conference, Leningrad—Moscow,
Summer 1963. [Translated into Czech.]

Reprinted as: Dialogu wschód-zachód C.D. *Wspólczesność*
(Warsaw), 9 no. 12 (1964), p. 4. [Translated from *Plamen* into
Polish.]

C378   THE CHALLENGE OF KIPLING. *Observer*, 29 March 1964,
p. 23. Review of *Kipling's Mind and Art*, edited by Andrew
Rutherford.

C379   *Transatlantic Review* (London—Princeton—New York), 15
(Spring 1964), 106-108. Review of *City of Night* by John Rechy.

C380   VISIONARY AMONG THE RATIONALISTS. *Observer*, 10
May 1964, p. 26. Review of *Beginning Again* by Leonard Woolf.

C381   MODERN MAN'S BURDEN? *Observer*, 31 May 1964, p. 27.
Review of *Science: The Glorious Entertainment* by Jacques Barzun.

C382   PARTY OF ONE—CONFESSIONS OF A ZOO-LOVER. *Holiday* (New York), June 1964, pp. 12, 16-18, 20, 22.

Reprinted as: Confessions of a Zoo Lover. *Reflections in a Writer's
Eye*, 1986.

C383   MERRIE ENGLAND. *Commentary* (New York), 37 (June 1964),
74-75. Review of *Sprightly Running* by John Wain. *See also* C321.

C384   MIĘDZYNARODOWA ANKIETA *Polityki* [*Polityka*'s International Questionnaire]. *Polityka* (Warsaw), 8 (13 June 1964),
p. 12. Statement on the Frankfurt trial of former Nazis for war-
time activities. [Translated into Polish.]

C385   GARDENS OF EDEN? *Observer*, 5 July 1964, p. 26. Review of
*The English Garden* by Edward Hyams.

C386   PASSIONATE MOCKERY. *Observer*, 19 July 1964, p. 23.
Review of *Chaos and Night* by Henry de Montherlant.

C387   THE DELIGHTS OF ABROAD. *Observer*, 27 September 1964,
p. 24. Review of *Away To It All* by William Sansom.

C388    WAITING FOR THE REAL SADE. *Observer*, 13 December 1964, p. 27. Review of *Justine* by the Marquis de Sade.

C389    BOOKS OF THE YEAR. *Observer*, 20 December 1964, p. 7. Wilson's choices for 1964: *Chaos and Night* by Henry de Montherlant, *The Soul of Kindness* by Elizabeth Taylor and *Modern Houses of the World* by Sherban Cantacuzino.

# 1965

C390    THE CONDITION OF THE NOVEL. *New Left Review*, no. 29 (January-February 1965), 19-40 (35-36). Statement made at the International Writers' Conference, Leningrad-Moscow, Summer 1963.

C391    DICKENS'S PRIVATE VOICE. *Observer*, 14 February 1965, p. 27. Review of *The Letters of Charles Dickens, 1820-1839*, Vol. 1, edited by Madeline House and Graham Storey and *Dickens from Pickwick to Dombey* by Steven Marcus.

C392    ZOLA BEFORE, DURING AND AFTER. *Times Literary Supplement*, 8 April 1965, p. 272. Review of *Zola Before the Rougon-Macquart* by John C. Lapp, *The Naturalist Novel* by Emile Zola, edited by Maxwell Geismar and *Pages d'exil* by Emile Zola, edited by Colin Burns. Unsigned.

C393    MRS THIRKELL IN EXILE. *Observer*, 18 April 1965, p. 26. Review of *The Road to Gundagai* by Graham McInnes.

C394    THE HORROR GAME. *Observer*, 30 May 1965, p. 27. Review of *Cabot Wright Begins* by James Purdy.

C395    SENSE AND SENSITIVITY. *Observer*, 27 June 1965, p. 22. Review of *A Dedicated Man* by Elizabeth Taylor and *A Day in the Dark* by Elizabeth Bowen.

C396    TRAVELLING COMPANIONS. *Observer*, 8 August 1965, p. 20. Review of *The Companion Guide to Venice* by Hugh Honour and *The Companion Guide to Rome* by Georgina Masson.

C397    INTELLECTUALS ON TAPE. *Observer*, 29 August 1965, p. 21. Review of *Under Pressure* by A. Alvarez.

C398    WHY DO I BOTHER? *Christian Action Journal*, Autumn 1965, pp. 2-5.

C399    LABOUR'S FIRST YEAR: A REVIEW OF THE GOVERN-MENT'S RECORD. *New Statesman*, 70 (15 October 1965), 557.

C400    JOURNEY TO JERUSALEM. *Observer*, 17 October 1965, p. 28. Review of *The Mandelbaum Gate* by Muriel Spark.

C401    BLOOD-BROTHERS AND SCARECROWS. *Observer*, 7 November 1965, p. 27. Review of *Dog Years* by Günter Grass and *A Wilderness of Mirrors* by Max Frisch.

        Reprinted in part as: Günter Grass. *Diversity and Depth in Fiction*, 1983.

C402    CLASS-ROOM DISTINCTIONS. *Observer*, 5 December 1965, p. 27. Review of *Dr Moberly's Mint-Mark* by Christopher Dilke, *Westminster School* by John Carleton and *The Manchester Grammar School*, edited by J.A. Graham and B.A. Phythian.

C403    TEAROOMS AND COTTAGES. *New Statesman*, 70 (10 December 1965), 936-937. Review of *Selected Letters* by Mark Gertler.

C404    BOOKS OF THE YEAR. *Observer*, 19 December 1965, p. 22. Wilson's choices for 1965: *The Companion Guide to Venice* by Hugh Honour, *The War of the Roses* by J.R. Lander and *The Looking Glass War* by John Le Carré.


                                1966

C405    THE ARTIST AS YOUR ENEMY IS YOUR ONLY FRIEND. *Southern Review* (Adelaide), 2 (1966), 101-114.

C406    GEORGE. *Adam International Review*, 31 nos. 310-312 (1966), 120-122. On George D. Painter.

C407    TROPICAL GREENE. *Guardian*, 28 January 1966, p. 8. Review of *The Comedians* by Graham Greene.

        Reprinted: *Manchester Guardian Weekly*, 3 February 1966, p. 10.

C408    TRAGI-COMEDY FROM AFRICA. *Observer*, 30 January

1966, p. 27. Review of *A Man of the People* by Chinua Achebe and *African English Literature: An Anthology*, edited by Anne Tibble.

C409 INSIGHTS INTO ISHERWOOD. *Observer*, 20 March 1966, p. 26. Review of *Exhumations* by Christopher Isherwood.

C410 MAKING WITH THE METAPHYSICS. *Observer*, 1 May 1966, p. 27. Review of *The Magus* by John Fowles.

Reprinted as: Fowles's Foul Fantasy. *Critic (Chicago)*, 25 (August-September 1966), 50-51.

C411 MOSAIC OF ITALIAN LIFE. *Observer*, 15 May 1966, p. 27. Review of *That Awful Mess on Via Merulana* by Carlo Emilio Gadda.

C412 SPEAKING OUT: ONLY FOOLS LAUGH AT THEIR WOES. *Saturday Evening Post* (New York), 21 May 1966, pp. 12, 16.

C413 SYMPHONY OF A THOUSAND PAGES. *Observer*, 12 June 1966, p. 26. Review of *Miss Mackintosh, My Darling* by Marguerite Young.

C414 FLORENCE-WORSHIP. *Observer*, 17 July 1966, p. 23. Review of *The Companion Guide to Florence* by Eve Borsook.

C415 RED PAINT AND SAWDUST. *Observer*, 11 September 1966, p. 27. Review of *The Decline of the West* by David Caute.

C416 EROS DENIED IN THE BRITISH MUSEUM. *Observer*, 16 October 1966, p. 26. Review of *Private Case—Public Scandal* by Peter Fryer.

C417 THE UNIVERSAL NOVELIST. *Observer*, 6 November 1966, p. 27. Review of *Tolstoy and the Novel* by John Bayley.

C418 BOOKS OF THE YEAR: SOME PERSONAL CHOICES. *Observer*, 18 December 1966, p. 23. Wilson's choices for 1966: *That Awful Mess on Via Merulana* by Carlo Emilio Gadda, *Italo Svevo* by P.N. Furbank and *A Roman Marriage* by Brian Glanville.

## 1967

C419    COSMOPOLITAN PAPERBACKS. *Observer*, 5 February 1967, p. 26. Review of *The New Writing in the U.S.A.*, edited by Donald Allen and Robert Creeley; *German Writing Today*, edited by Christopher Middleton; *Italian Writing Today*, edited by Raleigh Trevelyan; and *African Writing Today*, edited by Ezekiel Mphahlele.

C420    CHERRY OR BILBERRY PIE? *Observer*, 26 February 1967, p. 27. Review of *Class*, edited by Richard Mabey; *The Left*, edited by Gerald Kaufmann; *Confrontations with Judaism*, edited by Philip Longworth; and *The Computer in Society* by Brian Murphy.

C421    FEMININE IN-FIGHTER. *Observer*, 2 April 1967, p. 27. On *Pilgrimage* by Dorothy M. Richardson.

Reprinted as: Dorothy Richardson's *Pilgrimage*. *Diversity and Depth in Fiction*, 1983.

C422    CLASSIC OF THE RURAL PAST. *Observer*, 9 April 1967, p. 27. Review of *Fenland Chronicle* by Sybil Marshall.

C423    BETWEEN TWO ISLANDS. *Observer*, 30 April 1967, p. 27. Review of *The Mimic Men* by V.S. Naipaul.

C424    LOWER DEPTHS OF LITERATURE. *Observer*, 21 May 1967, p. 27. Review of *New Grub Street* by George Gissing.

Reprinted: *George Gissing: Critical Essays*. Ed. Jean-Pierre Michaux. London: Vision Press, 1981; New York: Barnes & Noble, 1981, pp. 123-125 (B54).

Reprinted as: Gissing's *New Grub Street*. *Diversity and Depth in Fiction*, 1983.

C425    PURDY PUSHES COMEDY PAST BLACKNESS. *Life* (New York), 2 June 1967, p. 8. Review of *Eustace Chisholm and the Works* by James Purdy.

C426    THE HUMANISM OF BECKETT. *Observer*, 16 July 1967, p. 20. Review of *No's Knife, Come and Go* and *Eh, Joe* by Samuel Beckett, *Samuel Beckett's Art* by John Fletcher and *Beckett at Sixty: A Festschrift*.

C427   NOVELIST AS CLUBMAN. *Observer*, 22 October 1967, p. 30. Review of *My Brother Evelyn and Other Profiles* by Alec Waugh.

C428   THE ICEMAN COMETH. *Observer*, 17 December 1967, p. 20. Review of *Henrik Ibsen* by Michael Meyer.

C429   CHARACTER AND THE NOVEL. *Nineteenth-Century Fiction* (Berkeley—Los Angeles), 22 (1967-1968), 195-199. Review of *Character and the Novel* by W.J. Harvey.

## 1968

C430   NOT ALL PURE MARAT-SADE. *Observer*, 3 March 1968, p. 29. Review of *Intellectuals Today* by T.R. Fyvel.

C431   EXPATRIATE EXTRAVAGANZA. *Observer*, 7 April 1968, p. 24. Review of *Tunc* by Lawrence Durrell.

C432   IN THE JANE AUSTEN TRADITION. *Observer*, 28 April 1968, p. 28. Review of *The Wedding Group* by Elizabeth Taylor.

C433   JANE AUSTEN BETWEEN THE LINES. *Observer Magazine*, 2 June 1968, pp. 23-24, 26-27, 29.

C434   THE TWO FACES OF BLOOMSBURY. *Observer*, 2 June 1968, p. 27. Review of *Bloomsbury* by Quentin Bell.

C435   THE HISTORICAL APPROACH. *Observer*, 21 July 1968, p. 22. Review of *The Victorian Debate* by Raymond Chapman.

C436   INVOLVEMENT: WRITERS REPLY. *London Magazine*, ns 8 no. 5 (August 1968). 5-19 (15-16).

C437   AUTOPSY ON A LONELY HEART. *Observer*, 22 September 1968, p. 30. Review of *My Father and Myself* by J.R. Ackerley.

C438   SEXUAL REVOLUTION. *Listener*, 80 (10 October 1968), 457-460. Broadcast talk (*see* G101).

C439   THE PURSUIT OF EVIL. *Observer*, 27 October 1968, p. 29. Review of *Poor Clare* by L.P. Hartley and *L.P. Hartley: The Collected Short Stories*.

C440    BOOKS OF THE YEAR: A PERSONAL CHOICE. *Observer*,
22 December 1968, p. 17. Wilson's choices for 1968: *The Armies of
the Night* by Norman Mailer, *Between* by Christine Brooke-Rose
and *Something To Answer For* by P.H. Newby.


## 1969


C441    IS THE NOVEL A DOOMED ART FORM? *English Literature
and Language* (Tokyo), 6 (1969), 1-31.

C442    POOR BIG RICH GIRL. *Observer*, 26 January 1969, p. 27.
Review of *Eva Trout* by Elizabeth Bowen.

C443    HOW THE OTHER HALF LIVED. *Observer*, 16 February
1969, p. 29. Review of *Charles Booth's London*, edited by Albert
Fried and Richard M. Ellman.

C444    GENTLEMEN AND PLAYERS. *Observer*, 18 May 1969, p. 30.
Review of *The Rise and Fall of the Man of Letters* by John Gross.

C445    EAST ANGLIAN ATTITUDES. *Observer*, 1 June 1969, p. 27.
Review of *Akenfield* by Ronald Blythe.

C446    IVY COMPTON-BURNETT. *Observer*, 31 August 1969, p. 20.
Eulogy.

Reprinted: *The Art of I. Compton-Burnett: A Collection of Critical
Essays*. Ed. Charles Burkhart. London: Gollancz, 1972, pp.
192-194 (B40).

C447    CITATIONS. *UEA Bulletin* (University of East Anglia,
Norwich), ns 1 no. 6 (September 1969), 124-148. Citations for
honorary degrees conferred upon Robert Ketton-Cremer, Sir
Nikolaus Pevsner, Sir Hugh Greene, Professor Charles Coulson
and Sir Alec Issigonis delivered by Wilson as Public Orator of the
University of East Anglia at the Congregation of June 1969.

C448    A NOVELIST FOR ALL SEASONS. *Observer*, 23 November
1969, p. 31. Review of *Charles Dickens: A Centenary Volume*,
edited by E.W.F. Tomlin; *The Letters of Charles Dickens,
1840-1841*, Vol. 2, edited by Madeline House and Graham Storey;
and *The Uncollected Writings of Charles Dickens*, edited by Harry
Stone.

C449 A NOVELIST'S PROGRESS. *Observer*, 14 December 1969, p. 30. Review of *Joyce Cary* by Malcolm Foster.

C450 BOOKS OF THE YEAR: A PERSONAL CHOICE. *Observer*, 21 December 1969, p. 17. Wilson's choices for 1969: *Eva Trout* by Elizabeth Bowen, *The Rise and Fall of the Man of Letters* by John Gross and *The New S.F.*, edited by Langdon Jones.

## 1970

C451 CULTURE AND CLASSLESSNESS. *Observer*, 1 March 1970, p. 33. Review of *Speaking To Each Other: About Society*, Vol. I; *About Literature*, Vol. II by Richard Hoggart.

C452 PEKING TO FIESOLE. *Observer*, 19 April 1970, p. 30. Review of *More Memoirs of an Aesthete* by Harold Acton.

C453 LIFE STUDIES. *Guardian*, 30 April 1970, p. 9. Review of *The English Novel from Dickens to Lawrence* by Raymond Williams.

Reprinted: *Manchester Guardian Weekly*, 9 May 1970, p. 18.

C454 PER I 70 ANNI DI SILONE. *Il Dramma* (Rome), 46 no. 5 (maggio 1970), 71-83 (83). Statement on the novels of Ignazio Silone on his 70th birthday. [Translated into Italian.]

C455 THE MACABRE WORLD OF YOUNG DICKENS. *Observer Magazine*, 17 May 1970, pp. 24-25. Pre-publication extract from *The World of Charles Dickens*, pp. 21-23, 27-30.

C456 CHARLES DICKENS: A FAILED MIDDLE-CLASS MARRIAGE. *Observer Magazine*, 24 May 1970, pp. 37-38, 41-43. Pre-publication extract from *The World of Charles Dickens*, pp. 248, 251-256.

C457 LIGHT AND DARK IN DICKENS. *Listener*, 83 (28 May 1970), 701-703. Broadcast talk (*see* G108).

C458 COURAGE AND CUNNING. *Observer*, 31 May 1970, p. 31. Review of *You Must Know Everything* by Isaac Babel.

C459 FIRST OF THE MODERNS? *Observer*, 21 June 1970, p. 31. Review of *George Meredith and English Comedy* by V.S. Pritchett and *The Letters of George Meredith*.

C460    DES VERITES POUR NOTRE SIECLE. *Le Monde* (Paris), 13
        juillet 1970, Supplement, p. IV. On Charles Dickens. [Translated
        into French by Marion Fabré.]

C461    MOLARS AND INCISORS. *Observer*, 19 July 1970, p. 24.
        Review of *Local Anaesthetic* by Günter Grass.

        Reprinted as: Günter Grass. *Diversity and Depth in Fiction*, 1983.

C462    DICKENS AND DOSTOEVSKY. *Dickensian*, 66 (September
        1970), Supplement, 41-61. *See also* B35.

        Reprinted: *Diversity and Depth in Fiction*, 1983.

C463    SEX IN NEVER NEVER LAND. *Observer*, 20 September 1970,
        p. 27. Review of *J.M. Barrie* by Janet Dunbar and *The Bright
        Twenties* by Cecil Roberts.

C464    IN THE GREAT TRADITION. *Observer*, 18 October 1970,
        p. 34. Review of *Dickens the Novelist* by F.R. and Q.D. Leavis.

C465    RIGHT ABOUT TURN. *Observer*, 22 November 1970, p. 30.
        Review of *What Became of Jane Austen?* by Kingsley Amis.

C466    BOOKS OF THE YEAR. *Observer*, 20 December 1970, p. 17.
        Wilson's choices for 1970: *Trespasses* by Paul Bailey, *Troubles* by
        J.G. Farrell and *The Big Dig* by Michael Orsler.


## 1971

C467    CHARLES DICKENS TODAY. *Adam International Review*, 35,
        nos. 346-348 (1971), 11-14.

C468    THE HEART OF EDITH DOMBEY. *Dickensian*, 67 (January
        1971), 45-47. Review of *The Moral Art of Dickens* by Barbara
        Hardy.

C469    IN DARKEST EAST ANGLIA. *Observer*, 10 January 1971,
        p. 27. Review of *Where Beards Wag All* by George Ewart Evans.

C470    THE FIRST AND THE LAST. *Observer*, 7 February 1971,
        p. 26. Review of *Dolores* and *The Last and The First* by Ivy
        Compton-Burnett.

C471    AESTHETE WITH A SWORD. *Observer*, 14 March 1971, p. 36. Review of *Sun and Steel* by Yukio Mishima.

C472    VISITOR'S LONDON. *Illustrated London News*, May 1971, pp. 31, 33-34. Extract from Introduction, *England* (B38).

C473    LM and KM. *Observer*, 4 July 1971, p. 28. Review of *Katherine Mansfield: The Memories of L.M.* [Leslie Moore].

C474    LITTLE NELL AND DERBY DAY. *Dickens Studies Newsletter* (Carbondale, IL), 2 (September 1971), 88-89.

C475    ONE MAN BAND. *Observer*, 10 October 1971, p. 32. Review of *The World of George Orwell*, edited by Miriam Gross.

C476    ISSYVOO AND HIS PARENTS. *Observer*, 24 October 1971, p. 36. Review of *Kathleen and Frank* by Christopher Isherwood.

C477    CONGREGATION 25 JUNE 1971. *UEA Bulletin* (University of East Anglia, Norwich), ns 4 no. 2 (November 1971), 1-16. Citations for honorary degrees conferred upon Professor Frances Yates, Dr Rex Richards, Sir Joseph Hutchinson and Sir John Hicks delivered by Wilson as Public Orator of the University of East Anglia.

C478    BOOKS OF THE YEAR. *Observer*, 19 December 1971, p. 17. Wilson's choices for 1971: *Los Angeles* by Reyner Banham and *The Survival of the English Countryside* by Victor Bonham-Carter.

## 1972

C479    RESPECTABLE AMERICANS. *Observer*, 11 June 1972, p. 29. Review of *In the Village* by Anthony Bailey.

C480    VIRGINIA AMONG THE WOLVES. *Observer*, 18 June 1972, p. 32. Review of *Virginia Woolf: A Biography*, Vol. I *Virginia Stephen* by Quentin Bell.

C481    BOOKS VERSUS BICEPS. *Observer*, 8 October 1972, p. 39. Review of *The Life To Come and Other Stories* by E.M. Forster.

C482    [CITATIONS.] *UEA Bulletin* (University of East Anglia, Norwich), ns 5 no. 2 (November 1972), 5-20. Citations for

honorary degrees conferred upon Sir Alfred Ayer, Brigadier
Ralph Bagnold, Sir Frederick Dainton and Robert Lowell delivered by Wilson as Public Orator of the University of East Anglia
at the Congregation of June 1972.

C483    RADICAL PARALLELS. *Observer*, 3 December 1972, p. 37.
Review of *The Really Interesting Question and Other Papers* by
Lytton Strachey.

C484    BOOKS OF THE YEAR. *Observer*, 17 December 1972, p. 25.
Wilson's choices for 1972: *The Needle's Eye* by Margaret Drabble
and *The Age of Neo-Classicism*, an exhibition catalogue.

C485    *Iowa Review* (Iowa City), 3 no. 4 (1972), 106-108. Rejected fragment from *As If By Magic*.


## 1973

C486    *Dickensian*, 69 (January 1973), 48-51. Review of *The Mystery of
Edwin Drood* by Charles Dickens, edited by Margaret Cardwell.

C487    ENGLISH INFLUENCE ON LITERATURE IN WESTERN
EUROPE HAS REACHED A LOW EBB. *Times*, 2 January
1973, pp. viii, xi.

C488    THE GLORY THAT WAS GREECE. *Observer*, 7 January
1973, p. 34. Review of *The Greek Revival* by J. Mordaunt Crook.

C489    LOCAL COLOUR. *Observer*, 21 January 1973, p. 34. Review of
*Aldeburgh Anthology*, edited by Ronald Blythe; *The Suffolk Land-
scape* by Norman Scarfe and *The Restless Ocean* by Neville
Blackburne.

C490    ROMANTIC MATERIALIST. *Observer*, 11 March 1973, p. 36.
Review of *The Wizard of the North* by Carola Oman.

C491    HOMAGE TO FIRBANK. *Observer*, 1 April 1973, p. 37.
Review of *Prancing Novelist* by Brigid Brophy.

C492    A SELF-MADE HEROINE. *Observer*, 20 May 1973, p. 36.
Review of *Dorothy Richardson: The Genius They Forgot* by John
Rosenberg.

C493    PUTTING US IN THE PICTURE. *Observer*, 29 July 1973,

p. 32. Review of *Courbet: The Studio of the Painter* by Benedict Nicolson and *Watteau: A Lady at Her Toilet* by Donald Posner.

C494 FOR THE NATION. *Observer*, 5 August 1973, p. 27. Review of *The National Trust Guide*, edited by Robin Fedden and Rosemary Joekes.

C495 A GIFT FOR WORDS AND HUMBUG. *New York Times Book Review*, 19 August 1973, pp. 3-4. Review of *G.K. Chesterton* by Dudley Barker.

C496 A MESSAGE FROM OUR NEW PRESIDENT. *Dickensian*, 69 (September 1973), 193-194. Message to the Dickens Fellowship.

C497 THE MAGIC AGE. *Vogue* (New York), 1 September 1973, pp. 290-291, 338, 340-341. Pre-publication extract from *As If By Magic*, pp. 143-154.

C498 CITIES OF DREADFUL NIGHT? *Observer*, 2 September 1973, p. 35. Review of *The Victorian City: Images and Realities*, edited by H.J. Dyos and Michael Wolff.

C499 BEATON'S JUNGLE BOOK. *Books and Bookmen*, 19 no. 1 (October 1973), 30-31. Review of *The Strenuous Years: Diaries 1945-55* by Cecil Beaton.

C500 MORALITY UNDER THE MICROSCOPE. *New Statesman*, 86 (26 October 1973), 602-603. Review of *Samuel Richardson: Dramatic Novelist* by Mark Kinkead-Weekes.

C501 A HIGH TALENT FLOGGING AN OLD GENRE. *New York Times Book Review*, 11 November 1973, p. 6. Review of *The Riverside Villas Murder* by Kingsley Amis.

C502 [CITATIONS.] *UEA Bulletin* (University of East Anglia, Norwich), ns 6 no. 2 (December 1973), 6-29. Citations for honorary degrees conferred upon Professor Cyril Clarke, Timothy Colman, Sir Gordon Cox, Professor J.H. Plumb and Claude Simon (*see also* A21). Delivered by Wilson as Public Orator of the University of East Anglia at the Congregation of June 1973.

C503 THE DRUID OF WESSEX. *Observer*, 2 December 1973, p. 34. Review of *John Cowper Powys* by Glen Cavaliero, *The Demon Within* by John A. Brebner and *Weymouth Sands* and *Rodmoor* by John Cowper Powys.

C504    BOOKS OF THE YEAR. *Observer*, 16 December 1973, p. 33. Wilson's choices for 1973: *Articles of Faith* by Ronald Hardwood, *A Distant Likeness* by Paul Bailey and *Samuel Richardson: Dramatic Novelist* by Mark Kinkead-Weekes.


## 1974


C505 ʾ   POLITICAL METAPHORS—1. THE POLITICS OF THE FAMILY. *Listener*, 91 (10 January 1974), 40-43 (41-42). *See also* G124.

C506    GRAVES OF ACADEME. *Spectator*, 232 (12 January 1974), 45. Review of *Wild Thyme, Winter Lightning* by Anne Mulkeen.

C507    POLITICAL METAPHORS—2. ART AND THE ESTABLISHMENT. *Listener*, 91 (17 January 1974), 78-80 (78). *See also* G126.

C508    THE LOWER DEPTHS. *Observer*, 3 February 1974, p. 30. Review of *The Born Exile* by Gillian Tindall.

Reprinted as: Gissing's *New Grub Street. Diversity and Depth in Fiction*, 1983.

C509    BATTLE FOR THE BM. *Observer*, 24 February 1974, p. 32. Review of *That Noble Cabinet* by Edward Miller.

C510    INTERNATIONAL CHILDREN'S BOOK DAY MESSAGES. *Horn Book*, 50 (April 1974), 229-230.

C511    CURIOUS PEACH. *Guardian*, 25 April 1974, p. 16. Review of *Conundrum* by Jan Morris.

Reprinted: *Guardian Weekly*, 4 May 1974, p. 22.

C512    PROGRESS DOWN THE MIDDLE. *Observer*, 12 May 1974, p. 37. Review of *From the Diary of a Snail* by Günter Grass.

C513    MONTHERLANT'S WORLDS. *New Statesman*, 87 (17 May 1974), 697-698. Review of *The Boys* by Henry de Montherlant, translated by Terence Kilmartin.

C514    FAUNTLEROY'S CREATOR. *Observer*, 2 June 1974, p. 33. Review of *Waiting for the Party: The Life of Frances Hodgson Burnett 1849-1924* by Ann Thwaite.

C515     A MAN FROM THE MIDLANDS. *Times Literary Supplement*, 12 July 1974, pp. 737-738. Review of *Arnold Bennett* by Margaret Drabble.

C516     DICKENS IN AMERICA. *Observer*, 25 August 1974, p. 23. Review of *The Letters of Charles Dickens: 1842-1843*, Vol. 3, edited by Madeline House, Graham Storey and Kathleen Tillotson.

C517     A LADY AND HER LIONS. *Observer*, 1 September 1974, p. 26. Review of *Ottoline at Garsington: Memoirs of Lady Ottoline Morrell*, edited by Robert Gathorne-Hardy.

C518     THE MYSTICAL YEARS. *Observer*, 15 September 1974, p. 28. Review of *Aldous Huxley: 1939-1963*, Vol. 2 by Sybille Bedford.

C519     VICTORIAN MORALITY. *Observer*, 17 November 1974, p. 33. Review of *Scholar Extraordinary* by Nirad C. Chaudhuri.

C520     THE GREAT CHAM. *Observer*, 24 November 1974, p. 33. Review of *Samuel Johnson* by John Wain.


## 1975

C521     DOSTOEVSKY REINSTATED. *Observer*, 26 January 1975, p. 29. Review of *Dostoevsky* by Leonid Grossman.

C522     [CITATIONS.] *UEA Bulletin* (University of East Anglia, Norwich), ns 7 no. 1 (February 1975), 5-32. Citations for honorary degrees conferred upon Professor Joseph Chatt, Denys Lasdun, Harold Pinter, Professor Guido Pontecorvo and Professor Joan Robinson delivered by Wilson as Public Orator of the University of East Anglia at the Congregation of June 1974.

C523     LOVE IN A COLD CLIMATE. *Observer*, 2 February 1975, p. 29. Review of *The Letters of J.R. Ackerley*, edited by Neville Braybrooke.

C524     ANATOMY OF A VILLAGE. *Observer*, 16 February 1975, p. 30. Review of *The Common Stream* by Rowland Parker.

C525     THE REFERENDUM CHOICE. *New Statesman*, 89 (30 May 1975), 718-719 (719). On Wilson's vote in the Common Market referendum.

C526 THOMAS MANN–ZUM HUNDERSTEN GEBURSTAG. ACHTZEHN ANTWORTEN AUF DIE FRAGEN: WAS BEDEUTET IHNEN THOMAS MANN, WAS VER-DANKEN SIE IHM? *Frankfurter Allgemeine Zeitung* (Frankfurt-am-Main), 31 Mai 1975, *Bilder und Zeiten*, pp. [1-4] ([3]). Statement on the occasion of Mann's centenary. [Translated into German.]

Reprinted as: Die Infragestellung seiner selbst. *Was halten Sie von Thomas Mann? Achtzehn Autoren antworten.* Ed. Marcel Reich-Ranicki. Frankfurt-am-Main: Fischer Taschenbuch Verlag, 1986, pp. 81-82.

C527 THE KIPLING DAEMON. *Observer*, 15 June 1975, p. 30. Review of *Kipling: The Glass, The Shadow and The Fire* by Philip Mason. *See also* C542.

C528 FROM ZULULAND TO BLOOMSBURY. *Observer*, 14 September 1975, p. 25. Review of *The Autobiography of William Plomer*.

C529 THE YOUNG VIRGINIA. *Observer*, 21 September 1975, p. 23. Review of *The Flight of the Mind: The Letters of Virginia Woolf 1888-1912*, edited by Nigel Nicolson; and *Virginia Woolf and Her World* by John Lehmann.

C530 THE EVELYN WAUGH PLAY. *Times Literary Supplement*, 3 October 1975, pp. 1116-1117. Review of *Evelyn Waugh: A Biography* by Christopher Sykes.

Reprinted as: Evelyn Waugh. *Diversity and Depth in Fiction*, 1983.

Reprinted: *Evelyn Waugh: The Critical Heritage.* Ed. Martin Stannard. London: Routledge & Kegan Paul, 1984, pp. 482-489 (B61).

C531 TOUR DE FORCE. *Observer*, 19 October 1975, p. 27. Review of *The Great Railway Bazaar* by Paul Theroux.

C532 FICTION AND THE BOOKER PRIZE. *Bookseller*, 22 November 1975, pp. 2448-2450. Announcement of award to Ruth Prawer Jhabvala for *Heat and Dust*.

C533 DREAMERS OF DREAMS. *Observer*, 23 November 1975, p. 31. Review of *Edward Burne-Jones* by Penelope Fitzgerald, *William Morris* by Jack Lindsay and *Edwardian Architecture*, edited by Alastair Service.

C534    BOOKS OF THE YEAR. *Observer*, 14 December 1975, p. 19. Wilson's choices for 1975: *Heat and Dust* by Ruth Prawer Jhabvala, *Gossip from the Forest* by Thomas Keneally and *The Great Railway Bazaar* by Paul Theroux.

C535    THE EYES OF THE PEACOCK. *Sunday Times Magazine* 14 December 1975, pp. 58-59, 61, 63. Story.

C536    WHICH MISS AUSTEN? *Observer*, 14 December 1975, p. 24. Review of *Jane Austen and the War of Ideas* by Marilyn Butler and *A Reading of Jane Austen* by Barbara Hardy.

C537    RICHARDSON'S *Clarissa*. *Horizon*, no. 17 (Winter 1975), 103-106.

Reprinted: *Diversity and Depth in Fiction*, 1983.


## 1976

C538    *As If By Magic*: ANGUS WILSON ON HIS OWN NOVEL. *Dutch Quarterly Review of Anglo-American Letters* (Assen), 6 (1976), 259-277.

Reprinted: *The Best of the DQR*. Ed. F. G. A. Maarts et al. Amsterdam: Rodopi, 1984 (B59).

C539    ANGUS WILSON ON DICKENS'S INFLUENCE. *Dickensian*, 72 (January 1976), 56-58. Text of banquet speech at 69th annual conference of the Dickens Fellowship, Broadstairs, May 1975.

C540    AN AREA OF PREJUDICE. *Observer*, 25 January 1976, p. 30. Review of *Everywhere Spoken Against* by Valentine Cunningham.

C541    MARY ANN INTO GEORGE. *Observer*, 7 March 1976, p. 27. Review of *George Eliot: The Emergent Self* by Ruby V. Redinger.

C542    *Critic* (Chicago), 34 (Spring 1976), 88-90. Review of *Kipling: The Glass, the Shadow and the Fire* by Philip Mason. *See also* C527.

C543    REMEMBRANCE OF THINGS PAST. *New York Times Book Review*, 11 April 1976, pp. 6-7. Review of *Monsieur Proust* by Céleste Albaret.

C544    ANIMAL MAGNETISM. *Observer*, 2 May 1976, p. 31. Review of *The Ark in the Park* by Wilfred Blunt and *London's Zoo: An Anthology* by Gwynne Vevers.

C545  BLOOMSBURY'S BEST. *Observer*, 6 June 1976, p. 29. Review of *Moments of Being: Unpublished Autobiographical Writings of Virginia Woolf*, edited by Jeanne Schulkind.

C546  HIGH LIVING AND HALITOSIS. *Observer*, 13 June 1976, p. 27. Review of *Ottoline* by Sandra Jobson Darroch.

C547  RETURN TO KIPLING'S INDIA. *Observer Magazine*, 20 June 1976, pp. 23, 25-26, 28, 30.

Reprinted (with additions) as: New and Old on the Grand Trunk Road. *Reflections in a Writer's Eye*, 1986.

C548  JOCK AND ADA. *Observer*, 11 July 1976, p. 23. Review of *John Galsworthy* by Catherine Dupré.

C549  GOODBYE TO SAPPHO. *Observer*, 5 September 1976, p. 23. Review of *Violet Trefusis* by Philippe Jullian and John Phillips.

C550  FUN WITH FACTS. *Observer*, 26 September 1976, p. 25. Review of *The Frank Muir Book* by Frank Muir.

C551  NORMAN'S CONQUESTS. *Observer*, 5 December 1976, p. 30. Review of *Norman Douglas* by Mark Holloway.

C552  BOOKS OF THE YEAR. *Observer*, 12 December 1976, p. 26. Wilson's choices for 1976: *Hotel de Dream* by Emma Tennant, *An Unreasonable Man* by Henrie Mayne and *The Frank Muir Book*.

C553  ALWAYS THERE. *Adam International Review*, 40 nos. 397-400 (1976-1977), 33. On the London Library.

## 1977

C554  THE QUEST FOR ROLFE. *Observer*, 16 January 1977, p. 21. Review of *Frederick Rolfe: Baron Corvo* by Miriam J. Benkovitz.

C555  REPUTATIONS REVISITED. *Times Literary Supplement*, 21 January 1977, pp. 66-67 (66). On the two most over- and under-rated books of the past 75 years.

C556 [Discussion of George Steiner's] "The Difficulties of Reading John Cowper Powys." *Powys Review* (Dyfed), no. 1 (Spring 1977), 11.

C557 JOHN COWPER POWYS AS A NOVELIST. *Powys Review* (Dyfed), no. 1 (Spring 1977), 13-25.

C558 MY OXFORD. *Encounter*, 48 (April 1977), 27-33.

Reprinted: *My Oxford*. Ed. Ann Thwaite. London: Robson, 1977, pp. 91-108 (B48).

C559 NOTTING HILL DREAMER. *Observer*, 3 April 1977, p. 26. Review of *The Condition of Muzak* by Michael Moorcock.

C560 EDNA LYALL SLEPT HERE. *Observer*, 24 April 1977, p. 25. Review of *The Oxford Literary Guide to the British Isles* by Dorothy Eagleton and Hilary Carnell.

C561 THE MODERN BULLY. *Observer*, 15 May 1977, p. 13.

C562 STRANGE BEDFELLOWS. *Observer*, 22 May 1977, p. 28. Review of *Children of the Sun* by Martin Green.

C563 THE APPEAL OF TURGENEV. *Observer*, 26 June 1977, p. 28. Review of *The Gentle Barbarian: The Life and Work of Turgenev* by V.S. Pritchett.

C564 POETRY AND THE PARTY LINE. *Observer*, 24 July 1977, p. 29. Review of *The Spiral Ascent* by Edward Upward.

C565 LIVING AND LOVING. *Observer*, 28 August 1977, p. 24. Review of *Blindness* by Henry Green.

Reprinted as: Henry Green. *Diversity and Death in Fiction*, 1983.

Reprinted: *Twentieth Century Literature* (Hempstead, NY), 29 (Winter 1983), 384-386.

C566 PLAIN MAN'S NOVELIST. Observer, 2 October 1977, p. 27. Review of *Thackeray: Prodigal Genius* by John Carey.

C567 MORAL IMPERATIVES. *Observer*, 13 November 1977, p. 28. Review of *Rebecca West: A Celebration*.

C568 THE RICH TASTE OF AFRICA. *Observer*, 11 December 1977,

p. 28. Review of *First Catch Your Eland* by Laurens van der Post and *The Anthropologist's Cook Book*, edited by Jessica Kuper.

C569 BOOKS OF THE YEAR: OBSERVER CONTRIBUTORS MAKE THEIR ANNUAL CHOICE. *Observer*, 18 December 1977, p. 21. Wilson's choices for 1977: *The Condition of Muzak* by Michael Moorcock and *Rebecca West: A Celebration*.

## 1978

C570 LADY BOUNTIFUL. *Observer*, 8 January 1978, p. 24. Review of *Lady Unknown: The Life of Angela Burdett-Coutts* by Edna Healey.

C571 DICKENS IN THE DOLDRUMS. *Observer*, 2 April 1978, p. 24. Review of *The Letters of Charles Dickens*, Vol. 4, edited by Kathleen Tillotson.

C572 REVALUATIONS. *Observer*, 23 April 1978, p. 30. Comment on the occasion of F.R. Leavis's death.

C573 *Dickensian*, 74 (May 1978), 110-111. Review of *Nicholas Nickleby* by Charles Dickens, edited by Michael Slater.

C574 THE STATE OF FICTION: A SYMPOSIUM. *New Review*, 5 no. 1 (Summer 1978), 14-76 (75-76).

C575 VICTORIAN SPECTACLES. *Observer*, 9 July 1978, p. 26. Review of *A View of Victorian Literature* by Geoffrey Tillotson.

C576 PAINTING AND HISTORY. *Observer*, 6 August 1978, p. 22. Review of *And When Did You Last See Your Father?* by Roy Strong.

C577 STATELY HOMES OF ENGLAND. *Observer*, 3 September 1978, p. 26. Review of *Life in the English Country House* by Mark Girouard, *Longleat* by David Burnett and *Burke's Guide to Country Houses: Ireland*, Vol. 1.

C578 REDISCOVERY OF ZOLA. *Observer*, 1 October 1978, p. 33. Review of *Garden of Zola* by Graham King and *Zola* by Joanna Richardson.

C579    THE BANNED BIOGRAPHY. *Observer*, 8 October 1978, p. 30.
Review of *Rudyard Kipling* by Lord Birkenhead.

C580    THE ALWAYS-CHANGING IMPACT OF VIRGINIA
WOOLF. *Studies in the Literary Imagination* (Atlanta), 11 no. 2
(Fall 1978), 1-9.

Reprinted as: Virginia Woolf (II). *Diversity and Depth in Fiction*,
1983.

C581    BOOKS OF THE YEAR: SOME PERSONAL CHOICES.
*Observer*, 17 December 1978, p. 33. Wilson's choices for 1978: *Life
in the English Country House by* Mark Girouard, *Sorry, Dad* by
Edward Blishen and *Live Bait* by Frank Tuohy.


## 1979

C582    WHAT THE DICKENS! *Observer*, 29 April 1979, p. 36. Review
of *Dickens* by Norman and Jeanne Mackenzie.

C583    EUROPEAN MASTERS. *Observer*, 13 May 1979, p. 37. Review
of *The Myth Makers* by V.S. Pritchett.

C584    BOZ IN THE LAND OF LIBERTY. *Observer*, 15 July 1979,
p. 36. Review of *Dickens on America and the Americans*, edited by
Michael Slater; and *Dickens on England and the English*, edited by
Malcolm Andrews.

C585    THE GULF TO EARL'S COURT. *Observer*, 22 July 1979,
p. 36. Review of *Arabia Through the Looking Glass* by Jonathan
Raban.

C586    DANCE OF DEATH. *Observer*, 30 September 1979, p. 37.
Review of *The Twyborn Affair* by Patrick White.

C587    LITERARY LANDSCAPES. *Observer*, 18 November 1979,
p. 38. Review of *A Writer's Britain* by Margaret Drabble.

C588    BOOKS OF THE YEAR. *Observer*, 9 December 1979, p. 35.
Wilson's choices for 1979: *Arabia Through the Looking Glass* by
Jonathan Raban, *The Twyborn Affair* by Patrick White and *The
Architects of London* by Alastair Service.

## 1980

C589    A HOUSE OF ARCHITECTS. *Observer*, 27 January 1980, p. 39. Review of *The Wyatts: An Architectural Dynasty* by John Martin Robinson.

C590    WONDERS OF THE SOUTH. *Observer*, 24 February 1980, p. 39. Review of *Separate Country* by Paul Binding.

C591    PASSENGERS TO INDIA. *Observer*, 2 March 1980, p. 38. Review of *Karma Cola* by Gita Mehta.

C592    MASTER OF MOCKERY. *Observer*, 20 April 1980, p. 39. Review of *The Shorter Strachey: Selected Essays of Lytton Strachey*, edited by Michael Holroyd and Paul Levy.

C593    A KIWI IN BOHEMIA. *Observer*, 11 May 1980, p. 38. Review of *The Life of Katherine Mansfield* by Anthony Alpers.

C594    RICHARD II AT WESTMINSTER. *Times*, 5 July 1980, p. 6. Pre-publication extract from *Setting the World on Fire*, pp. 35-44.

C595    CASTLES IN THE AIR. *Observer*, 26 October 1980, p. 28. Review of *Edwin Lutyens* by Mary Lutyens.

C596    A BIOGRAPHER IN SEARCH OF HIMSELF. *Michigan Quarterly Review* (Ann Arbor), 19 (Summer 1980), 427-429. Review of *The English Climate* by James Gindin.

C597    SIR ANGUS WILSON RETURNS: AN OLD ADMIRER SALUTES THE U.S.A. *Los Angeles Times*, 8 December 1980, p. V-2. [Syndicated.]

Reprinted as: America — A Celebration. *Reflections in a Writer's Eye*, 1986.

## 1981

C598    A LA RECHERCHE DE MARCEL PROUST. *Observer*, 1 March 1981, p. 31. Review of *Remembrance of Things Past* by Marcel Proust, translated by Terence Kilmartin.

Reprinted as: Pleasures of Proust: Celebrating a Classic—At Its Best. *Vogue* (New York), August 1981, pp. 350-351.

Reprinted as: Marcel Proust. *Diversity and Depth in Fiction*, 1983.

C599 WHEN THE GOING WAS GOOD. *Observer*, 22 March 1981, p. 32. Review of *Abroad* by Paul Fussell.

C600 THE GENESIS OF *Anglo-Saxon Attitudes*. *Books at Iowa* (Iowa City), 34 (April 1981), 3-8.

C601 A TOUCH OF THE PUB. *Observer*, 28 June 1981, p. 32. Review of *The Oxford Book of Short Stories*, edited by V.S. Pritchett.

C602 PARADISE LOST? *Observer*, 26 July 1981, p. 29. Review of *The Victorian Countryside*, edited by G.E. Mingay.

C603 THE MAKING OF A MASTER. *Observer*, 1 November 1981, p. 32. Review of *Flaws in the Glass* by Patrick White.

C604 BOOKS OF THE YEAR. *Observer*, 6 December 1981, p. 25. Wilson's choices for 1981: *Flaws in the Glass* by Patrick White and *Byzantium Endures* by Michael Moorcock.

## 1982

C605 A HANDFUL OF GEMS. *Observer*, 24 January 1982, p. 30. Review of *Katherine Mansfield: The Collected Short Stories*.

C606 A VOYAGE OF DISCOVERY. *Observer*, 14 February 1982, p. 33. Review of *The Wider Sea: A Life of John Ruskin* by John Dixon Hunt.

C607 HANDS ACROSS THE SEA. *Observer*, 7 March 1982, p. 32. Review of *Children of the Empire* by Gillian Wagner.

C608 ANTIQUE ROAD-SHOW. *Observer*, 4 April 1982, p. 32. Review of *Mortimer Wheeler* by Jacquetta Hawkes.

C609 TALES OF THE SOUTH. *Observer*, 30 May 1982, p. 30. Review of *Losing Battles, Delta Wedding* and *The Robber Bridegroom* by Eudora Welty.

C610 A BOOK IN MY LIFE. *Spectator*, 248 (26 June 1982), 29-30. On *The Harp and The Oak* by Hugh Massingham.

C611 RUGBY TO GREYFRIARS. *Observer*, 27 June 1982, p. 31. Review of *The Heirs of Tom Brown* by Isabel Quigly.

C612 MONUMENTS AND MEMORIALS. *Observer*, 18 July 1982, p. 31. Review of *Victorian Sculpture* by Benedict Read.

## 1983

C613 *HIM Monthly*, no. 57 (May 1983), 54. Review of *The Penguin Book of Homosexual Verse*, edited by Stephen Coote.

## 1984

C614 GREENE: FOUR SCORE YEARS AND THEN? Angus Wilson et al. *Times*, 7 September 1984, p. 10. Tribute to Graham Greene on his eightieth birthday.

C615 THE PICARESQUE IMAGINATION OF MICHAEL MOORCOCK. *Washington Post*, 23 December 1984, *Book World*, pp. 1, 13. Review of *The Laughter of Carthage* by Michael Moorcock.

Reprinted: *International Herald Tribune* (Paris), 12-13 January 1985, p. 12.

# D. TRANSLATIONS

## BULGARIAN

*Book:*

D1    *Anglo-saksonski nravi*. Plovdiv: Darzhavnov Izdatelstvo Christo G. Danov, 1986.

A translation by Krasimir Adazhieva and Julia Tosheva of *Anglo-Saxon Attitudes* with an introduction by Mikhail Grincharov.

## CZECHOSLOVAK

*Books:*

D2    *Anglosaský postoj*. Prague: SNKLU, 1960.

A translation by Jarmila Urbánková of *Anglo-Saxon Attitudes* with an afterword by Květa Marysková.

D3    *Svět Charlese Dickense*. Prague: Odeon, 1979.

A translation by Zdeněk Kirschner of *The World of Charles Dickens*.

D4    *Kdo by se taky smál*. Prague: Odeon, 1983.

A translation by Marta Staěková of *No Laughing Matter* with an afterword by Martin Hilský.

# DANISH

*Books:*

D5      "På det gale parti." *Noveller fra radioen*. Ed. Jørgen Claudi and Mogens Knudsen. Copenhagen: Steen Hasselbachs Forlag, 1953, pp. 57-66.

         A translation by Bendix Bech-Thostrup of 'The Wrong Set.'

         Reprinted: *40 dage og naetter: noveller fra radioen*. Copenhagen: Steen Hasselbachs Forlag, 1954.

D6      *Skarn og skarntyde*. Copenhagen: H. Hagerup, 1953.

         A translation by Mogens Boisen of *Hemlock and After*.

# DUTCH

*Books:*

D7      *Dolle kervel*. Amsterdam: De Arbeiderspers, 1954.

         A translation by Otto Nagtzaam of *Hemlock and After*.

D8      "Wat eten nijlpaarden?" *Meesters der engelse vertelkunst*. Amsterdam: J.M. Meulenhoff, 1958.

         A translation by Guus Sötemann of 'What Do Hippos Eat?'

         Reprinted: *Meesters der vertelkunst*. Amsterdam: J.M. Meulenhoff, 1959.

D9      *Het tweede leven van Meg Eliot*. Amsterdam and Antwerp: Uitgeverij Contact, 1960.

         A translation by M[aurits] Mok of *The Middle Age of Mrs Eliot*.

D10     *De oude mannen van de dierentuin*. Amsterdam: Uitgeverij Contact, 1963.

         A translation by M[aurits] Mok of *The Old Men at the Zoo*.

         Reprinted: Amsterdam: Uitgeverij Contact, 1968.

D11     "Inleiding." Sir Arthur Conan Doyle, *De terugkeer van Sherlock Holmes*. Amsterdam: Uitgeverij Contact, 1977.

         A translation by S. Vestdijk of 'Introduction' to *The Return of Sherlock Holmes*.

*Periodicals:*

D12    "Tokio: dag en nacht." *Elegance: Magazine voor mensen met smak* (Amsterdam), 16 no. 11 (november 1959), 66-71.

       A translation of 'Night and Day in Tokyo' (C208).

D13    "Het tweede leven van Meg Eliot." *Het Vrije Volk: Demokratish socialistich dagblad* (Amsterdam), 18 november 1960-6 mei 1961. [143 installments.]

       A translation by M[aurits] Mok of *The Middle Age of Mrs Eliot*.

# ESTONIAN

*Books:*

D14    *Halb seltskond*. Tallinn: Gaz.-Žurn. Izd., 1959.

       A translation by E. Roks of *The Wrong Set and Other Stories*.

D15    *Anglosaksi poosid*. Tallinn: Ėėsti raamat, 1970.

       A translation by Henno Rajandi of *Anglo-Saxon Attitudes*.

# FINNISH

*Book:*

D16    *Epäjumala haudassa*. Porvoo—Helsinki: Werner Söderström Osakeyhtiö, 1957.

       A translation by Mikko Kilpi of *Anglo-Saxon Attitudes*.

# FRENCH

*Books:*

D17    *La Ciguë et après*. Paris: Laffont, 1954.

       A translation by Marie Tadié of *Hemlock and After*.

       Reprinted: Paris: Union Générale d'Editions, 1983; Paris: Laffont, 1984.

D18    *Attitudes anglo-saxonnes*. Paris: Librarie Stock, 1957.

A translation by Claude Elsen of *Anglo-Saxon Attitudes* with an introduction by the translator.

Reprinted: Paris: Union Générale d'Editions, 1983; Paris: Laffont, 1984.

D19   *Les Quarante Ans de Mrs Eliot*. Paris: Stock, 1959.

A translation by Claude Elsen of *The Middle Age of Mrs Eliot*.

Reprinted: Paris: Union Générale d'Editions, 1983; Paris: Laffont, 1984.

D20   *Saturnales et autres nouvelles*. Paris: Librarie Stock, 1960.

A translation by Claude Elsen of selections from *The Wrong Set and Other Stories, Such Darling Dodos and Other Stories* and *A Bit Off the Map and Other Stories* with an introduction by the translator.

Reprinted: Paris: Laffont, 1984.

D21   *La Girafe et les vieillards*. Paris: Librarie Stock, 1963.

A translation by Anne-Marie Soulac of *The Old Men at the Zoo*.

D22   *L'Appel du soir*. Paris: Librarie Stock, 1965.

A translation by Marie-Alyx Revellat of *Late Call*.

Reprinted: Paris: Union Générale d'Editions, 1983; Paris: Laffont, 1984.

D23   *En jouant le jeu*. Paris: Librarie Stock, 1969.

A translation by Jean Autret of *No Laughing Matter*.

D24   *Le Monde de Charles Dickens*. Paris: Gallimard, 1972.

A translation by Suzanne Nétillard of *The World of Charles Dickens*.

D25   *Comme par magie*. Paris: Librarie Stock, 1976.

A translation by Anne-Marie Soulac of *As If By Magic* with an introduction by Raymond LasVergnas.

D26   *Embraser le monde*. Paris: Librarie Stock, 1981.

A translation by Anne-Marie Soulac of *Setting the World on Fire*.

*Periodicals:*

D27   "Zola en anglais." *Preuves* (Paris), no. 21 (novembre 1952), 45-48.

A translation by Christine Lalou of 'Appendix: Zola and His English and American Readers' (A3).

D28   "Saturnale." *Les Lettres Nouvelles* (Paris), 7 ns no. 5 (1 avril 1959), 14-22.

A translation by Claude Elsen of 'Saturnalia.'

D29   "Un peu déboussolé." *La Nouvelle Revue Française* (Paris), 14 (juillet 1959), 8-34.

A translation by Claude Elsen of 'A Bit Off the Map.'

D30   "Que mangent les hippopotames?" *La Revue de Paris*, 66 (aôut 1959), 42-51.

A translation by Claude Elsen of 'What Do Hippos Eat?'

D31   "Albert Camus." *La Nouvelle Revue Française* (Paris), 15 (mars 1960), 545-548.

A translation of 'Albert Camus, Humanist' (C248).

D32   "La Source." *Cahiers des Saisons* (Paris), (hiver 1965), 542-544.

A translation by Léo Dilé of an extract from *The Wild Garden* (A11, pp. 13-16).

D33   "John Cowper Powys." *Granit* (Paris) 1/2 (automne/hiver 1973), 13-15.

A translation by François Xavier Jaujard of 'John Cowper Powys' (C328).

D34   "Journal de Sri Lanka (I)." *Le Promeneur* (Paris), no. 24 (mi-décembre 1983), 13-15.

A translation by Bernard Turle of 'Sri Lankan Journal' (B58).

D35   "Journal de Sri Lanka (II)." *Le Promeneur* (Paris), no. 25 (mi-janvier 1984), 5-10.

A translation by Bernard Turle of 'Sri Lankan Journal' (B58).

# GERMAN

*Books:*

D36 *Späte Entdeckungen.* Wiesbaden: Insel-Verlag, 1957.

A translation by Alexander Koval of *Anglo-Saxon Attitudes.*

Reprinted: Reinbek bei Hamburg: Rowohlt Verlag, 1961; Berlin-Weimar: Aufbau Verlag, 1969, with an afterword by Klaus Schirrmeister; Frankfurt-am-Main: Suhrkamp Verlag, 1984.

D37 *Was für reizende Vögel: Geschichten aus England.* Frankfurt-am-Main: Insel-Verlag, 1958.

A translation by Hilde Spiel and Wolfgang von Einsiedel of selections from *The Wrong Set and Other Stories, Such Darling Dodos and Other Stories* and *A Bit Off the Map and Other Stories.*

Reprinted: Munich: Deutscher Taschenbuch Verlag, 1963.

D38 *Meg Eliot.* Wiesbaden: Insel-Verlag, 1960.

A translation by Helmut Lindemann of *The Middle Age of Mrs Eliot.*

Reprinted: Berlin-Weimar: Aufbau Verlag, 1969.

D39 "Mutters Sinn für Humor." *England Erzählt.* Frankfurt-am-Main: Fischer-Bücherei, 1960.

A translation by Hilde Spiel of 'Mother's Sense of Fun.'

D40 *Mehr Freund als Untermieter: Erzählung.* Frankfurt-am-Main: Insel-Verlag, 1961.

A translation by Hilde Spiel of 'More Friend than Lodger.'

D41 *Die Alten Männer im Zoo.* Frankfurt-am-Main: Insel-Verlag, 1962.

A translation by Peter Stadelmayer of *The Old Men at the Zoo.*

D42 *Später Ruf.* Zurich and Munich: Droemer-Knaur, 1966.

A translation by Ursula von Zedlitz [Ursula Hohenlohe] of *Late Call.*

Reprinted: Zurich and Munich: Droemer-Knaur, 1969; Berlin: Deutsche Buch-Gemeinschaft, 1967; Zurich: Neue Schweizer Bibliothek, 1969.

D43     *Kein Grund zum Lachen*. Zurich and Munich: Droemer-Knaur, 1969.

A translation by Maria Dessauer of *No Laughing Matter*.

* Reprinted: Zurich and Munich: Droemer-Knaur, 1973; Gütersloh: Bertelsmann, 1971; Stuttgart: Europäischer Buch-und-Phonoklub, 1971.

D44     "Rex Imperator." *Erkundungen: 23 englische Erzähler*. Ed. Hans Petersen. Berlin: Verlag Volk und Welt, 1971, pp. 25-38.

A translation by Gisela Petersen of 'Rex Imperator.'

Reprinted: Berlin: Verlag Volk und Welt, 1973.

D45     *England*. Zurich and Freiburg im Breisgau: Atlantis, 1975.

A translation of 'Introduction' to *England* (B38).

D46     *Wie durch Magie*. Zurich and Munich: Droemer-Knaur, 1975.

A translation by Werner Peterich of *As If By Magic*.

Reprinted: Stuttgart: Deutscher Bücherbund, 1976; Munich: Droemer-Knaur, 1976.

D47     *Bruchiges Eis*. Köln-Lövenich: Hohenheim Verlag, 1982.

A translation by Werner Peterich of *Setting the World on Fire*.

Reprinted: Frankfurt-am-Main: Suhrkamp Verlag, 1984.

D48     "Himbeermarmelade." *Shakespeares Muse: moderne Erzähler aus Grosbritannien*. Ed. Frank Auerbach. Stuttgart: Thienemanns, 1983, pp. 82-101.

A translation by Frank Auerbach of 'Raspberry Jam.'

D49     "Höhere Masstäbe." *English Short Stories (2)/Englische Kurzgeschicten (2)*. Munich: Deutscher Taschenbuch Verlag, 1986, pp. 71, 73, 75, 77, 79, 81, 83, 85, 87, 89.

A translation by Theo Schumacher of 'Higher Standards.'

D50     "Realpolitik." *Die englische Literatur in Text und Darstellung: 20. Jahrhundert II* (Band 10). Ed. Raimund Borgmeier and Bernhard Reitz. Stuttgart: Philipp Reclam jun. Verlag, 1986, pp. 357, 359, 361, 363.

A translation by Raimund Borgmeier of 'Realpolitik.'

*Periodicals:*

D51     "Realpolitik."   *Merkur*   (Stuttgart),   4   (Dezember   1950), 1289-1297.

A translation of 'Realpolitik.'

D52     "Totentanz." *Die Neue Furche: Monatsschrift für geistige auseinandersetzung* (Stuttgart), 6 (Mai 1952), 333-338 and 6 (Juni 1952), 397-402.

A translation of 'Totentanz.'

D53     "Meg Eliot." *Frankfurter Allgemeine Zeitung* (Frankfurt-am-Main), 14 März-6 Juli 1960. [94 installments.]

A translation by Helmut Lindemann of *The Middle Age of Mrs Eliot.*

## HUNGARIAN

*Book:*

D54     *Angloszász furcsaságok*. Budapest: Magvetö Kiadó, 1972.

A translation by Tibor Szilágyi of *Anglo-Saxon Attitudes*.

*Periodicals:*

D55     "Reálpolitika."   *Nagyvilág*   (Budapest),   6   (március   1961), 393-398.

A translation by Tamás Kéri of 'Realpolitik.'

D56     "Mit esznek a vízipacik?" *Nagyvilág* (Budapest), 9 (április 1964), 575-583.

A translation by László Nemes of 'What Do Hippos Eat?'

D57     "Családi   ebéd."   *Nagyvilág*   (Budapest),   26   (március   1981), 366-388.

A translation by László Nemes of extracts from *Setting the World on Fire*.

# ITALIAN

*Books:*

D58    *La cicuta e dopo.* Milan: Garzanti, 1956.

A translation by Eugenio Montale of *Hemlock and After.*

D59    *Prima che sia tardi.* Milan: Garzanti, 1957.

A translation by Carlo Rossi Fantonetti of *Anglo-Saxon Attitudes.*

D60    *Una signora di mezza età.* Milan: Garzanti, 1961.

A translation by Ugo Tolomei of *The Middle Age of Mrs Eliot.*

D61    *La parte sbagliata.* Milan: Garzanti, 1962.

A translation by Argia Michettoni of selections from *The Wrong Set and Other Stories, Such Darling Dodos and Other Stories* and *A Bit Off the Map and Other Stories.*

D62    *Vecchi allo zoo.* Milan: Garzanti, 1966.

A translation by Franca Cancogni of *The Old Men at the Zoo.*

D63    *Per gioco ma sul serio.* Milan: Feltrinelli Editore, 1969.

A translation by Paola Ojetti of *No Laughing Matter.*

Reprinted: Milan: Club degli editori, 1971.

D64    *Per chi suona la cloche: Un album degli anni venti.* Milan: Adelphi, 1974.

A translation by Adriana Monti of *For Whom the Cloche Tolls.*

*Periodicals:*

D65    "Realpolitik." *Inventario* (Milan), 4 no. 2 (marzo-aprile 1952), 82-87.

A translation by Joyce M. Hansford Brusa of 'Realpolitik.'

D66    "Totentanz." *Nuovi argomenti* (Rome), no. 1 (marzo-aprile 1953), 160-180.

A translation by Lidia Storoni of 'Totentanz.'

D67　　　"Ai margini." *L'Illustrazione italiana* (Milan), febbraio 1958, pp. 73-80, 82-86.

A translation by Carlo Rossi Fantonetti of 'A Bit Off the Map.'

D68　　　"Una vicenda di interesse storico." *L'Illustrazione italiana* (Milan), settembre 1958, pp. 79-80, 82, 84, 86-87.

A translation by Carlo Rossi Fantonetti of 'A Story of Historical Interest.'

## JAPANESE

*Books:*

D69　　　*Warui nakama; Nire-no-ki.* Tokyo: Nanundō, 1960.

A translation by Kazuo Sakamoto and Shōzō Kizumi of *The Wrong Set and Other Stories* and 'Heart of Elm' from *Such Darling Dodos and Other Stories*.

D70　　　*Warui nakama.* Tokyo: Hakusuisha, 1968.

A translation by Adio Kudō and Yasushi Suzuki of *The Wrong Set and Other Stories*.

D71　　　*Waraigoto ja maiyo.* Tokyo: Kodansha, 1973.

A translation by Kazue Serizawa of *No Laughing Matter*.

D72　　　*Wo Wiruson.* Tokyo: Shueisha, 1977.

A translation by Eizo Hikawa of *Anglo-Saxon Attitudes* with a translation of *The Ordeal of Gilbert Pinfold* by Evelyn Waugh.

D73　　　*Dikkenzu no sekai.* Tokyo: Eihōsha, 1979.

A translation by Masaie Matsumura of *The World of Charles Dickens*.

D74　　　"Vikutoria-chô no kokoro." *Shārokku Homuzu o yomu: Suiri shosetsu e no pasupoto, Ellery Queen hoka.* Tokyo: Kodansha, 1981, pp. 157-175.

A translation by Tsukasa Kobayashi and Akane Higashiyama of 'Introduction' to *The Return of Sherlock Holmes*.

# NORWEGIAN

*Books:*

D75     *Frisk luft og andre noveller.* Oslo: J.W. Cappelens Forlag, 1957.

A translation by Eivind Haug of selections from *The Wrong Set and Other Stories.*

D76     "Slike fortryllende fossiler." *England forteller: Britiske og irske noveller.* Ed. Kristian Smidt. Oslo: Den norske bokklubben, 1970, pp. 485-504.

A translation by Eivind Haug of 'Such Darling Dodos' with a prefatory note by Kristian Smidt.

# POLISH

*Books:*

D77     *Anglosaskie pozy.* Warsaw: Czytelnik, 1958.

A translation by Adam Klimowicz of *Anglo-Saxon Attitudes* with an afterword by the translator.

D78     *Dojrzałpe lata Pani Eliot.* Warsaw: Czytelnik, 1963.

A translation by Adam Klimowicz of *The Middle Age of Mrs Eliot.*

D79     "Nieodpowiednie towarzystwo." *Życie innych ludzi: Opowiadania angielskie.* Warsaw: Pánstwowy Instytut Wydawniczy, 1967, pp. 201-214.

A translation by Agnieszka Glinczanka of 'The Wrong Set.'

D80     *Późne wstawanie.* Warsaw: Czytelnik, 1967.

A translation by Cecylia Wojewoda of *Late Call.*

D81     *Co jedza hipopotamy: Opowiadania.* Warsaw: Pánstwowy Instytut Wydawniczy, 1972.

A translation by Henryk Krzeczkowski of selections from *The Wrong Set and Other Stories, Such Darling Dodos and Other Stories* and *A Bit Off the Map and Other Stories.*

D82     *Bardziej przyjaciel niz lokator: Opowiadania.* Warsaw: Ksiąska & Wiedza, 1976.

A translation by Henryk Krzeczkowski of *A Bit Off the Map and Other Stories*.

*Periodicals:*

D83    "Mapa obłędu." *Nowa Kultura* (Warsaw), 9 no. 17 (1958), 4-6.

A translation by Henryk Józefowicz of 'A Bit Off the Map.'

D84    "Pisarze a prasa." *Życie literackie* (Cracow), 41 (1958), 2, 9.

A translation by Leszek Elektorowicz of Wilson's contribution to *The Author and the Public* (B13).

D85    "Muszę wiedzieć." *Walka Młodych* (Warsaw), 10 no. 48 (1958), 6.

A translation by Jerzy Segel of 'A Bit Off the Map' (extract).

D86    "Złe towarzystwo." *Nowa Kultura* (Warsaw), 11 no. 6 (1960), 6.

A translation by K. Klinger of 'The Wrong Set.'

D87    "Przyjaciel niż lokator." *Kronika Beskidzka* (Bielsko-Biała), 6 (1961), 3-12.

A translation by Henryk Józefowicz of 'More Friend than Lodger.'

D88    "Trafiła kosa na kamień." *Panorama Północy* (Olsztyn), 6 no. 18 (1962), 14.

A translation by Z. Sołtynska of a story by Wilson.

D89    "Papa." *Wiedza i Życie* (Warsaw), 6 (1968), 30-32.

A translation by J. Grytner of 'The Men with Bowler Hats.'

D90    "Przeciw tyranii krytków." *Odra* (Wrocław), 9 no. 4 (1969), 29-32.

A translation by Tadeusz Rybowski of 'If It's New and Modish Is It Good?' (C276).

D91    "Realpolitik." *Kierunki* (Warsaw), 16 no. 34 (1971), 7.

A translation by Henryk Krzeczkowski of 'Realpolitik.'

# PORTUGESE

*Books:*

D92     *Depois da cicuta.* Lisbon: Portugália Editora, 1961.

A translation by Mário Henrique Leiria of *Hemlock and After* with an introduction by Luis de Sousa Rebelo.

D93     *Os velhos do jardim zoológico.* Rio de Janeiro: Ediçoes Bloch, 1968.

A translation by Thomáz Newlands Neto of *The Old Men at the Zoo* with an introduction by P.A. Nascimento Silva.

D94     [Statement on Vietnam.] *Vietname: Os escritores tomam posição.* Lisbon: Editora Ulìsseìa, 1968, p. 196.

A translation by Orlando Neves of Wilson's contribution to *Authors Take Sides on Vietnam* (B32).

D95     *A meia-idade da Sra Eliot.* Lisbon: Portugália Editora, 1976.

A translation by José António Machado of *The Middle Age of Mrs Eliot.*

D96     *A revelação da Sra Eliot.* Rio de Janeiro: Livraria Francisco Alves Editora, 1982.

A translation by José Eduardo Ribeiro Moretzsohn of *The Middle Age of Mrs Eliot.*

# ROMANIAN

*Books:*

D97     *Chemare tîrzie.* Bucharest: Editura pentru literaturǎ universalǎ, 1968.

A translation by Ady Florea and Nicolae Minei of *Late Call.*

D98     *Atitudini anglo-saxone.* Bucharest: Editurii Univers, 1985.

A translation by Georgeta Pǎdureleanu of *Anglo-Saxon Attitudes* with an introduction by Mircea Pǎdureleanu.

# RUSSIAN

*Book:*

D99    *Mir Čarl'za Dikkensa.* Moscow: Progress, 1975.

A translation by R. Pomeranceva and V. Hakitonov of *The World of Charles Dickens.*

# SERBO-CROAT

*Books:*

D100    *Anglosaksonski maniri.* Belgrade: Prosveta, 1961.

A translation by Hamo Džabić of *Anglo-Saxon Attitudes.*

Reprinted: Belgrade: Prosveta, 1963.

D101    *Starci u zoološkom vrtu.* Belgrade: Prosveta, 1964.

A translation by Zĭvojin Simić of *The Old Men at the Zoo* with an introduction by Aleksandar V. Stefanović.

# SPANISH

*Books:*

D102    *La madurez de la señora Eliot.* Santiago de Chile and Buenos Aires: Editorial del Nuevo Extremo, 1960.

A translation by Jorge Onfray and Wilfredo Reyes of *The Middle Age of Mrs Eliot.*

D103    *Actitudes anglosajonas.* Barcelona: Editorial Seix y Barral, 1961.

A translation by Micaela Mata and José M. Aroca of *Anglo-Saxon Attitudes.*

D104    *Después de la cicuta.* Buenos Aires: Compañía General Fabril Editora, 1961.

A translation by Ana Teresa Weyland of *Hemlock and After.*

D105    *Los viejos del zoo.* Barcelona: Plaza & Janés, 1962.

A translation by Jorge Ferrer-Vidal of *The Old Men at the Zoo*.

Reprinted: Barcelona: Círculo de Lectores, 1969.

D106    *La mala gente*. Barcelona: Ediciones G.P., 1964.

A translation by Mary Rowe of *The Wrong Set and Other Stories*.

D107    *Los siete pecados capitale*. Buenos Aires: Compañía General Fabril Editora, 1964.

A translation by Marta I. Guastavino of 'Envy,' *The Seven Deadly Sins* (B20).

D108    *Aquellos adorables tipos raros*. Barcelona: Plaza & Janés, 1965.

A translation by Jorge Ferrer-Vidal of *Such Darling Dodos and Other Stories*.

D109    *Que me llamen tarde*. Barcelona: Editorial Seix y Barral, 1968.

A translation by Georgina Regás of *Late Call*.

D110    [Statement on Vietnam.] *Los Intellectuales ante el Vietnam: Dos preguntas sobre la guerra en el Vietnam, contestadas por intellectuales de varias naciones*. Madrid-Barcelona: Alfaguara, 1968, pp. 211-212.

A translation of Wilson's contribution to *Authors Take Sides on Vietnam* (B32).

D111    *Las malas compañías*. Madrid: Altea, Taurus, Alfaguara, 1984.

A translation by Barbara McShane and Javier Alfaya of *The Wrong Set and Other Stories*.

D112    *Prendiendo fuego al mundo*. Madrid: Altea, Taurus, Alfaguara, 1985.

A translation by Juan Basabe of *Setting the World on Fire*.

D113    *Los viejos del zoo*. Madrid: Altea, Taurus, Alfaguara, 1986.

A translation by Barbara McShane and Javier Alfaya of *The Old Men at the Zoo*.

# SWEDISH

*Books:*

D114    *Giftdryck.* Stockholm: P.A. Norstedt & Söners Forlag, 1953.
A translation by Jane Lundblad of *Hemlock and After.*

D115    *Dåligt sällskap och andra noveller.* Stockholm: P.A. Norstedt &
Söners Forlag, 1956.
A translation by Aida Törnell of *The Wrong Set and Other
Stories.*

D116    *Britter emellan.* Stockholm: P.A. Norstedt & Söners Forlag, 1958.
A translation by Göran Salander of *Anglo-Saxon Attitudes.*

D117    *Efter sommaren.* Stockholm: P.A. Norstedt & Söners Forlag,
1961.
A translation by Göran Salander of *The Middle Age of Mrs Eliot.*

D118    "Ett taktlóst besök." *Modern Engelsk Berättarkonst.* Ed. Lars
Bjurman. Delfin No. 240. Stockholm: Aldus/Bonniers Förlag,
1966, pp. 67-74.
A translation by Mårten Edlund of 'A Visit in Bad Taste.'

# E. INTERVIEWS

Place of publication is London unless otherwise indicated. For radio and television interviews, *see* G.

E1     Strating, J.J. "Interview met Angus Wilson." *Literair Paspoort* (Amsterdam), 8 (oktober 1953), 211-214.

E2     Anon. "Wij spraken met Angus Wilson, engels schrijver." *Het Vaderland* (The Hague), 7 november 1956.

E3     Millgate, Michael. "Angus Wilson." *Paris Review* (New York), no. 17 (Autumn-Winter 1957), 88-105.

Reprinted: *Writers at Work: The "Paris Review" Interviews*. lst ser. Ed. Malcolm Cowley. New York: Viking Press, 1957, pp. 251-266; London: Secker & Warburg, 1958, pp. 225-238; Harmondsworth: Penguin, 1979, pp. 251-266.

Reprinted: *Books and Bookmen*, 3 no. 8 (May 1958), 14-16.

Reprinted as: "Wywiady [Interview]." *Nowa Kultura* (Warsaw), 9 no. 23 (1958), 8. [Extract translated into Polish.]

Reprinted as: "Une conversation avec Angus Wilson." *Cahiers des Saisons* (Paris), 40 (hiver 1965), 532-538. [Extract translated into French by Léo Dilé.]

Reprinted as: "Angus Wilson: The Art of Fiction." *Critical Essays on Angus Wilson*, ed. Jay L. Halio, pp. 39-48 (J86).

E4     Reve, G.K. van het. "Interview met Angus Wilson." *Tirade* (Amsterdam), 15 december 1957, pp. 350-353.

E5      Gillon, Diana. " 'Raspberry Jam' Puts Angus on the Map."
        *Reynolds News & Sunday Citizen*, 21 September 1958, p. 6.

E6      Bay, André. "Angus Wilson." *La Revue de Paris*, 66 (août 1959),
        40-42. [In French.]

E7      "Angus Wilson o sobie i swojej twórczości [Angus Wilson on Him-
        self and His Work]." *Nowa Kultura* (Warsaw), 11 no. 28 (1960), 8.
        [Translated into Polish from French.]

E8      Wilson, Angus and William Sansom. "How They Write and Why
        They Do It." *Queen*, 15 March 1960, pp. 143-144.

E9      Taylor, Barbara Ann. "If You Can't Afford the Best, Try To Be
        Amusing." *Evening Standard*, 9 November 1961, p. 21. Article
        based on an interview.

E10     Kermode, Frank. "Myth, Reality and Fiction." *Listener*, 68 (30
        August 1962), 311-313. *See also* G51.

        Reprinted as: "House of Fiction: Interview with Seven English Nov-
        elists." *Partisan Review* (New York), 30 (Spring 1963), 61-82
        (68-70).

        Reprinted as: "The House of Fiction: Interviews with Seven Novel-
        ists." *The Novel Today: Contemporary Writers on Modern Fiction*.
        Ed. Malcolm Bradbury. Manchester: Manchester University Press,
        1977; London: Fontana/Collins, 1977; Totowa, NJ: Rowman & Lit-
        tlefield, 1977, pp. 111-135 (119-122).

E11     Sandvad, Else. "Det er i dramaet, ikke i romanen det foregaar [It's
        Happening in Drama, Not the Novel]." *Information* (Copen-
        hagen), 10 September 1962, p. 5. Interview at the Writers' Confer-
        ence, Edinburgh.

E12     Dick, Kay. "Portrait: Angus Wilson's Countryside." *Ramparts*, 3
        (November 1964), 5-6, 8. Article based on an interview.

E13     Poston, Lawrence, III. "A Conversation with Angus Wilson."
        *Books Abroad* (Norman, OK), 40 (Winter 1966), 29-31.

E14     Foster, William. "The Butterfly Who Thinks." *Scotsman*
        (Edinburgh), 29 July 1967, *Week-End Scotsman*, p. 3. Article based
        on an interview.

E15     Grosvenor, Peter. "Don't Laugh Too Much! Advice from 'Nice
        but Nasty' Angus Wilson." *Daily Express*, 8 August 1967, p. 6.

E16 Coleman, Terry. "Angus Wilson's Attitudes." *Manchester Guardian*, 29 August 1967, p. 4. Article based on an interview.

E17 Leeson, Bob. "I'm a Radical but Cannot Cut My Links with the Past." *Morning Star*, 17 May 1968, p. 4.

E18 Drescher, Horst W. "Angus Wilson—An Interview." *Die Neueren Sprachen* (Frankfurt-am-Main), 17 (Juli 1968), 351-356.

E19 Narita, Shigehisa. "A Reformer, Not a Revolutionary: Angus Wilson Talks on Novels and Novelists." *Eigo Sei Nen* (Tokyo), 115 (1 December 1969), 752-759.

E20 Oka, Teruo. "An Interview with Angus Wilson." *Japan Radio Magazine* (Tokyo), December 1969, pp. 4-13. [Accompanied by a Japanese translation.]

E21 Biles, Jack I. "An Interview in London with Angus Wilson." *Studies in the Novel* (Denton, TX), 2 (Spring 1970), 76-87.

Reprinted: *Critical Essays on Angus Wilson*, ed. Jay L. Halio, pp. 48-59 (J86).

E22 Stockwood, June. "The Potent Appeal of Dickens: An Interview with Angus Wilson." *Harper's Bazaar* (New York), May 1970, pp. 18-19.

E23 Jebb, Julian. "Angus Wilson in the World of Charles Dickens." *Vogue*, London edn., June 1970, pp. 133-134.

E24 Geracimos, Ann. "An Anglo-Saxon Attitude." *International Herald Tribune* (Paris), 1 December 1970, p. 16.

E25 Zielinski, Mary. "Angus Wilson: A Genial Leprechaun Who Writes a Bit." *Daily Iowan* (Iowa City), 3 December 1971, p. 6. Article based on an interview.

E26 Anon. "Cred in tulburatorul azi [I Believe in the Stirring Present Day]." *Cronica* (Bucharest), 7 no. 12 (March 1972), 13, 16.

E27 McDowell, Frederick P.W. "An Interview with Angus Wilson." *Iowa Review* (Iowa City), 3 (Fall 1972), 77-105.

Reprinted: *Diversity and Depth in Fiction*, 1983 .

E28 Fernandez, Diane and Patrick Reumaux. "Angus Wilson parle de Dickens." *Quinzaine littéraire* (Paris), 155 (1-15 janvier 1973), 5-6.

E29    Moorcock, Michael. "Angus Wilson Talks to Michael Moorcock."
       *Books and Bookmen*, 18 no. 8 (May 1973), 22-28.

E30    Devlin, Tim. "Angus Wilson and the Art of the Unexpected."
       *Times*, 30 May 1973, p. 18. Article based on an interview.

E31    Hall, John. "Anglo-Indian Attitudes." *Guardian*, 2 June 1973,
       p. 10.

E32    Veen, Adriaan van der. "Praten met Angus Wilson: 'Ik heb niets
       tegen snobs.' " *NRC Handelsblad* (Rotterdam), 15 juni 1973, *Cul-
       tureel Supplement*, p. 1.

E33    Anon. "Is Your Family at War?" *Radio Times*, 8-14 December
       1973, pp. 25-26. *See also* G124.

E34    Firchow, Peter. "Angus Wilson." *The Writer's Place: Interviews on
       the Literary Situation in Contemporary Britain*. Minneapolis: Uni-
       versity of Minnesota Press, 1974, pp. 331-352.

E35    Raban, Jonathan. "Profile: Angus Wilson." *New Review*, 1 (April
       1974), 16-24.

E36    Grant, Patricia K. "Angus Wilson, 'British Novelist,' Eludes
       Categories." *Sunday Sun* (Baltimore), 10 November 1974, pp. 1,
       26. Article based on an interview.

E37    Barfoot, C.C. "Interview with Angus Wilson." *Dutch Quarterly
       Review of Anglo-American Letters* (Assen), 6 (1976), 279-290.

E38    Bennett, Peter and Denis Lemon. "Interview: Angus Wilson." *Gay
       News*, no. 92 (8-21 April 1976), 17-18.

E39    Robinson, Robert. "Wilson Stories." *Listener*, 95 (4 March 1976),
       283. *See also* G134.

E40    Bradbury, Malcolm. "Angus Wilson in Conversation with
       Malcolm Bradbury." Literature Study Aids Series. British Coun-
       cil, 1977. Transcript of a taped recording (F12).

E41    Toomey, Philippa. "Angus Wilson: A Busy Man for a Writer Who
       Is 'Not Popular.' " *Times*, 16 November 1977, p. 22. Article based
       on an interview.

E42    Shenker, Israel. "Angus Wilson, Biographer." *New York Times
       Book Review*, 12 March 1978, pp. 1, 36-37.

E43 Brata, Sasthi. "A Life in the Day of Angus Wilson." *Sunday Times Magazine*, 20 August 1978, p. 46. Article based on an interview.

E44 Anon. "U-M Writer-in-Residence a 'Pratfall' Expert." *Ann Arbor News*, 7 October 1979, p. F4. Article based on an interview.

E45 deJongh, Nicholas. "A Novel View Through a Child's Eye." *Guardian*, 28 June 1980, p. 11. Article based on an interview.

E46 Lewis, Peter. "Angus Wilson's Attitudes." *Sunday Telegraph*, 29 June 1980, p. 9.

E47 Hayman, Ronald. "Angus Wilson in Interview." *Books and Bookmen*, 25 no. 10 (July 1980), 17-20.

E48 Sage, Lorna. "Doing What Dickens Did." *Observer*, 6 July 1980, p. 27. Article based on an interview.

E49 Bigsby, Christopher. "An Interview with Angus Wilson." *Literary Review*, November 1980, pp. 33-38.

Reprinted: *The Radical Imagination and the Liberal Tradition: Interviews with Novelists*. Ed. Heide Ziegler and Christopher Bigsby. London: Junction Books, 1982; Atlantic Highlands, NJ: Humanities Press, 1982, pp. 231-259.

E50 Horgan, Daniel. "Knighted Author Is Prof at UD." *Evening Journal* (Wilmington), 7 November 1980, p. B2. Article based on an interview.

E51 Sinkler, Rebecca. "Two Bloomin' Successes, Late." *Philadelphia Inquirer*, 9 November 1980, p. 14-I. Article based on an interview.

E52 Barber, Michael. "A Talk with Angus Wilson." *New York Times Book Review*, 16 November 1980, pp. 41-42.

E53 Christian, George. "Sir Angus Looks Back." *Houston Chronicle*, 14 December 1980, pp. 44, 51. Article based on an interview.

E54 Draine, Betsy. "An Interview with Angus Wilson." *Contemporary Literature* (Madison, WI), 21 (Winter 1980), 1-14.

Reprinted: *Interviews with Contemporary Writers, Second Series, 1972-82*. Ed. L.S. Dembo. Madison: University of Wisconsin Press, 1983, pp. 270-283.

E55 Cartano, Tony. "Angus Wilson, un vieux snob ésthetique." *Magazine littéraire* (Paris), nos. 172-173 (mai 1981), 88-90.

E56 M., D. "Novelist Recalls His First Words." *University Times* (University of Pittsburgh), 22 October 1981, pp. 4, 10. Article based on an interview.

E57 Mallet, Gina. "A Literary Knight To Remember." *Toronto Star*, 25 October 1981, p. F8.

E58 Sachs, Sylvia. "Good Knight! English Author in Residence at Pitt." *Pittsburgh Press*, 22 November 1981, p. G-6. Article based on an interview.

E59 Sciullo, Diane. "Profile: Sir Angus Wilson, Visiting Mellon Professor." *Pitt News* (University of Pittsburgh), 23 November 1981, pp. 2-3. Article based on an interview.

E60 Fisher, Ruth D. "A Conversation with Sir Angus Wilson." *Four Quarters* (Philadelphia), 31 (Summer 1982), 3-22.

E61 Suchert, Debbie. "British Professor Recounts Many Achievements as Fiction Writer." *Current* (University of Missouri—St Louis), 7 October 1982, pp. 8-9. Article based on an interview.

E62 Rice, Patricia. "A Writer for Warm Seasons." *St Louis Post-Dispatch*, 29 November 1982, *Everyday Magazine*, p. 5D. Article based on an interview.

E63 Kissane, Joseph. "Talking with Angus Wilson." *Twentieth Century Literature* (Hempstead, NY), 29 (Summer 1983), 142-150.

E64 Moorcock, Michael. "Under Observation." *Radio Times*, 10-16 September 1983, pp. 80-82. Article based on an interview.

E65 Anon. "The Old Man at the Zoo: Angus Wilson." *L'Ane* (Paris), no. 13 (novembre-décembre 1983), pp. 39-40. [In French.]

E66 Mullinax, Gary. "Writer Enjoys Traveling, Savors Stays in Delaware." *News Journal* (Wilmington), 8 December 1983, pp. D1, D12. Article based on an interview.

E67 Ingham, Zita. "An Interview with Sir Angus Wilson." *Sonora Review* (University of Arizona, Tucson), 8 (1984), 80-86.

E68 Minnen, C.L. van. "Enkele vragen aan Angus Wilson." *Wildgroei* (Leiden), 6 (maart/april 1984), 18-20. [In Dutch with Wilson's responses in English.]

E69 Bradley, Steve. "A Complex and Talented Man." *Bury Free Press* (Bury St Edmunds), 29 June 1984, p. 10. Article based on an interview.

E70 Mandrake. "Sir Angus Honouring His Missing Companions." *Sunday Telegraph*, 8 July 1984, p. 8. Article based on an interview.

E71 Mayers, Darrel. "Visiting Writer from England Finds Subjects in Dark Side of Childhood." *Arizona Daily Wildcat* (University of Arizona, Tucson), 24 September 1984, p. 8. Article based on an interview.

E72 Tully, Jacqui. "Author Angus Wilson Maintains Healthy Career at 71." *Arizona Daily Star* (Tucson), 26 September 1984, p. 1C. Article based on an interview.

E73 Biles, Jack I. "Some Words More, Some Years Later: A Talk with Angus Wilson." *Critical Essays on Angus Wilson*. Ed. Jay L. Halio. Boston: Hall, 1985, pp. 59-69 (J86).

E74 Shaw, John. "Sir Angus Wilson Yields to Lure of South of France." *Daily Telegraph*, 29 August 1985, p. 15. Article based on an interview.

E75 Fallowell, Duncan. "An Englishman Abroad." *Time Out*, 16-22 January 1986, pp. 12-13.

Reprinted as: "From Bexhill-on-Sea to St-Rémy-de-Provence Angus Wilson Comes to Rest in France." *Sydney Morning Herald*, 1 March 1986, *Good Weekend Magazine*, pp. 46-50.

E76 Foster, William. "Writer with a Sense of Evil." *Scotsman* (Edinburgh), 22 February 1986, *Week-End Scotsman*, p. 2. Article based on an interview.

# F. RECORDINGS

F1    "Angus Wilson." Long-playing record. Recorded 25 October 1960, Hollywood, California. Readings from *Hemlock and After, The Middle Age of Mrs Eliot, Anglo-Saxon Attitudes* and Once a Lady (complete) from *A Bit off the Map and Other Stories*. Verve Records, 1961. MG-V 15023.

F2    "The English Novel Today: Dickens to Snow." Taped recording. Recorded 1960, Berkeley, California. New York: Jeffrey Norton, 1974. Cassette #C23074. Available at University of Iowa.

F3    "My Life and Yours." Taped recording of a lecture at the University of Chicago, 9 November 1960. University of Chicago Library Archives, Chicago, Illinois 60637.

F4    "Before Publication: Angus Wilson Reads from His New Novel *Late Call*." Taped recording of BBC broadcast, 21 September 1964 (*see* G67). The British Library, National Sound Archive, 29 Exhibition Road, London SW7 2AS. #M 113 W.

F5    Interview with Michael Ratcliffe on *Late Call*. Taped recording of BBC broadcast, 11 November 1964 (*see* G68). The British Library, National Sound Archive, 29 Exhibition Road, London SW7 2AS. #M 124 W.

F6    "Angus Wilson: An Interview by John H. Raleigh." Taped recording. New York: Jeffrey Norton, 1967. Cassette #23077.

F7    "The Bloomsbury Group." Taped recording. Recorded 1967,

Berkeley, California. New York: Jeffrey Norton, 1974. Cassette #C23076. Available at University of Iowa.

F8    Interview with Professor Frederick P. W. McDowell, 1971. Phonotape. University of Iowa Manuscript Collection 199. *See also* E27 and H18*e*(15).

F9    "Dickens and the Modern City." Taped recording of a lecture at the University of Iowa, Iowa City, 20 October 1971. University of Iowa Manuscript Collection 199. *See also* H18*e*(9).

F10   "Angus Wilson, Novelist." Interview with Andrew Joynes. Taped recording. Profile, BBC Topical Tapes Series, [1973]. The British Library, National Sound Archive, 29 Exhibition Road, London SW7 2AS. #LP35354.

F11   "Dickens." A.E. Dyson and Angus Wilson. Taped recording. Approach to Literary Criticism Series, Sussex Tapes International. Holt Information Systems, 383 Madison Avenue, New York, N. Y. 10017. Cassette #F12006. *See also* B46.

F12   "Angus Wilson in Conversation with Malcolm Bradbury." Taped recording. Literature Study Aids Series, 1977. The British Council, 65 Davies Street, London W1Y 2AA. *See also* E40.

F13   "Jane Austen: Prudence versus Courage." Taped recording of a lecture at the Sunday Evening Seminar Series "Confronting Changing Expectations: Insights from Literature, Art and Theology," 19 September 1980. Christ Church Christiana Hundred, Greenville, Delaware 19807. Available at University of Iowa.

F14   "Changing Careers in Mid-Life." Creative Aging Series. Taped recording of KWMU broadcast, 14 November 1982 (*see* G154). Continuing Education—Extension, College of Arts and Sciences, University of Missouri—St Louis, 8001 Natural Bridge Road, St Louis, Missouri 63121. Available at University of Iowa.

F15   "Angus Wilson on Angus Wilson." Taped recording of a lecture at Drew University, 30 September 1983. Media Resource Center, Drew University Library, Madison, N. J. 07940.

F16   "The Strange Ride of Rudyard Kipling." Taped recording of a lecture at the Sunday Evening Seminar Series "A Quest There Is: Reflections on the Search for Religious Meaning," 13 November

1983. Christ Church Christiana Hundred, Greenville, Delaware 19807.

F17    "Angus Wilson on Angus Wilson." Taped recording of a lecture at the 6th P.E.N. Writers' Day, London, 24 March 1984. The British Library, National Sound Archive, 29 Exhibition Road, London SW7 2AS. #T 6973 W.

F18    What Do Hippos Eat? and extracts from *The Old Men at the Zoo, No Laughing Matter* and *As If By Magic*. Taped recording of Wilson reading from his works with brief comments, 26 September 1984. Taped recording. University of Arizona, Poetry Center, 1086 North Highland Avenue, Tucson, Arizona 85719. For use at the Poetry Center or with written permission of the author.

F19    "What Do Hippos Eat?" Videotape of Wilson reading, 26 November 1984. University of Arizona, Poetry Center, 1086 North Highland Avenue, Tucson, Arizona 85719. For use at the Poetry Center or with written permission of the author.

# G. Broadcast Talks, Radio and Television Interviews and Discussions, Radio and Television Productions

\*  designates radio programmes held at the British Library, National Sound Archive, 29 Exhibition Road, London SW7.

\#  designates radio programmes held at the BBC Sound Archives, Broadcasting House, London W1. These archives are organised primarily as a service for broadcasting.

‡  designates television programmes held at the National Film Archive, 81 Dean Street, London W1.

The following abbreviations are used:

    ABC  A.B.C. Television
    ATV  Associated Television
    BBC  British Broadcasting Corporation
    CBC  Canadian Broadcasting Corporation
    ITA  Independent Television Authority
    ITV  Independent Television

## 1947

G1      30 August. "Realpolitik" (story). BBC Third Programme. *See also* H1*c*(1).

G2          20 September. "Full Steam Ahead" (story). BBC Home Service.

## 1950

G3          8 August. "Sense and Sensibility in Recent Writing." BBC
            Third Programme. Repeated 26 September. *See also* C30 *and*
            H1*a*(1).

G4          2 December. "What the Londoner Doesn't Know." BBC Gen-
            eral Overseas Service.

## 1951

G5          18 February. "A Visit in Bad Taste" (story; read by Wilson).
            BBC Third Programme. Repeated 23 February. *See also*
            H1*c*(2).

G6          22 March. "Broken Promise: The English Novel 1912-1922."
            BBC Third Programme. Repeated 25 March. *See also* C36 *and*
            H1*a*(2).

G7          27 March. "Presenting Angus Wilson" (interview). BBC radio,
            London, and European Service (Swedish Programme).

## 1952

G8          25 November. "The Seven Deadly Sins and the Contemporary
            World: No. 7, 'Sloth.' " BBC Home Service. *See also* H1*a*(3).

G9          30 October. *Chronique des Lettres et des Arts*: "Zola in England."
            BBC European Service (French Programme). *See also* C54.

G10         2 December. "Skeletons and Assegais: Family Reminiscences"
            (drama with commentary read by Wilson). BBC Third Pro-
            gramme. Repeated 4 December and 31 December 1952 and
            1 July 1953. *See also* C301 *and* H1*c*(3).

G11         21 December. *New Soundings* ("Higher Standards" read by
            Wilson). BBC Third Programme. Repeated 27 December. *See
            also* C58.

## 1953

G12    14 June. "The Bi-centenary of the British Museum: II—The Reading Room." BBC Third Programme. *See also* C71 *and* H1*a*(4).

## 1954

G13    14 April. *Literary Opinion*: No. 1, "The Death of the Novel" (with Kathleen Nott, F.W. Bateson and John Holloway; Wilson on the future of the English novel). BBC Third Programme. *See also* C86 *and* H1*b*(1).

G14    8 May. *The Long View*: "The Satirist & Society." BBC radio, London Calling Asia. *See also* H1*a*(5).

## 1955

G15    12 January. *Question Time* (participant). BBC radio, London Calling Asia.

G16    26 January. *Question Time* (participant). BBC radio, London Calling Asia.

G17    25 May. *Question Time* (participant). BBC radio, London Calling Asia.

G18    15 June. *Question Time* (participant). BBC radio, London Calling Asia.

G19    7 December. *Question Time* (participant). BBC radio, London Calling Asia.

G20    28 December. *Question Time* (participant). BBC radio, London Calling Asia.

## 1956

G21    6 April. *Week-end Review* (interview). BBC radio, London Calling Asia.

G22    23 April. "Left in the Middle" (drama with commentary read by

Wilson). BBC Third Programme. Repeated 26 April and 30 October. *See also* H1c(4a)-(4b).

G23     16 June. *Stage and Screen* (interview in French). BBC radio, London.

G24     29 June. "Angus Wilson" (interview in Swedish). BBC radio, European Service (Swedish Programme).

G25     31 July. "Writers and the Public" (extract from Wilson's address to the Congress of the International P.E.N. Clubs). BBC Home Service, and Northern Ireland. *See also* B13 *and* I43.

G26     19 August. "What I Believe." BBC radio, London Calling Asia.

G27     28 September. *Highlight*: "The Third Programme's Anniversary Programme" (co-author). BBC television.

G28     30 September-5 October. "The Memoirs of Mrs Cramp, Being Episodes in the Life of the Wife of a Professional Writer" (drama). BBC Third Programme. Six-part serial. *See also* H1c(5)-(10).

## 1957

G29     25 February. *Meeting Writers* (interview). BBC European Service (Norwegian Programme). Repeated, Home and European Services, 4 March; European Service (German Programme), 30 May.

G30     7 March. *Modern Reading*: "Writing Novels and Short Stories". BBC radio, London Calling Asia, 7 March.

G31     8 March. *Week-end Review*: "A Catalogue for the British Museum." BBC radio, London Calling Asia. *See also* C268.

G32     4 May. *Recent Novels* (discussion on *Justine* by Lawrence Durrell, *Room at the Top* by John Braine, *The Comforters* by Muriel Spark and *Seize the Day* by Saul Bellow with Frank Kermode and Christopher Salmon). BBC Third Programme. Repeated 7 May. *See also* H1b(2).

G33     12 October. *Week-end Review*: "Writers at P.E.N. — The 1957 Congress." BBC radio, London Calling Asia.

G34    20 October. *Sunday Night Theatre*: "The Mulberry Bush" (drama). BBC television. *See also* H1c(11) *and* H18c(2c).

*#G35    31 October. "A Biographical Portrait of Norman Douglas" (participant). BBC Third Programme.

*#G36    22 December. *Asian Club*: "The Writer & His Times." BBC radio, London Calling Asia, 22 December. *See also* H1b(3).

## 1958

G37    8 January. *Books To Read* (participant). BBC General Overseas Service.

## 1959

G38    12 March. *Books and Writers* (interview). BBC European Service (Finnish Programme).

G39    17 March. *The World We Live In* (participant). BBC General Overseas Service.

G40    6 September. "Angus Wilson on His Novels" (interview with John Bowen). BBC Third Programme. Repeated 12 October. See also H1b(4).

‡G41    20 September. *Armchair Theatre*: "After the Show" (drama based on the story). ITA—ABC. *See also* H14(1), H18b(1) *and* H18c(4).

## 1960

G42    20 November. *Armchair Theatre*: "The Stranger" (drama). ITA—ABC. *See also* H14(2).

## 1961

G43    4 February. *The World of Books*: "Such Darling Dodos" (story). BBC Home Service, all regions.

G44    9 March. "Is English Literature Parochial? Views on Present

Day English Literature." BBC European Service (Italian Programme). [In Italian and in English.]

G45     25 September. *Tonight* (interview with Derek Hart on *The Old Men at the Zoo*). BBC1.

G46     27 September. *New Comment* (interview with John Bowen on *The Old Men at the Zoo*). BBC Third Programme. Repeated, *Conversations from "New Comment"*, Third Programme, 23 December. *See also* H1*b*(5).

*#G47     29 September. "Fiction and Reality" (interview with Frank Kermode). BBC Third Programme.

G48     17 October. *Bookstand: A Critical Survey of Books and Writers*: "Charles Dickens" (participant). BBC1.

## 1962

G49     7 February. *Bookstand: A Critical Survey of Books and Writers*: "Joseph Conrad" (participant). BBC1.

G50     30 March. *Woman's Hour*: "A Favourite Short Story— 'Realpolitik' " (chosen and introduced by John Braine). BBC Light Programme. *See also* H1*c*(12).

G51     2 April. "Myth, Reality and Fiction" (discussion with Frank Kermode). BBC Third Programme. *See also* E10 *and* H1*b*(6).

G52     27 June. *Bookstand: A Critical Survey of Books and Writers*: "Iris Murdoch" (participant). BBC1.

*G53     22 August. *New Comment*: "The Writers' Conference at the Edinburgh Festival" (with David Coate, Norman Mailer and Muriel Spark, chaired by John Bowen). BBC Third Programme. *See also* H1*b*(7).

G54     1 September. *The World of Books*: "The Contemporary Novel— The Writers' Conference at the Edinburgh Festival" (with Kushwant Singh and Norman Mailer, chaired by David Daiches). BBC Home Service, all regions. Repeated 15 October as "Does the Novel Matter?" BBC Third Programme, Home Service, all regions. *See also* H1*b*(8)-(9).

G55    9 October. "Human Drama in the Works of John Cowper Powys." BBC Third Programme.

G56    3 December. "Evil in the English Novel: 1. The Central Tradition—Richardson to Jane Austen." BBC Third Programme. Repeated 28 March 1964. *See also* C338 *and* H1a(6).

G57    10 December. "Evil in the English Novel: 2. The Central Tradition—George Eliot to Virginia Woolf." BBC Third Programme. *See also* C342 *and* H1a(7).

G58    17 December. "Evil in the English Novel: 3. Outside The Central Tradition." BBC Third Programme. *See also* C344 *and* H1a(8).

G59    21 December. *The Masters*: "Joseph Conrad" (participant). BBC Home Service, all regions. *See also* H1b(10).

G60    22 December. "Evil in the English Novel: 4. Evil in The Novel Today." BBC Third Programme. *See also* C346 *and* H1a(9).

## 1963

G61    1 February. *That Reminds Me* (participant). BBC radio, Midlands.

G62    25 February. *The Learning Stage*: "Talking About Books" (interview). CBC radio.

G63    31 March. *Armchair Theatre*: "The Invasion" (drama). ITA—ABC. *See also* H14(3).

## 1964

*#G64    31 August. *The Masters*: "Graham Greene: A Radio Portrait" (participant). BBC General Overseas Service.

G65    5 September. *Writer's World*: "The Incestuous Muse" (author). BBC2.

*#G66    7 September. *The Masters*: "Angus Wilson: A Radio Portrait" (narrated by V.S. Naipaul, with Joanna Kilmartin, Marghanita Laski, Bentley Bridgewater, John Wain and John Bowen;

extracts from *The Wild Garden* read by Wilson; extracts from "Realpolitik" and "Mother's Sense of Fun"). BBC General Overseas Service.

*G67    21 September. *Before Publication*: "Angus Wilson Reads from His New Novel *Late Call*." BBC Third Programme. *See also* F4 and H1*c*(13).

*G68    11 November. *New Comment* (interview with Michael Ratcliffe on *Late Call*). BBC Third Programme. Repeated, *Conversations from "New Comment"*, 28 December. *See also* F5 *and* H1*b*(11).

G69    15 November. *Not So Much a Programme, More a Way of Life* (participant). BBC1. Repeated 20 December.


## 1965


G70    5 January. *Woman's Hour*: "Talks of Books and Writers" (interview with Joan Yorke on *Late Call*). BBC Light Programme. Repeated, *Home for the Day*: "My Heroines," BBC Home Service, Midlands and Northern Ireland, 7 February. *See also* H1*b*(12).

G71    4 April. *Not So Much a Programme, More a Way of Life* (participant). BBC1.

G72    26 May. *Take It Or Leave It*: "Preference and Prejudice Towards Books and Writers" (panel member). BBC2.

G73    31 May. *For Sixth Forms*: "Modern Novelists, No. 4" (interview). BBC1, all regions.

G74    2 June. *Take It Or Leave It* (panel member). BBC2.

G75    21 July. *Take It Or Leave It* (panel member). BBC2.

G76    28 July. *Take It Or Leave It* (panel member). BBC2.

G77    12 October. *Take It Or Leave It* (panel member). BBC2.

G78    26 October. *Take It Or Leave It* (panel member). BBC2.

G79    1 November. *Study Session*: "Shorthand Dictation" (extract from

*The Middle Age of Mrs Eliot*). BBC Third Network. Repeated, BBC Third Network, 3 November and 8 November; repeated, BBC Home Service, all regions, 27 November.

G80   16 November. *Ten O'Clock News and Comment*: "The South Africa Brain Boycott" (interview). BBC Home Service, all regions.

G81   21 November. *The Reputation Makers* (Wilson interviews Cyril Connolly). ATV.

G82   28 November. *The Reputation Makers* (Wilson interviews Milton Shulman). ATV.

G83   5 December. *The Reputation Makers* (Wilson interviews Robert Pitman). ATV.

G84   12 December. *The Reputation Makers* (Wilson interviews Kenneth Tynan). ATV.

G85   19 December. *The Reputation Makers* (Wilson interviews Penelope Gilliatt). ATV.

G86   26 December. *The Reputation Makers* (Wilson interviews Donald Zec). ATV.


## 1966

G87   2 January. *The Reputation Makers* (Wilson interviews Philip Purser). ATV.

G88   29 July. *Holiday Books in Paperback*: "*The Ordeal of Gilbert Pinfold* and Other Works by Evelyn Waugh" (with Eleanor Bron and Denis Norden, chaired by Julian Mitchell). BBC Home Service, all regions. *See also* H1*b*(13).

*#G89   5 November. "George Devine (1910-1966): A Tribute to The Actor-Manager-Producer" (participant). BBC Third Programme. *See also* H1*b*(14).

G90   23 December. *Late Night Line-Up: Criticism, Discussion, Diversion*: "Writing for the B.B.C." (participant). BBC2.

## 1967

G91      8 March. *Late Night Line-Up: Criticism, Discussion, Diversion*: "The Influence of Television on Literature" (participant). BBC2.

G92      10 May. *The Lively Arts: Review of the Arts in the Making*: "*The Mimic Men* by V.S. Naipaul" (with Karl Miller). BBC Third Network. *See also* H1b(15).

G93      1 August. *Take It Or Leave It* (panel member). BBC2.

G94      8 August. *Take It Or Leave It* (panel member). BBC2.

G95      5 October. "Crazy Crowd" (story dramatised by Nesta Pain). BBC Radio 3. *See also* H1c(14).

\*#G96      11 October. *The Lively Arts: Review of the Arts in the Making* (interview with Frank Kermode on *No Laughing Matter*). BBC Third Programme. *See also* H1b(16).

G97      23 November. *Personal Column* (telephone interview from the University of California at Berkeley with Tom Wisdom). BBC radio, Midlands.

## 1968

G98      3 August. *Take It Or Leave It* (panel member). BBC2.

G99      10 August. *Take It Or Leave It* (panel member). BBC2.

G100      31 August. *Saturday Evening* (interview). CBC radio.

G101      10 September. *Contrast*: "The Sex War." BBC1. *See also* C438.

G102      30 September. *Home This Afternoon*: "After the Hemlock" (interview with Rene Cutforth). BBC Radio 4.

## 1969

G103      24 February. *Desert Island Discs* (interview). BBC Radio 4.

G104      22 March. *Release*: "Twenty Years as a Published Writer." BBC2.

G105    11 May. *Spectrum*: "Writers on Four" (interview with Lindsay Evans; discussion with Christopher Logue, Margaret Drabble and Nell Dunn). BBC Radio 4, Wales.

G106    1 November. *Saturday Night Theatre*: "Late Call" (novel dramatised by Eric Ewens). BBC Radio 4. Repeated 3 November. *See also* H1c(15).

## 1970

G107    15 May. "What the Dickens!" (quiz programme participant). BBC Radio 4. *See also* H1b(17).

G108    26 May. "Charles Dickens 1812-1870: A Celebration" (author). BBC1. Repeated, BBC2, 24 June. *See also* C457.

#G109    3 June. *Now Read On: Books and Writers, News and Reviews* (interview with Jonathan Raban on Charles Dickens). BBC Radio 4. *See also* H1b(18).

G110    23 August. "Dickens in 1970" (lecture). BBC Radio 3. *See also* B36 *and* H1a(10).

*#G111    20 November. *Any Questions?* (on modern plays and novels; participant). BBC Radio 4.

## 1971

G112    10 January. *Omnibus*: "The Road to the Left—Essay on George Orwell" (participant). BBC1.

G113    10 February. *Now Read On: Books and Writers, News and Reviews* (participant). BBC Radio 4. *See also* H1b(19).

G114    2 May. *Omnibus*: "Marcel Proust—In Search of Lost Time" (participant). BBC1. Repeated 7 September 1973.

G115    28 May. *PM: News Magazine* (interview with Sue MacGregor on the opening of "The Book Bang Exhibition"). BBC Radio 4.

G116    2 June. *Now Read On: Books and Writers, News and Reviews* (interview with Derek Parker on "The Book Bang Exhibition"). BBC Radio 4. *See also* H1b(20).

#G117    7 June. *Books and Writers* (interview with James Mellen on "The Book Bang Exhibition"). BBC European service.


## 1972

G118    2 May. *Study on 3—Perspective*: "Do Books Matter?" (participant in a National Book League debate). BBC Radio 3. *See also* H1*b*(21).


## 1973

*#G119   25 May. *Arts Commentary* (interview with Julian Jebb on *As If By Magic*). BBC Radio 3. *See also* H1*b*(22).

G120    30 June. *Woman's Hour*: "Learning's Little Tribute" (story). BBC Radio 4.

G121    2 August. *Kaleidoscope* (interview on *For Whom the Cloche Tolls*). BBC Radio 4. Repeated 4 August.

G122    2 October. *PM Reports*: "The British as Book Buyers" (interview). BBC Radio 4.

G123    12 October. *The Book Programme* (participant). BBC2. Repeated 14 October.

G124    9 December. "Political Metaphors—1. The Politics of The Family" (with Frank Kermode). BBC Radio 3. *See also* C505 *and* E33.

G125    11 December. *Kaleidoscope* (interview with Peter France on the John Cowper Powys revival). BBC Radio 4. Repeated 15 December. *See also* H1*b*(23).

G126    16 December. "Political Metaphors—2. Art and the Establishment" (with Frank Kermode). BBC Radio 3. *See also* C507.


## 1975

G127    14 January. *The Book Programme* (on Rudyard Kipling). BBC2.

G128    1, 8, 15 and 22 March. "Late Call" (novel dramatised by Dennis

Potter). BBC2. Repeated 1, 8, 15 and 22 May 1976. Four-part serial. *See also* H1*c*(16)-(19).

G129　　4 August. *Read All About It* (choosing the paperbacks of the week). BBC1.

G130　　24 August. *The World This Weekend* (interview with Tony Wilkinson on the annual conference of the Campaign for Homosexual Equality). BBC Radio 4. *See also* H1*b*(24).

G131　　19 November. *Kaleidoscope* (interview with Michael Oliver on awarding the Booker Prize and on current fiction writers). BBC Radio 4. *See also* H1*b*(25).

*G132　　18 December. "Jane Austen: Some Bicentennial Reflections." BBC Radio 3. Repeated 25 March 1976. *See also* H1*a*(11).

*#G133　　28 December. "Drawing Tears Out of the Stone: An Appreciation of the Novels of Henry Green (1905-1973)" (participant). BBC Radio 3. Repeated 3 January 1976. *See also* H1*b*(26).

## 1976

G134　　2 March. *The Book Programme* (interview with Robert Robinson). BBC2. Repeated, *Pick of the Week*, BBC Radio 4, 5 March. *See also* E39.

G135.　　27 May. *Afternoon Theatre*: "The Little Companion" (story dramatised by John Graham). BBC Radio 4. *See also* H1*c*(20).

*G136　　3 June. *Afternoon Theatre*: "Heart of Elm" (story dramatised by John Graham). BBC Radio 4. *See also* H1*c*(21).

*G137　　10 June. *Afternoon Theatre*: "Et Dona Ferentes" (story dramatised by John Graham). BBC Radio 4. *See also* H1*c*(22).

*G138　　17 June. *Afternoon Theatre*: "Crazy Crowd" (story dramatised by John Graham). BBC Radio 4. *See also* H1*c*(23).

G139　　8 July. *Call My Bluff* (participant). BBC2.

G140　　15 July. *Call My Bluff* (participant). BBC2.

G141   28 October. *First Impressions: The Book Programme* (participant). BBC2.

G142   30 December. *Something to Declare*: "Writers and Travellers on the Pleasures and Perils of Journeys" (participant). BBC Radio 4.

## 1977

G143   3 January. *Writers' Houses*: "Angus Wilson Lives Here" (interview with Antonia Fraser at Bradfield St George, Suffolk). BBC2.

G144   7 April. *The Book Programme*: "The Year of the Penguin" (participant; on the Silver Jubilee of 1935). BBC2.

*G145   6 November. "Wilson on Kipling" (interview with Jonathan Raban on *The Strange Ride of Rudyard Kipling*). BBC Radio 3. Repeated 11 March 1978. *See also* H1*b*(27).

## 1980

G146   3 March. Interview with James Gindin. University of Michigan Radio Stations WUOM/WVGR.

G147   29 June. *The South Bank Show* (interview with Melvyn Bragg; extracts from his work read by Wilson). ITV—London Weekend Television.

*#G148   3 July. *PM* (interview with Joan Bakewell on *Setting the World on Fire* and on being knighted). BBC Radio 4.

G149   7 July. *Kaleidoscope* (interview with Michael Billington on *Setting the World on Fire*). BBC Radio 4. *See also* H1*b*(28).

## 1981

G150   19 March. *Les Dialogues de France-Culture*: "Le roman en question" (with Jean-Louis Curtis). Radio France-Culture.

G151   27 March. *Apostrophes* (with Bernard Pivot). Deuxième chaine—Antenne 2 télévision.

*G152    22 August. *Novels Up To Now*: "No. 6, Figures in the Carpet" (interview with Anthony Curtis on the problem of using ancient myths in contemporary novels). BBC Radio 4. Repeated 6 February 1982. *See also* H1b(29).

## 1982

G153    20 June. *Bookshelf* (biographical feature; interview with Frank Delaney). BBC Radio 4. *See also* H1b(30).

G154    14 November. *Creative Aging*: "Changing Careers in Mid-Life" (interview with Ray Buchan and Jean Eberle). University of Missouri—St Louis Radio Station KWMU. *See also* F14.

## 1983

G155    15, 22, 29 September and 6, 13 October. "The Old Men at the Zoo" (novel dramatised by Troy Kennedy Martin). BBC2. Repeated, A&E Cable, New York, 18 and 25 February, 4, 11 and 18 March 1985. Five-part serial. *See also* H1c(24)-(28).

#G156   23 December. "Cabin'd, Cribb'd, Confin'd" (documentary profile of William Golding; participant). BBC radio 3. *See also* H1b(31).

## 1984

G157    29 February. *The Other Half*: "No. 4, Sir Angus Wilson and Tony Garrett" (biographical feature; interview with John Pitman). BBC1.

G158    7 March. *Matinées littéraires*: "Trois grands romanciers d'ailleurs." Radio France-Culture.

# H. Manuscripts, Working Papers and Letters

H1    British Broadcasting Corporation
H2    British Library, Reference Division
H3    Brotherton Library, Leeds
H4    Churchill College, Cambridge
H5    Columbia University
H6    Eton College
H7    Hall-Carpenter Archives
H8    King's College, Cambridge
H9    New York Public Library, Berg Collection
H10    Northamptonshire Record Office
H11    Oxford University, Bodleian Library
H12    Royal Society of Literature
H13    Secker & Warburg, Ltd
H14    Thames Television
H15    University College, University of London
H16    University of Durham
H17    University of East Anglia
H18    University of Iowa
H19    University of Reading
H20    University of Sussex
H21    Viking Penguin Inc.

# H1     BRITISH BROADCASTING CORPORATION

*a. Broadcast Talks*

Scripts are held by the Written Archives Centre, Caversham Park, Reading RG4 8TZ. *See* G. for programme details.

(1)    8 August 1950. "Sense and Sensibility in Recent Writing." Microfilm of typescript with autograph revisions. 11 leaves. *See also* C30.

(2)    22 March 1951. "Broken Promise: The English Novel 1912-1922." Microfilm of typescript with autograph revisions. 10 leaves. *See also* C36.

(3)    25 November 1952. "The Seven Deadly Sins and the Contemporary World: No. 7, 'Sloth.' " Microfilm of typescript with autograph revisions. 10 leaves.

(4)    14 June 1953. "The Bi-centenary of the British Museum: II—The Reading Room." Microfilm of typescript with autograph revisions. 10 leaves. *See also* C71.

(5)    8 May 1954. "The Satirist & Society." Microfilm of typescript. 4 leaves.

(6)    3 December 1962. "Evil in the English Novel: 1. The Central Tradition—Richardson to Jane Austen." Microfilm of typescript with autograph corrections not in Wilson's hand. 9 leaves. *See also* C338.

(7)    10 December 1962. "Evil in the English Novel: 2. The Central Tradition—George Eliot to Virginia Woolf." Microfilm of typescript with autograph corrections not in Wilson's hand. 7 leaves. *See also* C342.

(8)    17 December 1962. "Evil in the English Novel: 3. Outside the Central Tradition." Microfilm of typescript with autograph corrections not in Wilson's hand. 10 leaves. *See also* C344.

(9)    22 December 1962. "Evil in the English Novel: 4. Evil and the Novelist." Microfilm of typescript with autograph corrections not in Wilson's hand. 9 leaves. *See also* C346.

(10) 23 August 1970. "Dickens in 1970." Microfilm of typescript. 22 leaves. *See also* B36.

(11) 18 December 1975. "Jane Austen: Some Bicentennial Reflections." Microfilm of typescript. [i], 9 leaves.

## b. Radio Reviews and Discussions

Scripts (3(a), 14, 22(a), 26(a) and 31) are held by the Sound Archives, Broadcasting House, London W1. All other scripts are held by the Written Archives Centre, Caversham Park, Reading RG4 8TZ. *See* G. for programme details and titles of books reviewed.

(1)   14 April 1954. *Literary Opinion*: No. 1. Microfilm of typescript. [i], 15 leaves.

(2)   4 May 1957. *Recent Novels*. Microfilm of typescript. 26 leaves.

(3)   22 December 1957. *Asian Club*: "The Writer & His Times." (a)  Typescript (carbon), 9 leaves; (b)  microfilm of typescript. [i], 7 leaves.

(4)   6 September 1959. "Angus Wilson on His Novels." Microfilm of typescript. 10 leaves.

(5)   27 September 1961. *New Comment*. Microfilm of typescript. [i], 7 leaves.

(6)   2 April 1962. "Myth, Reality and Fiction." Microfilm of typescript. 17 leaves. *See also* E10.

(7)   22 August 1962. *New Comment*: "The Writers' Conference at the Edinburgh Festival." Microfilm of typescript. 17 leaves.

(8)   1 September 1962. *The World of Books*: "The Contemporary Novel— The Writers' Conference at the Edinburgh Festival." Microfilm of typescript. 17 leaves.

(9)   15 October 1962. "Does the Novel Matter?" Microfilm of typescript. 17 leaves.

(10)  21 December 1962. *The Masters*: "Joseph Conrad." Microfilm of typescript. [i], 9 leaves.

(11)  11 November 1964. *New Comment*. Microfilm of typescript. 11 leaves.

(12)  5 January 1965. *Woman's Hour*: "Talks of Books and Writers." Microfilm of typescript. 6 leaves.

(13)  29 July 1966. *Holiday Books in Paperback*. Microfilm of typescript. 23 leaves.

(14) 5 November 1966. "George Devine (1910-1966): A Tribute to the Actor-Manager-Producer." Typescript (mimeo); [i], 20 leaves.

(15) 10 May 1967. *The Lively Arts: Review of the Arts in the Making.* Microfilm of typescript. [i], 15 leaves.

(16) 11 October 1967. *The Lively Arts: Review of the Arts in the Making.* Microfilm of typescript. 18 leaves.

(17) 15 May 1970. "What the Dickens!" Microfilm of typescript. 24 leaves.

(18) 3 June 1970. *Now Read On: Books and Writers, News and Reviews.* Microfilm of typescript. [i], 15 leaves.

(19) 10 February 1971. *Now Read On: Books and Writers, News and Reviews.* Microfilm of typescript. 22 leaves.

(20) 2 June 1971. *Now Read On: Books and Writers, News and Reviews.* Microfilm of typescript. 24 leaves.

(21) 2 May 1972. *Study on 3—Perspective*: "Do Books Matter?" Microfilm of typescript. 15 leaves.

(22) 25 May 1973. *Arts Commentary.* (a) Typescript (mimeo), 12 pages on 6 leaves; (b) microfilm of typescript. 22 leaves.

(23) 11 December 1973. *Kaleidoscope.* Microfilm of typescript. 16 leaves.

(24) 24 August 1975. *The World This Weekend.* Microfilm of typescript. 3 leaves.

(25) 19 November 1975. *Kaleidoscope.* Microfilm of typescript. 16 leaves.

(26) 28 December 1975. "Drawing Tears Out of a Stone: An Appreciation of the Novels of Henry Green (1905-1973)." (a) Typescript (mimeo), [i], 26 leaves; (b) microfilm of typescript. [i], 26 leaves.

(27) 6 November 1977. "Wilson on Kipling." 15 leaves.

(28) 7 July 1980. *Kaleidoscope.* [i], 14 leaves.

(29) 22 August 1981. *Novels Up to Now*: "No. 6, Fgures in the Carpet." Microfilm of typescript. [i], 12 leaves.

(30)  20 June 1982. *Bookshelf*. Microfilm of typescript. [i], 8 leaves.

(31)  23 December 1983. "Cabin'd, Cribb'd, Confin'd." Photocopy of the typescript; 37 leaves.


### c. Radio and Television Productions

Scripts (1, 2, 4(a), 12 and 13) are held by the Written Archives Centre; (3, 4(b), 5-10, 14 and 20-23) by the Play Library, Broadcasting House, Portland Place, London W1; and (11, 15-19 and 24-28) by the Television Script Unit, Television Centre, Wood Lane, London W1Z 7RJ. *See* G. for programme details.

(1)  REALPOLITIK (G1)
     30 August 1947. Microfilm of typescript. [i], 9 leaves.

(2)  A VISIT IN BAD TASTE (G5)
     18 February 1951. Microfilm of typescript with autograph revisions. 9 leaves.

(3)  SKELETONS AND ASSEGAIS: FAMILY REMINISCENCES (G10)
     2 December 1952. Microfiche of typescript with autograph revisions (microfiche). [ii], 36 frames.

(4)  LEFT IN THE MIDDLE (G22)
     23 April 1956. (a) Microfilm of typescript. [i], 42 leaves; (b) microfiche of typescript with autograph revisions. [ii], 42 frames. *See also* H18*c*(3).

(5)  THE MEMOIRS OF MRS CRAMP (G28)
     30 September 1956. Episode I. Microfiche of typescript with autograph revisions not in Wilson's hand. [i], 11 frames.

(6)  THE MEMOIRS OF MRS CRAMP (G28)
     1 October 1956. Episode II. Microfiche of typescript with autograph revisions not in Wilson's hand. [iii], 14 frames.

(7)  THE MEMOIRS OF MRS CRAMP (G28)
     2 October 1956. Episode III. Microfiche of typescript with autograph revisions not in Wilson's hand. [iii], 12 frames.

(8)  THE MEMOIRS OF MRS CRAMP (G28)
     3 October 1956. Episode IV. Microfiche of typescript with autograph revisions not in Wilson's hand. [iii], 15 frames.

(9) THE MEMOIRS OF MRS CRAMP (G28)
4 October 1956. Episode V. Microfiche of typescript with autograph revisions not in Wilson's hand. [iii], 13 frames.

(10) THE MEMOIRS OF MRS CRAMP (G28)
5 October 1956. Episode VI. Microfiche of typescript with autograph revisions not in Wilson's hand. [iii], 17 frames.

(11) THE MULBERRY BUSH (G34)
20 October 1957. *Sunday Night Theatre.* (a) Rehearsal script. Typescript (mimeo). [i], 92 leaves; also on microfilm. (b) Microfilm of typescript (camera script). [ii], 83 leaves. *See also* H18*c*(2c).

(12) REALPOLITIK (G50)
30 March 1962. *Woman's Hour*: A Favourite Short Story. Microfilm of typescript. [i], 9 leaves.

(13) LATE CALL (G67)
21 September 1964. *Before Publication*: Angus Wilson Reads from His New Novel. Microfilm of typescript. 11 leaves.

(14) CRAZY CROWD (G95)
5 October 1967. Dramatised by Nesta Pain. (a) Typescript (mimeo) with autograph revisions. [i], 28 pages on 28 leaves. (b) Typescript (mimeo) with autograph revisions. [i], 28 pages on 28 leaves.

(15) LATE CALL (G106)
1 November 1969. Dramatised by Eric Ewens. (a) Typescript (mimeo) with autograph revisions. [iii], 60 pages on 60 leaves. (b) Typescript (mimeo). [i], 60 pages on 60 leaves.

(16) LATE CALL (G128)
1 March 1975. Dramatised by Dennis Potter. Part One. Camera script. Typescript (mimeo). [vi], 85 leaves; also on microfilm.

(17) LATE CALL (G128)
8 March 1975. Dramatised by Dennis Potter. Part Two. Camera script. Typescript (mimeo). [vi], 90 leaves; also on microfilm.

(18) LATE CALL (G128)
15 March 1975. Dramatised by Dennis Potter. Part Three. Camera script. Typescript (mimeo). [vi], 85 leaves; also on microfilm.

(19) LATE CALL (G128)
22 March 1975. Dramatised by Dennis Potter. Part Four. Camera script. Typescript (mimeo). [vii], 87 leaves; also on microfilm.

(20) THE LITTLE COMPANION (G135)
27 May 1976. Dramatised by John Graham. Typescript (mimeo). [i],
34 pages on 34 leaves.

(21) HEART OF ELM (G136)
3 June 1976. Dramatised by John Graham. Typescript (mimeo). [i],
33 pages on 17 leaves.

(22) ET DONA FERENTES (G137)
10 June 1976. Dramatised by John Graham. (a) Typescript (mimeo)
with autograph revisions. [i], 35 pages on 18 leaves. (b) Typescript
(mimeo). [i], 35 pages on 18 leaves.

(23) CRAZY CROWD (G138)
17 June 1976. Dramatised by John Graham. (a) Typescript (mimeo)
with autograph revisions. [i], 43 pages on 43 leaves. (b) Typescript
(mimeo) with autograph revisions. [i], 43 pages on 43 leaves.

(24) THE OLD MEN AT THE ZOO (G155)
15 September 1983. Dramatised by Troy Kennedy Martin. Episode
One: "A Tall Story." Post-production script. Typescript (photocopy).
[ii], 104 leaves; also on microfilm.

(25) THE OLD MEN AT THE ZOO (G155)
22 September 1983. Dramatised by Troy Kennedy Martin. Episode
Two: "Godmanchester's Plan." Post-production script. Typescript
(photocopy). [ii], 102 leaves; also on microfilm.

(26) THE OLD MEN AT THE ZOO (G155)
29 September 1983. Dramatised by Troy Kennedy Martin. Episode
Three: "Exodus." Post-production script. Typescript (mimeo). [ii],
102 leaves; also on microfilm.

(27) THE OLD MEN AT THE ZOO (G155)
6 October 1983. Dramatised by Troy Kennedy Martin. Episode Four:
"Armageddon." Post-production script. Typescript (mimeo). [ii], 115
leaves; also on microfilm.

(28) THE OLD MEN AT THE ZOO (G155)
13 October 1983. Dramatised by Troy Kennedy Martin. Episode
Five: "The Year of the Yeti." Post-production script. Typescript
(mimeo). [ii], 103 leaves; also on microfilm.

*d. Correspondence*

Correspondence is held by the Written Archives Centre, Caversham Park, Reading RG4 8TZ

Miscellaneous correspondence from Wilson to BBC personnel from 1950. Correspondence to Mr Baker-Smith, Mrs Bray, Peggy Caird, Donald Carne-Ross, Christopher, Douglas Cleverdon, Terence Cooper, Philip French, Kay Fuller, Ian Grimble, Anna Kallin, R.E. Keen, Ludovic Kennedy, Owen Leeming, Margaret Lyons, Gerard Mansell, John Morris, P.H. Newby, Miss Pearce, Rose Mary Sands, Anthony Thwaite and Mary Treadgold. Correspondence less than twenty years old is restricted, and some correspondence from Wilson not under this rule has been restricted by request.

## H2    BRITISH LIBRARY, REFERENCE DIVISION
### Department of Manuscripts, Great Russell Street, London WC1

### THE MULBERRY BUSH (A6)

*a. Drama*

Mimeographed copy of second version. 104 pages on 104 leaves. Copy submitted to the Lord Chamberlain's office for licencing for performance. Licence 8973 granted 9 March 1956.

*b. Correspondence*

One typed letter signed from Wilson to Christopher Logue. Dated 17 December 1968. Add. Mss. 62542.

## H3    BROTHERTON LIBRARY, UNIVERSITY OF LEEDS
### Leeds LS2 9JT

*Ralph Abercrombie Papers*. Two letters from Wilson to Ralph Abercrombie. Dated 14 October 1952 and postmark 7 May 1968.

*"London Magazine" Archive*. Five letters from Wilson to Alan Ross, editor of *London Magazine*. Dated 19 April 1970—postmark 20 December 1976.

# H4          CHURCHILL COLLEGE LIBRARY, CAMBRIDGE
### Churchill Archives Centre, Cambridge CB3 0DS

*Cecil Roberts Papers.* Two letters from Wilson to Cecil Roberts. Dated 24 June 1968 and 8 July 1974.

# H5          COLUMBIA UNIVERSITY
### Rare Book and Manuscript Library, Butler Library, New York, N. Y. 10027

*Curtis Brown Manuscript Collection.* Correspondence from Wilson to Curtis Brown Ltd, some undated, 1960-1967. Three autograph letters signed; seven typed letters signed; one autograph postcard signed.

*James Oliver Brown Manuscript Collection.* Correspondence from Wilson to James Oliver Brown, 1978-1985. One autograph letter signed; four typed letters signed; one autograph note signed; two autograph postcards signed.

*Cushman Manuscript Collection.* Correspondence from Wilson to John Cushman, 1967-1977. One autograph letter signed; two typed letters signed.

*Hoopes Manuscript Collection.* Correspondence from Wilson to Ned E. Hoopes. One autograph postcard signed. Dated 27 March 1963.

*Moers Manuscript Collection.* Correspondence from Wilson to Ellen Moers, 1960-[1973]. Three typed letters signed.

# H6          ETON COLLEGE, SCHOOL LIBRARY
### Windsor, Berkshire SL4 6HB

*Eton College Literary Society Collection.* Correspondence from Wilson to Quintin Hoare, Piers Rodgers, Simon Hornblower, Philip Mansel, Timothy Shawcross, Crispin Hasler, Mark Southern and Jonathan Bond, 1956-1981. Twelve autograph letters signed.

*Susan Hill Collection.* One typed letter signed from Wilson to Susan Hill. 198—.

**H7**                **HALL-CARPENTER ARCHIVES**
67/69 Cowcross Street, London EC1
Mailing address: BM Archives, London WC1N 3XX.

Correspondence from Wilson as an honorary Vice-president of the Campaign for Homosexual Equality protesting the personnel policies of British Home Stores. Four typed letters signed. 9 February 1976 (two letters) and 19 March 1976 (two letters).


**H8**                **KING'S COLLEGE, CAMBRIDGE**
Cambridge CB2 1ST

*E.M. Forster Papers*. Letter from Wilson to E.M. Forster. Undated.


**H9**    **NEW YORK PUBLIC LIBRARY (ASTOR, LENOX AND TILDEN FOUNDATIONS), BERG COLLECTION OF ENGLISH AND AMERICAN LITERATURE**
Fifth Avenue at 42nd Street, New York, N. Y. 10018

*a. Short Stories*

(1)  TEARS, IDLE TEARS
Autograph manuscript. 1 leaf, 1 page. Notes related to the story.

(2)  UNION REUNION (A1)
Autograph manuscript. 38 pages on 21 leaves. Accompanied by a postcard from Wilson about the manuscript.


*b. Radio Drama*

LEFT IN THE MIDDLE (G22)
Typescript (mimeo) with holograph revisions not in Wilson's hand. [i], 42 pages. Signed by the producer, Louis MacNeice.


*c. Non-fiction*

[STATEMENT ON VIETNAM] (B32)
Typescript. 1 leaf, 1 page.

*d. Correspondence*

Two letters to Cecil Woolf. Dated 3 July [1966] and 12 July 1966. With
other correspondence and material related to Wilson's statement in *Authors
Take Sides on Vietnam* (B32).

Two postcards to Leonard Clark. Postmark 2 March 1970 and 2 May 1970.


## H10    NORTHAMPTONSHIRE RECORD OFFICE
### Delapré Abbey, London Road, Northampton NN5
### 9AW

*Northampton Arts Association (Literature Group).* One letter from Wilson,
1965.


## H11    OXFORD UNIVERSITY, BODLEIAN LIBRARY
### Oxford OX13 BG

Two letters from Wilson, 1968 and undated.


## H12        ROYAL SOCIETY OF LITERATURE
### 1 Hyde Park Gardens, London W2 2LT

Correspondence from Wilson dating from his acceptance of a Fellowship in
the Royal Society of Literature in 1958.


## H13        SECKER & WARBURG, LTD
### 54 Poland Street, London W1V 3DF

Archives on deposit at the University of Reading, Whiteknights, Reading
RG6 2AE. Consultation by permission and prior appointment only.
Correspondence with Wilson from 1950. Readers reports by Wilson.
Uncatalogued.


## H14        THAMES TELEVISION
### Thames Television House, Programme Documentation
### Archive, 306-316 Euston Road, London NW1 3BB

*Television Drama*

(1)  AFTER THE SHOW (G41)
     20 September 1959. Camera script. Typescript (mimeo). [ii], 56 leaves.

(2)  THE STRANGER (G42)
     20 November 1960. Rehearsal script. Typescript (mimeo). [iii], 61 leaves.

(3)  THE INVASION (G63)
     31 March 1963. Camera script. Typescript (mimeo). [iv], 61 leaves.


H15     UNIVERSITY COLLEGE, UNIVERSITY OF
                    LONDON
           Gower Street, London WC1E 6BT

*Alex Comfort Papers*. Letter from Wilson to Alex Comfort, 1951.


H16             UNIVERSITY OF DURHAM
     University Library, Palace Green Section, Palace Green
                    DH1 3RN

*Plomer Collection*. Three letters from Wilson to William Plomer. Dated 4 October 1952, postmark 28 June 1953 and 11 November 1960.


H17             UNIVERSITY OF EAST ANGLIA
        Office of the Vice Chancellor, Norwich NR4 7TJ

Typescripts of two citations for honorary degrees conferred upon Sir Hedley Atkins at the Congregation of September 1968 and Professor T.A. Bennet-Clark at the Congregation of October 1968 delivered by Wilson as Public Orator of the University of East Anglia.


H18                UNIVERSITY OF IOWA
        University of Iowa Libraries, Special Collections, Iowa
                    City, Iowa 52242

The following is a summary listing compiled with the assistance of Mr Robert A. McCown, Head, Special Collections and Manuscripts Librarian. For a detailed description of the collection purchased in 1968, *see*

Frederick P. W. McDowell and E. Sharon Graves, *The Angus Wilson Manuscripts in the University of Iowa Libraries* (Iowa City: Friends of the University of Iowa Libraries, 1969). *See also* Frederick P. W. McDowell, "The Angus Wilson Collection," *Books at Iowa*, 10 (April 1969), 9-18, 20, 23. Papers acquired after 1968, consisting for the most part of works published since 1970, are being catalogued.

Manuscripts are arranged as follows: *a*. Novels; *b*. Short Stories; *c*. Radio, Stage and Television Drama; *d*. Non-Fiction; *e*. Essays, Lectures and Reviews; *f*. Reading Notes and Miscellaneous; *g*. Correspondence.

*a. Novels*

(1)  HEMLOCK AND AFTER (A4)
     Autograph manuscript. Seven notebooks, including one notebook of preliminary notes. 443 pages on 379 leaves.

(2)  ANGLO-SAXON ATTITUDES (A7)
     (a) Autograph manuscript. Sixteen notebooks, including one notebook of a preliminary version of Chapter One and five notebooks of preliminary notes. 520 pages on 566 leaves. (b) Typescript.

(3)  THE MIDDLE AGE OF MRS ELIOT (A9)
     Autograph manuscript. Thirteen notebooks, including two notebooks of preliminary notes. 640 pages on 710 leaves.

(4)  GOAT AND COMPASSES
     Unfinished novel. (a) Autograph manuscript. Three notebooks. 51 pages on 51 leaves. (b) Typescript. 40 pages on 40 leaves. (c) Typescript. (d) Typescript (carbon) of one chapter, published as My Husband Is Right (C281). 30 pages on 30 leaves.

(5)  THE OLD MEN AT THE ZOO (A10)
     (a) Twelve notebooks, including two notebooks of early versions of Parts I and II. 603 pages on 636 leaves with additional pages. (b) Five scripts for the television dramatisation by Troy Kennedy Martin.

(6)  LATE CALL (A12)
     (a) Autograph manuscript. Nine notebooks, including one notebook of preliminary notes. 451 pages on 638 leaves and additional notes. (b) Typescript with autograph revisions. 424 pages. (c) Typescript. (d) Typescript. 53 pages on 53 leaves.

Chap. V.

*A page from Wilson's* Late Call *notebooks.*
*By permission of Sir Angus Wilson and the University of Iowa Libraries, Special Collections.*

(7)  NO LAUGHING MATTER (A14)
(a) Autograph manuscript. Nineteen notebooks, including four note-books of preliminary notes. 796 pages on 859 leaves and additional notes. (b) Typescript. (c) Proofs.

(8)  AS IF BY MAGIC (A17)
(a) Autograph manuscript. (b) Typescript. (c) Typescript.  12 leaves. Rejected episode published in *The Iowa Review* (C485).

(9)  SETTING THE WORLD ON FIRE (A20)
(a) Autograph manuscript. (b) Typescript. (c) Miscellaneous notes, notes on fashion and revolutionaries, and miscellaneous journals and newspaper clippings.

*b.  Short Stories*

(1)  AFTER THE SHOW (A8)
Autograph manuscript. One notebook. 20 pages on 20 leaves.

(2)  A BIT OFF THE MAP (A8)
Autograph manuscript. Two notebooks. 55 pages on 55 leaves.

(3)  CHRISTMAS BRINGS MEMORIES
Unfinished story. Autograph manuscript. 11 pages on 11 leaves.

(4)  CHRISTMAS DAY IN THE WORKHOUSE (A2)
Autograph manuscript. One notebook. 27 pages on 27 leaves.

(5)  CRAZY CROWD (C2)
Autograph manuscript. One notebook. 35 pages on 35 leaves.

(6)  DIVIDED WORSHIP
Story fragment. Autograph manuscript. 5 pages on 4 leaves.

(7)  AN ELEPHANT NEVER FORGETS (C39)
Autograph manuscript with preliminary notes. 18 pages on 10 leaves.

(8)  ET DONA FERENTES (A1)
Autograph manuscript. One notebook. 36 pages on 18 leaves.

(9)  THE EYES OF THE PEACOCK (C534)
Autograph manuscript and typescript. 23 pages on 23 leaves.

(10) A FLAT COUNTRY CHRISTMAS (C34)
Autograph manuscript. One notebook. 12 pages on 12 leaves.

(11) HEART OF ELM
Autograph notes for a preliminary version. 2 pages on 2 leaves.

(12) HOLIDAY LESSONS
Autograph manuscript. 14 pages on 13 leaves.

(13) I DOUBLE DARE YOU
Autograph manuscript. 5 pages on 5 leaves.

(14) LEARNING'S LITTLE TRIBUTE (A2)
Autograph manuscript. One notebook. 16 pages on 18 leaves.

(15) A LITTLE COMPANION (A2)
Autograph manuscript. One notebook. 9 pages on 9 leaves.

(16) LIVE AND LET DIE
Autograph manuscript. 15 pages on 10 leaves.

(17) THE MEN WITH BOWLER HATS (C66)
Autograph manuscript. 14 pages on 14 leaves.

(18) MORE FRIEND THAN LODGER (C181)
(a) Autograph manuscript. Three notebooks. 54 pages on 54 leaves.
(b) Typescript.

(19) MORE THAN A VANLOAD
Story fragment. Autograph manuscript. 1 page on 1 leaf.

(20) MOTHER'S SENSE OF FUN (C1)
Autograph manuscript. One notebook. 16 pages on 16 leaves.

(21) MUMMY TO THE RESCUE (A2)
Autograph manuscript. One notebook. 13 pages on 13 leaves.

(22) NECESSITY'S CHILD (A2)
Autograph manuscript. One notebook. 13 pages on 7 leaves.

(23) NO FUTURE FOR OUR YOUNG
Autograph manuscript. 20 pages on 16 leaves.

(24) ONCE A LADY (C182)
(a) Autograph manuscript. One notebook. 27 pages on 27 leaves.
(b) Typescript.

(25) THE PENDULUM'S SWUNG TOO FAR
Unfinished story. Autograph manuscript. 13 pages on 7 leaves.

(26)  RASPBERRY JAM (A1)
Autograph manuscript. One notebook. 31 pages on 36 leaves.

(27)  REALPOLITIK (C3)
Autograph manuscript. One notebook. 6 pages on 6 leaves.

(28)  REX IMPERATOR (C8)
Autograph manuscript. One notebook. 16 pages on 8 leaves.

(29)  A SAD FALL (A8)
Autograph manuscript. One notebook. 24 pages on 24 leaves.

(30)  SATURNALIA (A1)
Autograph manuscript. One notebook. 8 pages on 8 leaves.

(31)  SIGNIFICANT EXPERIENCE (A1)
Autograph manuscript. One notebook. 34 pages on 18 leaves.

(32)  SISTER SUPERIOR (A2)
Autograph manuscript. One notebook. 20 pages on 19 leaves.

(33)  A STORY OF HISTORICAL INTEREST (A1)
Autograph manuscript. One notebook. 17 pages on 20 leaves.

(34)  SUCH DARLING DODOS (C13)
Autograph manuscript. One notebook. 20 pages on 19 leaves.

(35)  TEN MINUTES TO TWELVE (A8)
Autograph manuscript. One notebook. 28 pages on 28 leaves.

(36)  TOTENTANZ (A2)
Autograph manuscript. One notebook. 12 pages on 15 leaves.

(37)  UNWANTED HEROINE (C83)
Autograph manuscript. 26 pages on 22 leaves.

(38)  WHAT DO HIPPOS EAT?
Autograph manuscript of two preliminary versions. 6 pages on 5 leaves.

(39)  WHO FOR SUCH DAINTIES? (B1)
Autograph manuscript. 4 pages on 3 leaves.

(40)  WITH IT
Autograph manuscript. 17 pages on 11 leaves.

## c. Radio, Stage and Television Drama

(1)  SKELETONS AND ASSEGAIS (G10)
Autograph manuscript.

(2)  THE MULBERRY BUSH (A6)
(a) Autograph manuscript. Eight notebooks, including three note-books of early versions (entitled *Sheep and Goats*) and preliminary notes. 328 pages on 237 leaves. (b) Typescript. (c) Television script (G34).

(3)  LEFT IN THE MIDDLE (G22)
(a) Autograph manuscripts. Two versions. (b) Script.

(4)  AFTER THE SHOW (G41)
Television script. 78 pages on 78 leaves. *See also* H14(1).

(5)  THE STRANGER (G42)
(a) Autograph manuscript. (b) Typescript. *See also* H14(2).

(6)  THE INVASION (G63)
(a) Autograph manuscript. 26 pages on 21 leaves. (b) Typescript. *See also* H14(3).

(7)  DANCE OF DEATH
Autograph manuscript. Television script (unproduced) based on Totentanz. 32 pages on 23 leaves.

(8)  A SLAP ALL AROUND
Autograph manuscript. Television script (unproduced) based on Sister Superior. 27 pages on 27 leaves.

## d. Non-Fiction

(1)  EMILE ZOLA: AN INTRODUCTORY STUDY OF HIS NOVELS (A3)
Autograph manuscript. Eleven notebooks. 207 pages on 297 leaves.

(2)  THE WILD GARDEN OR SPEAKING OF WRITING (A11)
(a) Autograph manuscript. Three notebooks. 147 pages on 147 leaves. (b) Typescript.

(3)  TEMPO: THE IMPACT OF TELEVISION ON THE ARTS (A13)
Autograph manuscript. One notebook. 40 pages on 40 leaves.

(4)  THE WORLD OF CHARLES DICKENS (A16)
Autograph manuscript. Notebooks.

(5)  THE STRANGE RIDE OF RUDYARD KIPLING (A19)
(a) Autograph manuscript. Eleven notebooks, including two notebooks of notes. (b) Typescript. (c) Miscellaneous notes, correspondence, British Library book request slips and library permissions
correspondence.

*e. Essays, Lectures and Reviews*

(1)  ADELAIDE SPEECH (C405)
Autograph manuscript. 39 pages on 25 leaves.

(2)  [BEAVERBROOK'S ENGLAND] (C300)
Autograph manuscript. 6 pages on 6 leaves.

(3)  THE BOOKS I READ (C273)
Autograph manuscript. 3 pages on 3 leaves.

(4)  BREADTH AND DEPTH IN THE NOVEL
Autograph manuscript. Lecture delivered at Morley College,
London, 13 November 1956. Published in part as: Diversity and
Depth in the Novel (C213). 17 pages on 11 leaves.

(5)  THE BRITISH MUSEUM (C126)
Autograph manuscript. 29 pages on 29 leaves.

(6)  CHANNEL ISLANDS
Autograph manuscript. Notes for an article (*see* A22). 5 pages on
3 leaves.

(7)  [The DAY BEFORE YESTERDAY] (C35)
(a) Autograph manuscript. (b) Typescript.

(8)  DICKENS AND THE AGE OF NATURALISM
Typescript.

(9)  DICKENS AND THE MODERN CITY
Typescript. 25 pages on 25 leaves. Transcript of a recording of a
lecture delivered 20 October 1971 at the University of Iowa. *See also*
F9.

(10) [DICKENS'S PRIVATE VOICE] (C391) [1965]
Autograph manuscript.

(11) GUILT AND INNOCENCE IN THE WORKS OF CHARLES DICKENS
Autograph manuscript.

(12) ENVY (B20)
Autograph manuscript. 13 pages on 8 leaves.

(13) HOW IT IS TO BE A WRITER
Autograph manuscript. Notes for an article or lecture. 12 pages on 8 leaves.

(14) MR HUXLEY'S SPLIT MIND (C53)
Autograph manuscript.

(15) AN INTERVIEW WITH ANGUS WILSON (E27)
(a) Typescript. 46 leaves. (b) Revised transcript. 46 leaves. Photocopy of transcript with written comments by McDowell and Wilson. (c) List of questions submitted to Wilson before the interview with his written comments. 11 leaves. *See also* A21.

(16) INTRODUCTION TO THE SELECTED STORIES OF W. SOMERSET MAUGHAM (B31)
Autograph manuscript. 4 pages on 4 leaves.

(17) JOHN COWPER POWYS
Autograph manuscript. Notes for a broadcast. 5 pages on 3 leaves. *See also* G55.

(18) JOURNEY TO MY MOTHER'S LAND (C269 and C270)
Autograph manuscript. 83 pages on 60 leaves. [1961]

(19) [THE LAST AMATEURS] (C279)
Autograph manuscript.

(20) [NEW NOVELS] (C7)
Autograph manuscript.

(21) [NEW NOVELS] (C9)
Autograph manuscript.

(22) THE NOVELS OF WILLIAM GODWIN (C40)
Autograph manuscript. 18 pages on 16 leaves.

(23) [NUNC DIMITTIS] (C62)
Autograph manuscript.

(24) PETTY'S NOVEL
Autograph manuscript. Notes (*see* B12). 3 pages on 3 leaves.

(25) [PROUST AS A SET BOOK] (C15)
Autograph manuscript. 4 pages on 4 leaves.

(26) PUBLIC LECTURE [ON THE NOVEL]
Autograph manuscript. 12 pages on 7 leaves.

(27) [REASONS FOR ACCEPTING A POST AT EAST ANGLIA]
(C371)
Autograph manuscript. 4 pages on 4 leaves.

(28) SAMUEL BUTLER AND HIS INFLUENCE (C187)
Typescript.

(29) [SHORT STORIES] (C12)
Autograph manuscript.

(30) [THE STATUS OF S.F.] (C271)
Autograph manuscript.

(31) TELEVISION
Autograph manuscript. 5 pages on 5 leaves.

(32) [TELEVISION PROGRAMMES]
Autograph manuscripts. Notes for reviews. 42 pages on 25 leaves.

(33) [THE VIKING PORTABLE DICKENS] (B57)
Autograph manuscript. Notes.

(34) VISITING KRUSHCHEV AT THE BLACK SEA (C365)
Autograph manuscript. 7 pages on 7 leaves.

(35) WHY DO I BOTHER? (C398)
Autograph manuscript (incomplete). 1 page on 1 leaf.

(36) [ZOLA AND THE ENGLISH READER] (C25)
Autograph manuscript.

(37) [ZOLA BEFORE, DURING AND AFTER] (C392)
Autograph manuscript.

(38) ZOLA IN ENGLAND (C54)
Autograph manuscript. Published as: Influence grandissante de Zola
en Angleterre. 5 pages on 5 leaves. *See also* G9.

(39)  ZOLA
      Autograph manuscript. Lecture. 12 pages on 9 leaves.

*f.  Reading Notes and Miscellaneous*

(1)   JANE AUSTEN
      Autograph manuscript. Notes. 45 pages on 26 leaves.

(2)   CHARLES DICKENS
      Autograph manuscript. Notes. 7 pages on 7 leaves.

(3)   DOSTOEVSKY'S *POSSESSED*
      Autograph manuscript. Notes.

(4)   [E.M. FORSTER AND VIRGINIA WOOLF]
      Autograph manuscript. Notes on *A Room with a View, Howards End,
      A Passage to India,* and *Mrs Dalloway* and *The Waves.*

(5)   NOTES ON A VISIT TO JAPAN
      Autograph manuscript. 3 pages on 3 leaves.

(6)   HUGH WALPOLE
      Autograph manuscript. Notes. 18 pages on 36 leaves.

*g.  Correspondence*

Miscellaneous correspondence from Wilson to Lady Cynthia Asquith, Mrs
Bernstein, O.M. Brack, Jr, Peter Burton, John Gerber, Frank Hamlin,
Miss Harrison, Mary Kivlin, John Leggett, Frederick P. W. McDowell,
Frank Paluka, John Pattison, Alan Ross, John Senhouse, Dennis Shaw and
George Starbuck comprising thirty-six letters or postcards. Miscellaneous
correspondence to Wilson.

H19               UNIVERSITY OF READING
                Whiteknights, Reading RG6 2AE

*British Council Correspondence File.* One letter from Wilson, 1965.

H20               UNIVERSITY OF SUSSEX
        University of Sussex Library, Falmer, Brighton BN1
                          9QL

Two letters from Wilson to Leonard Woolf. Dated 1962 and 1965.

# H21                  VIKING PENGUIN INC.
### 40 West 23rd Street, New York, N. Y. 10010

*a. Essay*

[AN OLD ADMIRER SALUTES THE U.S.A.] (C597)

Typescript. 5 pages on 5 leaves with holograph revisions not in Wilson's hand.

*b. Correspondence*

Correspondence from and to Wilson.

*Note*: The autograph manuscripts in one notebook of AUNT CORA (C27), HEART OF ELM (A2) and WHAT DO HIPPOS EAT? (C4) were purchased by Alan Jenkins in 1954. *See* "Hemlock—and Before," *Spectator*, 193 (17 September 1954), 331.

# I. Foreign Editions and Reprints. Braille Editions and Talking Books. Works Misattributed. Reported Speech. Communications to the Press. Extracts from Letters. Announced but not Published

## FOREIGN EDITIONS AND REPRINTS

I1    "Some Japanese Observations—II." *Some Japanese Observations*. Ed. with notes in Japanese by Keiichi Harada. Tokyo: Kaibunsha, 1958, pp. 8-20. Reprint of C190.

I2    *A Bit off the Map and Other Stories*. Ed. with notes and an introduction in Japanese by Tsutomu Ueda. Kenkyusha Pocket English Series. Tokyo: Kenkyusha, 1959.

    Contents: A Bit off the Map — A Flat Country Christmas — More Friend than Lodger

I3   *After the Show and Other Stories.* Ed. with notes and an introduction
     in Japanese by Kaneo Kawada. Kenkyusha Pocket English Series.
     Tokyo: Kenkyusha, [1959].

     Contents:  After the Show — Once a Lady — Ten Minutes to Twelve

I4   "The Two Faces of Japan." *Selected Readings in Current English.* Ed.
     Kioyaki Murata. Tokyo: Obunsha, 1959, pp. 16-25. Reprint of C231.

I5   *Such Darling Dodos.* Ed. with an introduction and notes in Japanese
     by Koichi Yajima. Hokuseido English Texts. Tokyo: Hokuseido
     Press, 1962.

     Contents:  A Little Companion — Learning's Little Tribute — Rex
     Imperator — Such Darling Dodos

I6   *After the Show.* Ed. C. Buddingh. Cahiers voor letterkunde voor het
     voortgezet onderwijs. Amsterdam: J.M. Meulenhoff, 1968.

I7   "Higher Standards." *English Short Stories (2)/Englische Kurz-
     geschicten (2).* Munich: Deutscher Taschenbuch Verlag, 1968, pp. 70,
     72, 74, 76, 78, 80, 82, 84, 86, 88. *See also* D49.

I8   *The World of Charles Dickens.* Haarlem: Uitgeverij J.H. Gottmer/
     London: Secker & Warburg, 1970.

I9   "The Men with Bowler Hats." *Read and Relate: 20 Stories for Repro-
     duction, Précis-writing, Discussion, Debating, Listening Comprehen-
     sion.* Ed. John R. Ashton. Berlin: Cornelsen-Velhagen und Klasing,
     1971.

I10  *The World of Charles Dickens.* New Delhi: Heritage Publishing/
     London: Secker & Warburg, 1980.

I11  "The Wrong Set." *20-seiki Igiri tanpen-shu/Twentieth Century British
     Authors.* Ed. Kazushi Kuzumi. Tokyo: Kinseido, 1981, Vol. II,
     pp. 46-60.

I12  "Raspberry Jam." *Modern British Stories II: Wilson, Spark, Wain,
     Lessing, Sillitoe.* Ed. with notes in Japanese by Nobuo Matsumoto.
     Tokyo: Eihōsha, 1984, pp. 9-34.

I13  "Higher Standards." *Modern English Short Stories III: From Bates to
     Swift.* Ed. Hans-Christian Oeser. Stuttgart: Philipp Reclam jun.
     Verlag, 1986, pp. 41-51.

I14  "Realpolitik." *Die Englische Literatur in Text und Darstellung: 20 Jahrhundert II* (Band 10). Ed. Raimund Borgmeier and Bernhard Reitz. Stuttgart: Philipp Reclam jun. Verlag, 1986, pp. 356, 358, 360, 362.

# BRAILLE EDITIONS AND TALKING BOOKS

The National Library for the Blind, Cromwell Road, Bredbury, Stockport SK6 2G.

I15  *Such Darling Dodos and Other Stories*. Secker & Warburg, 1950. Two volumes. Braille.

I16  *Hemlock and After*. Secker & Warburg, 1952. Four volumes. Braille.

I17  *Anglo-Saxon Attitudes*. Secker & Warburg, 1956. Seven volumes. Braille.

I18  *A Bit Off the Map and Other Stories*. Secker & Warburg, 1957. Three volumes. Braille.

I19  *The Middle Age of Mrs Eliot*. Secker & Warburg, 1958. Seven volumes. Braille.

I20  *The Old Men at the Zoo*. Secker & Warburg, 1961. Six volumes. Braille.

I21  *Late Call*. Secker & Warburg, 1964. Six volumes. Braille.

I22  *No Laughing Matter*. Secker & Warburg, 1967. Ten volumes. Braille.

I23  *The World of Charles Dickens*. Secker & Warburg, 1970. Six volumes. Braille.

I24  *As If By Magic*. Secker & Warburg, 1973. Nine volumes. Braille.

I25  *Setting the World on Fire*. Secker & Warburg, 1980. Four volumes. Braille.

Cassette Library for the Blind and Handicapped (Calibre), Aylesbury, Bucks HP20 1HU.

126  *The Middle Age of Mrs Eliot.* On thirteen cassettes. Talking book.

National Library Service for the Blind and Physically Handicapped, The Library of Congress, 1291 Taylor Street N. W., Washington, D. C. 20542

127  *Such Darling Dodos and Other Stories.* Secker & Warburg, 1950. Two volumes. Braille. BRA 7863.

128  *Late Call.* Secker & Warburg, 1964. Four volumes. Braille. BR 316.

129  *The World of Charles Dickens.* Viking, 1970. Disc. 16 sides. TB 3728.

130  *As If By Magic.* Viking, 1974. Ten volumes. Braille. BRA 13994.

131  *The Strange Ride of Rudyard Kipling: His Life and Works.* Viking, 1978. Four cassettes. RC 14967.

132  *The Penguin Book of English Short Stories* edited by Christopher Dolley. Penguin, 1967. Five volumes. Braille. BR 1493. Includes Raspberry Jam.

Illinois Regional Library for the Blind and Physically Handicapped, 1055 West Roosevelt Road, Chicago, Illinois 60608

133  *No Laughing Matter.* Viking, 1967. 13 volumes. Braille. BIL-950.

Recording for the Blind, The Anne T. Macdonald Center, 20 Roszel Road, Princeton, N. J. 08540

134  George Meredith, *The Egoist,* with an afterword by Angus Wilson. New American Library—Signet Books, 1963. Five cassettes. TC0429.

135  Emile Zola, *L'Assomoir,* with an afterword by Angus Wilson. New American Library, 1962. Five cassettes. TKO898.

136  Charles Dickens, *Great Expectations,* with an afterword by Angus Wilson. New American Library—Signet Books, 1963. Five cassettes. TBO279.

# WORKS MISATTRIBUTED

I37   *Acting Material for Dramatic Classes.* Comp. Angus Wilson. London: Pitman & Sons, 1934. *The National Union Catalogue Pre-1956 Imprints,* London: Mansell, 1980, Vol. 666, p. 381.

I38   *Home-made Lighting Apparatus for the Amateur Stage.* London: Yearbook Press, n.d.; London: H.F.W. Deane & Sons, [1936?]. *The National Union Catalogue Pre-1956 Imprints,* London: Mansell, 1980, Vol. 666, p. 381.

I39   "The Foundation of Modern Japan." *Spectator,* 167 (12 December 1941), 550-551. Stanton (M15), p. 1002.

I40   "Sugared Almonds." *Nation and Athenaeum,* 35 (26 July 1924 [*sic,* i.e., 1942]), 535-537. Stanton (M15), p. 999.

I41   *All About Photographing Shows with Your Camera.* London and New York: Focal Press, 1953. *The National Union Catalogue Pre-1956 Imprints,* London: Mansell, 1980, Vol. 666, p. 381.

I42   *Stage Lighting for the Amateur Producer.* London: Pitman, 1961. *The National Union Catalogue 1956 through 1967,* Totowa, NJ: Rowman and Littlefield, 1972, Vol. 123, p. 5; *The American Book Publishing Record, Cumulative 1950-1977,* New York: Bowker, 1978, Vol. 8, p. 1035.

# REPORTED SPEECH

I43   "Writers and the Public: Report on the XXVII Congress of International P.E.N." *P.E.N. News,* no. 193 (October 1956), 15-22 (16-17). Extract from Wilson's speech to the Congress (as broadcast transcription). *See also* G25.

I44   Holloway, John. "Reflections on English Intellectual Culture." *Listener,* 77 (19 January 1967), 85-86, 88-89 (89). Wilson quoted from remarks at the International Writers' Conference, Leningrad—Moscow, Summer 1963.

I45   "Man of Our Time: Angus Wilson." *Sunday Times,* 31 August 1969, p. 9.

I46   "The London Birthday Dinner." *Dickensian,* 70 (May 1974), 137-139. Report with quotations on Wilson's address to the Dickens Fellowship, 7 February 1974.

I47 "Annual Luncheon, 1984—Sir Angus Wilson's Introduction of the Guest Speaker." *Kipling Journal*, 58 (September 1984), 8-9. Report with quotations on Wilson's address to the Kipling Society, 3 May 1984.

I48 "British Bookstore To Be Tried for Obscenity." *New York Native*, 16-22 September 1985, p. 12. Wilson quoted, ex officio, as President of the Royal Society of Literature protesting the seizure of materials at the London bookshop, "Gay's the Word."

## COMMUNICATIONS TO THE PRESS SIGNED BY ANGUS WILSON

I49 "Zola and His Characters." *Times Literary Supplement*, 30 October 1953, p. 693. Letter to the editor taking issue with a review of F.W.J. Hemmings's *Emile Zola. See also* C73.

I50 "Hungarian Writers on Trial." *Times*, 29 October 1957, p. 11. Signed T.S. Eliot, E.M. Forster, C.P. Snow and others including Angus Wilson. Letter to the editor supporting Hungarian writers.

I51 "Homosexual Acts: Call To Reform Law." *Times*, 7 March 1958, p. 11. Signed Isaiah Berlin, C. Day Lewis, J.B. Priestley and others including Angus Wilson. Letter to the editor supporting the Wolfenden Report.

I52 *Lolita. Times*, 23 January 1959, p. 11. Signed Rosamond Lehmann, Iris Murdoch, V.S. Pritchett and others including Angus Wilson. Letter to the editor protesting the possible suppression of Vladimir Nabokov's novel in England.

I53 "Spanish Prisoners." *Times*, 1 March 1960, p. 11. Signed Rosamond Lehmann, John Osborne, C.P. Snow and others including Angus Wilson. Letter to the editor protesting the arrest of Luis Goytisolo and other Spanish writers.

I54 "Dr Agostinho Neto." *Times*, 2 October 1961, p. 13. Letter to the editor urging the release of the Angolan poet.

I55 "Talk of America." *Times*, 12 February 1962, p. 11. Letter to the editor on relations with the United States.

I56 "Pressure Against South Africa." *Times*, 22 June 1962, p. 13. Signed Ritchie Calder, Jeremy Thorpe and others including Angus Wilson.

Letter to the editor urging economic sanctions and an arms embargo on South Africa.

I57 "Evil in the English Novel." *Listener*, 69 (24 January 1963), 169. Letter to the editor in response to readers' letters (10 January, pp. 74-75 and 17 January, p. 127).

I58 "The Wild Garden." *Times Literary Supplement*, 28 November 1963, p. 933. Reply to "Getting Themselves Taped," an unsigned review of *The Wild Garden* (L490).

I59 "Mr Angus Heriot." *Times*, 10 February 1964, p. 14. An obituary tribute.

I60 "Mihajlo Mihajlov." *Times*, 23 March 1965, p. 13. Signed W.H. Auden, Stephen Spender, Rebecca West and others including Angus Wilson. Letter to the editor protesting the arrest and imprisonment of the Yugoslavian writer and teacher.

I61 "Evelyn Waugh." *Spectator*, 216 (29 April 1966), 524. An obituary tribute.

I62 "Rights Denied to Soviet Jews." *Times*, 27 June 1966, p. 11. Signed Kingsley Amis, Iris Murdoch, Herbert Read, John Wain and others including Angus Wilson. Letter to the editor protesting the Soviet Government's denial of cultural and religious rights to Soviet Jews.

I63 "Restrictions in South Africa." *Times*, 12 July 1967, p. 9. Letter to the editor appealing for the return of passport to playwright Athol Fugard.

I64 "Bursaries." *Times Literary Supplement*, 21 March 1968, p. 293. Letter to the editor as Chairman of the Arts Council on grants to writers, in reply to a letter from Sasthi Brata (14 March 1968, p. 269).

I65 "Obscene Publications." *Times Literary Supplement*, 27 June 1968, p. 679. Letter to the editor on the Arts Council Conference on obscene publications.

I66 "Bury St Edmunds Abbey." *Times*, 10 August 1968, p. 9. Signed Angus Wilson, Benjamin Britten, Francis Meynell and others. Letter to the editor protesting the possible demolition of old houses built into Abbey ruins.

I67 *Dickens Studies Newsletter*, 3 no. 1 (March 1972), 25. Letter to the editor in support of the London Library.

I68 "Writers and the Closed Shop." *Times Literary Supplement*, 25 April 1975, p. 440. Signed Margaret Drabble, William Golding, J.B. Priestley and others including Angus Wilson. Statement on proposed legislation regarding printing and the trade unions.

I69 "Money and the Arts." *Times*, 3 August 1981, p. 11. Letter to the editor protesting the Arts Council's possible closure of the New Fiction Society.

## EXTRACTS FROM LETTERS

I70 McDowell, Frederick P. W. "An Exchange of Letters and Some Reflections on *As If By Magic*." *Twentieth Century Literature*, 29 (Summer 1983), 231-235 (232-233). Extract of letter to the author, 24 July 1974.

I71 Rabinovitz, Rubin. *The Reaction Against Experiment in the English Novel, 1950-1960*. New York and London: Columbia University Press, 1967, pp. 66-67. Extracts from two letters to the author.

I72 Walker, D.P. et al. "Talking about Angus Wilson." *Twentieth Century Literature*, 29 (Summer 1983), 115-150 (132-133). Two postcards to Clive Sinclair, 11 August 1980 and 28 February 1983.

## ANNOUNCED BUT NOT PUBLISHED

I73 "Zola et Tolstoï." *Roman* (St-Paul, Alpes-Maritimes), no. 1 (janvier 1951).

# PART II: WORKS ABOUT ANGUS WILSON

# J. BOOKS AND ARTICLES

J1    Adams, Stephen. "High Class Camp: Angus Wilson and Iris Murdoch." *The Homosexual as Hero in Contemporary Fiction.* London: Vision Press; New York: Barnes & Noble, 1980, pp. 156-181.

J2    Allen, Walter. *The Novel Today.* London: British Council, 1960, pp. 29-32.

J3    ———. *Tradition and Dream: The English and American Novel from the Twenties to Our Time.* London: Phoenix House; *The Modern Novel in Britain and the United States.* New York: Dutton, 1964, pp. 270-274.

J4    ———. "Wilson." *The Short Story in English.* Oxford: Clarendon Press; New York: Oxford University Press, 1981, pp. 289-295.

J5    Allsop, Kenneth. *The Angry Decade: A Survey of the Cultural Revolt of the Nineteen-Fifties.* London: Peter Owen, 1958, pp. 26, 28, 158, 172, 186.

J6    Anderson, Lindsay. "The Court Style." *At the Royal Court: 25 Years of the English Stage Company.* Ed. Richard Findlater. London: Amber Lane Press, 1981, pp. 143-148 (143-144). On *The Mulberry Bush.*

J7    Anon. "Uncommitted Talents." *Times Literary Supplement,* 29 August 1952, Special Section, "Fresh Minds at Work: Reflections on the Practice of Letters Among the Younger Generation at Home & Overseas," p. iii.

J8     ——. "Boring Modern Novels?" *Listener*, 51 (29 April 1954), 726.

J9     ——. "Three Names That Sell." *Tatler*, 14 January 1959, pp. 74-75.

J10    ——. "The Workaday World That the Novelist Never Enters." *Times Literary Supplement*, 9 September 1960, Special Section, "The British Imagination," p. vii.

Reprinted: *The British Imagination: A Critical Survey from "The Times Literary Supplement"*. London: Cassell; New York: Athenaeum, 1961, pp. 13-19 (18-19).

J11    ——. "The Uses of Comic Vision: A Concealed Social Point in Playing for Laughs." *Times Literary Supplement*, 9 September 1960, p. ix.

Reprinted: *The British Imagination: A Critical Survey from "The Times Literary Supplement"*. London: Cassell; New York: Athenaeum, 1961, pp. 20-26 (25-26).

J12    ——. "The Dark Side." *Listener*, 68 (27 December 1962), 1076.

J13    ——. *Iowa Writers' Workshop Newsletter*, Fall-Winter 1971-72, pp. 1-3.

J14    ——. "England's Last Man of Letters." *Observer*, 7 August 1983, p. 7.

J15    Antonini, Giacomo. "Uno scrittore come personaggio." *La Fiera letteraria* (Rome), 5 ottobre 1952, pp. 1-2.

J16    Arban, Dominique. "Mon tunnel sous La Manche." *La Revue de Paris*, 65 no. 6 (juin 1958), 103-112 (110-111).

J17    ——. "Une entreprise d'exhumation." *Cahiers des Saisons* (Paris), 40 (hiver 1965), 520-524.

J18    Aury, Dominique. "Une doublure d'argent." *Cahiers des Saisons* (Paris), 40 (hiver 1965), 527-529.

J19    Bailey, Paul. "Meg and Sylvia." *Twentieth Century Literature* (Hempstead, NY), 29 (Summer 1983), 219-222.

J20    Baldwin, Dean. "The English Short Story in the Fifties." *The English Short Story 1945-1980: A Critical History*. Ed. Dennis Vannatta. Boston: Twayne, 1985, pp. 63-65.

BOOKS AND ARTICLES     J31

J21 Barnes, John. "Politics and the English Novel: Post-War Britain As Seen Through the Eyes of Contemporary Novelists in This Country." *Crossbow*, 10 (January-March 1967), 36-38.

J22 Beachcroft, T.O. *The Modest Art: A Survey of the Short Story in English*. London: Oxford University Press, 1968, pp. 217, 222, 223.

J23 Bergonzi, Bernard. "The Ideology of Being English"/"Between Nostalgia and Nightmare." *The Situation of the Novel*. Critical Essays in Modern Literature Series. London: Macmillan; Pittsburgh: University of Pittsburgh Press, 1970, pp. 56-79 (66)/149-187 (151-161, 183).

Reprinted: "Between Nostalgia and Nightmare." *Critical Essays on Angus Wilson*, ed. Jay L. Halio, pp. 122-130 (J86).

J24 Billy, Ted. "*Setting the World on Fire*: Phaethon's Fall and Wilson's Redemption." *Critical Essays on Angus Wilson*. Ed. Jay L. Halio. Boston: Hall, 1985, pp. 192-202.

J25 Binding, Paul. "Angus Wilson." *Isis* (Oxford), 12 May 1965, pp. 12-14.

J26 Bodelsen, Anders. "Attituder i det klasseløse samfund: Angus Wilson, en glaedesløs satiriker [Attitudes in a Classless Society: Angus Wilson, A Joyless Satirist]. *Aktuelt* (Copenhagen), 14 October 1959, p. 8.

J27 Blehl, Victor F. "Look Back at Anger." *America* (New York), 103 (16 April 1960), 64-65.

J28 Bomans, Godfried. "De tijd van Dickens." *The World of Charles Dickens*. Haarlem: Uitgeverij J.H. Gottmer; London: Secker & Warburg, 1970. 15-page insert. *See also* I8.

J29 Bowen, John. "One Man's Meat: The Idea of Individual Responsibility." *Times Literary Supplement*, 7 August 1959, Special Section, "British Books Around the World," pp. xii-xiii.

J30 Bradbury, Malcolm. "The Short Stories of Angus Wilson." *Studies in Short Fiction* (Newberry, SC), 3 (Winter 1966), 117-125.

J31 ———. "Our Writers Today: Who They Are—How They Live (II)." *Encounter*, 36 no. 3 (March 1971), 15-26 (16).

157

J32    ——. "The Fiction of Pastiche: The Comic Mode of Angus Wilson." *Possibilities: Essays on the State of the Novel.* London: Oxford University Press, 1973, pp. 211-230.

Reprinted: *Critical Essays on Angus Wilson*, ed. Jay L. Halio, pp. 139-155 (J86).

J33    ——, ed. "Introduction." *The Novel Today: Contemporary Writers on Modern Fiction.* Manchester: Manchester University Press; Totowa, NJ: Rowman & Littlefield, 1978, pp. 7-21 (18-19).

J34    ——. "Coming Out of the Fifties." *Twentieth Century Literature* (Hempstead, NY), 29 (Summer 1983), 179-189.

J35    ——. "Superman of Letters." *Times*, 11 August 1983, p. 6.

J36    Brenner, Jacques. "Hier et demain." *Cahiers des Saisons* (Paris), 40 (hiver 1965), 530-532.

J37    Breuer, Hans-Peter. "In Defense of Imagination: Angus Wilson's Three Critical Biographies." *Critical Essays on Angus Wilson.* Ed. Jay L. Halio. Boston: Hall, 1985, pp. 218-227.

J38    [Brown, Craig.] "Very Liberal Novelist. Survivors: A Profile of Sir Angus Wilson, Tireless Innovator." *Spectator*, 15 June 1985, pp. 15-16.

J39    Browne, Terry. *Playwrights' Theatre: The English Stage Company at the Royal Court Theatre.* London: Pitman, 1975, pp. 17-18, 25, 30, 103, 112. On *The Mulberry Bush*.

J40    Burden, Robert. "The Novel Interrogates Itself: Parody and Self-Consciousness in Contemporary English Fiction." *The Contemporary English Novel.* Ed. Malcolm Bradbury and David Palmer. London: Edward Arnold; New York: Holmes & Meier, 1979, pp. 133-155.

J41    Burgess, Anthony. "Other Kinds of Massiveness." *The Novel Now: A Guide to Contemporary Fiction.* New York: Norton, 1967, pp. 93-105 (102-105).

J42    Burns, Alan and Charles Sugnet, ed. *The Imagination on Trial: British and American Writers Discuss Their Working Methods.* London and New York: Allison and Busby, 1981, pp. 109, 116, 161.

J43  Byatt, A.S. "People in Paper Houses: Attitudes to 'Realism' and 'Experiment' in English Postwar Fiction." *The Contemporary English Novel*. Ed. Malcolm Bradbury and David Palmer. London: Edward Arnold; New York: Holmes & Meier, 1979; New Delhi: Arnold-Heinemann, 1980, pp. 19-41.

Reprinted: *Critical Essays on Angus Wilson*, ed. Jay L. Halio, pp. 170-175 (J86).

J44  Cockshut, A.O.J. "Favoured Sons: The Moral World of Angus Wilson." *Essays in Criticism* (Oxford), 9 (January 1959), 50-60.

J45  Cooper, Lettice. "The New Novelists: An Enquiry." *London Magazine*, 5 no. 11 (November 1958), 17-21 (18).

J46  Cox, C.B. "The Humanism of Angus Wilson: A Study of *Hemlock and After*." *Critical Quarterly* (Hull), 3 (Autumn 1961), 227-237.

J47  ——. "Angus Wilson: Studies in Depression." *The Free Spirit: A Study of Liberal Humanism in the Novels of George Eliot, Henry James, E.M. Forster, Virginia Woolf, Angus Wilson*. London: Oxford University Press, 1963, pp. 117-153.

Reprinted: *Critical Essays on Angus Wilson*, ed. Jay L. Halio, pp. 81-97 (J86).

J48  Craig, David. *The Real Foundations: Literature and Social Change*. London: Chatto & Windus, 1973, pp. 259-262.

J49  Curtis, Jean-Louis. "Tradition et aventure." *Cahiers des Saisons* (Paris), 40 (hiver 1965), 515-516.

J50  —— et al. "Portrait d'Angus Wilson." *Cahiers des Saisons* (Paris), 40 (hiver 1965), 515-544.

J51  Davies, Alistair and Peter Saunders. "Literature, Politics and Society." *Society and Literature 1945-1970*. Ed. Alan Sinfield. The Context of Literature Series. London: Methuen, 1983, pp. 13-50 (34-39, 41-42).

J52  Delpech, Jeanine. "Les masques d'Angus Wilson." *Les Nouvelles littéraires* (Paris), 10 avril 1969, p. 3.

J53  Dollimore, Jonathan. "The Challenge of Sexuality." *Society and Literature 1945-1970*. Ed. Alan Sinfield. The Context of Literature series. London: Methuen, 1983, pp. 51-85 (74-75).

J54    Drabble, Margaret. "Margaret Drabble on the Novels of Angus Wilson." *Mademoiselle* (New York), August 1975, pp. 94, 106.

J55    ———. "Paper Back Writer: Margaret Drabble on Angus Wilson." *Sunday Times Magazine*, 24 February 1980, p. 81.

J56    ———. "No 'Idle Rentier': Angus Wilson and the Nourished Literary Imagination." *Studies in the Literary Imagination* (Atlanta), 13 (Spring 1980), 119-129.

       Reprinted: *Critical Essays on Angus Wilson*, ed. Jay L. Halio, pp. 182-192 (J86).

J57    Edelstein, Arthur. "Angus Wilson: The Territory Behind." *Contemporary British Novelists*. Ed. Charles Shapiro. Carbondale and Edwardsville: Southern Illinois University Press, 1966, pp. 144-161. *See also* K7.

J58    Elsen, Claude. "Un Misanthrope sans amertume." *Cahiers des Saisons* (Paris), 40 (hiver 1965), 517-520.

J59    Engelborghs, Maurits. "Kroniek: Engelse letteren: Werk van Angus Wilson." *Dietsche Warande en Belfort* (Antwerp), 102 (1957), 181-189.

J60    Escudié, Danielle. *Deux aspects de l'aliénation dans le roman anglais contemporain, 1945-1965: Angus Wilson et William Golding.* Paris: Didier, 1975. *See also* K10.

J61    Faulkner, Peter. "Values in the Novel." *Question*, no. 9 (December 1975), 50-61.

J62    ———. *Humanism in the English Novel.* London: Elek Books; New York: Barnes & Noble, 1976, pp. 184-190.

J63    ———. *Angus Wilson: Mimic and Moralist.* London: Secker & Warburg; New York: Viking Press, 1980.

J64    Fletcher, John. "Women in Crisis: Louise and Mrs Eliot." *Critical Quarterly* (Hull), 15 (Summer 1973), 157-170.

       Reprinted as: "Women in Crisis: *The Grass* and *The Middle Age of Mrs Eliot.*" *Claude Simon and Fiction Now.* London: Calder & Boyars, 1975, pp. 135-155.

J65    Fletcher, Mary Dell. "Wilson's 'Raspberry Jam.'" *Explicator* (Washington, DC), 40 (Spring 1982), 49-51.

J66 Ford, George H. "Dickens in the 1960s." *Dickensian*, 66 (May 1970), 163-182 (174-176). Comments on Dickens's influence on Wilson.

J67 Fraser, G.S. "Cultural Nationalism in the Recent English Novel." *The Cry of Home: Cultural Nationalism and the Modern Writer*. Ed. H. Ernest Lewald. Knoxville: University of Tennessee Press, 1972, pp. 22-38 (32-36).

J68 ———. *The Modern Writer and His World: Continuity and Innovation in Twentieth-Century English Literature*. London: Verschoyle, 1953, pp. 127-129; rev. edn. New York and Washington: Praeger, 1965, pp. 152-155, 243-244.

J69 Fredman, Alice Green. "Angus Wilson: Literary Critic and Biographer." *Twentieth Century Literature* (Hempstead, NY), 29 (Summer 1983), 195-206.

J70 Gardner, Averil. "The Early Years of Angus Wilson." *Twentieth Century Literature* (Hempstead, NY), 29 (Summer 1983), 151-161. Chapter 1 of J71.

J71 ———. *Angus Wilson*. Twayne's English Authors Series. Boston: Hall—Twayne Publishers, 1985.

J72 Gillie, Christopher. "The Shape of Modern Fiction: Angus Wilson's *No Laughing Matter*." *Delta* (Amsterdam), 43 (juni 1968), 18-23.

J73 Gindin, James. "The Reassertion of the Personal." *Texas Quarterly* (Austin), 1 no. 4 (Winter 1958), 126-134.

J74 ———. "Comedy in Contemporary British Fiction." *Papers of the Michigan Academy of Science, Arts, and Letters* (Ann Arbor), 44 (1959), 389-397.

J75 ———. "Angus Wilson's Qualified Nationalism." *Postwar British Fiction: New Accents and Attitudes*. Berkeley and Los Angeles: University of California Press, 1962, pp. 145-164.

J76 ———. "The Fable Begins to Break Down." *Wisconsin Studies in Contemporary Literature* (Madison), 8 (Winter 1967), 1-18.

J77 ———. "Angus Wilson." *Harvest of a Quiet Eye: The Novel of Compassion*. Bloomington: Indiana University Press, 1971, pp. 277-304.

Reprinted: *Critical Essays on Angus Wilson,* ed. Jay L. Halio, pp. 155-169 (J86).

J78 Glage, Liselotte. "Angus Wilsons *The Old Men at the Zoo.*" *Germanisch-Romanische Monatsschrift* (Heidelberg), nf 26 (1976), 185-199.

J79 Graecen, Robert. "Social Class in Post-War English Fiction." *Southern Review* (Baton Rouge), ns 4 (January 1968), 142-151.

J80 Gransden, K.W. *Angus Wilson.* British Council and National Book League's Writers and Their Work Series no. 208. London: Longmans, Green, 1969.

J81 Haan, Jacques den. "Dollekervel en de Nasleep." *Een Leven als een oordeel.* Amsterdam: J.M. Meulenhoff/De Bezige Bij, 1968, pp. 284-290.

J82 Hahn, Thomas. "Medievalism, Make-Believe, and Real Life in Wilson's *Anglo-Saxon Attitudes.*" *Mosaic* (Winnipeg), 12 (Summer 1979), 115-134.

J83 Halio, Jay L. "The Novels of Angus Wilson." *Modern Fiction Studies* (West Lafayette, IN), 8 (Summer 1962), 171-181.

J84 ——. *Angus Wilson.* Writers and Critics Series. Edinburgh and London: Oliver & Boyd, 1964.

J85 ——. "Childhood and After." *Books and Bookmen,* 10 no. 4 (January 1965), 41-44, 48. Chapter 9 of J84.

J86 ——, ed. *Critical Essays on Angus Wilson.* Critical Essays on Modern British Literature Series. Boston: Hall, 1985.

J87 ——. "Angus Wilson: An Overview." Introduction to *Critical Essays on Angus Wilson,* pp. 1-19 (J86).

J88 Hall, James B. and Joseph Langland, ed. "Comment." *The Short Story.* New York: Macmillan, 1956, pp. 314-315. *See also* B66.

J89 Haule, James M. "*Setting the World on Fire*: Angus Wilson and the Problem of Evil." *Twentieth Century Literature* (Hempstead, NY), 28 (Winter 1982), 453-466.

J90 Herrick, Jim. "Angus Wilson." *New Humanist,* 96 (January 1981), 67-70.

J91     Hidalgo, Pilar. "Nonmimetic Devices in Angus Wilson's Later Fiction." *Anglo-American Studies* (Salamanca), 3 no. 1 (1983), 39-48.

J92     Higdon, David Leon. "Angus Wilson, *Late Call*, 'A Strange Gale of Memories' "/"Angus Wilson, *Anglo-Saxon Attitudes*, 'Echoes of Memory.' " *Shadows of the Past in Contemporary British Fiction.* London: Macmillan; Athens (GA): University of Georgia Press, 1984, pp. 39-50/137-151.

J93     Hobsbaum, Philip. "Anglo-Saxon Satirist." *Western Daily Press* (Bristol), 12 April 1961, p. 8.

J94     Hope, Francis. "Faces in the Novel." *Twentieth Century*, 173 (Autumn 1964), 56-61 (58).

J95     ——. "The Intellectual Left." *Encounter*, 27 (October 1966), 60-68 (67).

J96     Hutton, Kurt. "In a Suffolk Garden." *Tatler*, 1 April 1959, pp. 21-23.

J97     Ivaseva, Valentina V. "Literary Encounters." *Anglo-Soviet Journal* (London), 35 (December 1974), 26-31.

J98     ——. "Tri vstrechi s anglici [Three Meetings with Englishmen]. *Vestnik Moskovskogo Universiteta* (Moscow), 1 (1967), 80-87.

J99     Jacque, Valentina. "English Short Stories in Russia." *Soviet Literature* (Moscow), 1 (1963), 153-157.

J100     Jacquin, B. "Angus Wilson." *Le Roman en Grande-Bretagne depuis 1945.* Ed. Jean Ruer et al. Paris: Presses Universitaires de France, 1981, pp. 231-242. [In French.]

J101     Jaidev. "Introductions—I. Angus Wilson: Connoisseur of Hells." *Sunday Standard* (Bombay), 23 November 1980, p. 6.

J102     ——. "Angus Wilson—Fine Blend of Fantasy, Theatre and Fiction." *National Herald* (New Delhi), 31 July 1983, p. 3.

J103     ——. "The Function of *The Idiot* Motifs in *As If By Magic*." *Twentieth Century Literature* (Hempstead, NY), 29 (Summer 1983), 223-230.

Reprinted: *Critical Essays on Angus Wilson,* ed. Jay L. Halio, pp. 176-182 (J86).

J104   Jenkins, Alan. "Hemlock—And Before." *Spectator,* 193 (17 September 1954), 331.

J105   Jullian, Philippe. "Cinq croquis d'Angus Wilson." *Cahiers des Saisons* (Paris), 40 (hiver 1965), 538-541.

J106   ———. "Angus Wilson." *Les Nouvelles littéraires* (Paris), 12 décembre 1957, p. 7.

J107   Jump, John D. "The Recent British Novel." *Manchester Literary and Philosophical Society Proceedings,* 101 (1959), 23-38 (31-34).

J108   Katona, Anna. "Angus Wilson's Fiction and Its Relation to the English Tradition." *Acta Litteraria Academiae Scientiarum Hungaricae* (Budapest), 10 (1968), 111-127.

J109   Kaufmann, R.J. "On the Supersession of the Modern Classic Style." *Modern Drama* (Toronto), 2 (February 1960), 358-369 (367-368). On *The Mulberry Bush.*

J110   ———. "The British Public Psyche: An Analytical Sketch." *Massachusetts Review* (Amherst), 3 (Spring 1962), 521-538 (535-536).

J111   Kermode, Frank. "Foreword." *Anglo-Saxon Attitudes.* New York: New American Library—Signet Books, 1963, pp. vii-xvi.

J112   Kissane, Joseph, ed. Angus Wilson Issue. *Twentieth Century Literature* (Hempstead, NY), 29 (Summer 1983), 113-249.

J113   Koljević, Svetozar. "Putevi savremenog engleskog romana [Directions in the Contemporary English Novel]." *Delo za zdravje* (Ljubljana), 8 (1962), 870-889.

J114   Krzeczkowski, Henryk. "Przeciw podstarzałej lekkomyślności [Against Aging Forgetfulness]." *Po namyśle.* Cracow: Wydawnictwo ZNAK, 1977, pp. 90-95. On *Late Call.*

J115   Kums, Guido. "Reality in Fiction: *No Laughing Matter.*" *English Studies* (Lisse), 53 (December 1972), 523-531.

J116   ———. *Fiction, or the Language of Our Discontent: A Study of the*

*Built-in Novelist in Novels by Angus Wilson, Lawrence Durrell and Doris Lessing.* European University Studies—Series XIV, Vol. 140. Frankfurt-am-Main: Peter Lang, 1985, pp. 15-45. On *No Laughing Matter.*

J117    Laing, Stuart. "Novels and the Novel." *Society and Literature 1945-1970.* Ed. Alan Sinfield. The Context of Literature Series. London: Methuen, 1983, pp. 235-259 (235, 245-246, 248, 254).

J118    Leech, Clifford. "The Theme of Destitution in Twentieth Century Literature." *Indian Journal of English Studies* (Calcutta), 3 (1962), 89-105 (101-102).

J119    Lindberg, Margaret. "Angus Wilson: *The Old Men at the Zoo* As Allegory." *Iowa English Yearbook* (Des Moines), (Fall 1969), 44-48.

J120    Maack, Annegret. "Angus Wilsons Auseinandersetzungen mit Charles Dickens." *Literatur in Wissenschaft und Unterricht* (Universität Kiel, B.R.D.), 12 (1979), 267-286.

J121    McDowell, Frederick P. W. "The Angus Wilson Collection." *Books at Iowa* (Iowa City), 10 (April 1969), 9-18, 20, 23.

J122    ——. "An Exchange of Letters and Some Reflections on *As If By Magic.*" *Twentieth Century Literature* (Hempstead, NY), 29 (Summer 1983), 231-235.

J123    ——. "Chaos and the Forms of Order in *Setting the World on Fire.*" *Twentieth Century Literature* (Hempstead, NY), 29 (Summer 1983), 236-248.

J124    McEwan, Neil. "Angus Wilson: *No Laughing Matter.*" *The Survival of the Novel: British Fiction in the Later Twentieth Century.* London: Macmillan; Totowa, NJ: Barnes & Noble, 1981, pp. 60-77.

J125    McGivering, J.H. "Discussion Meetings." *Kipling Journal,* 45 (December 1978), 11-14.

J126    McSweeney, Kerry. "The Novels of Angus Wilson." *Wascana Review* (Regina, Sask.), 12 no. 2 (Fall 1977), 3-24.

J127    ——. "Angus Wilson: Diversity, Depth, and Obsessive Energy." *Four Contemporary Novelists: Angus Wilson, Brian Moore, John Fowles, V.S. Naipaul.* Kingston and Montreal: McGill-Queen's University Press, 1983, pp. 9-53. Reprint with revisions of J126.

J128 ——. "Angus Wilson's Critical Writings." *Twentieth Century Literature* (Hempstead, NY), 29 (Summer 1983), 207-218.

J129 ——, ed. *Diversity and Depth in Fiction: Selected Critical Writings of Angus Wilson.* London: Secker & Warburg, 1983; New York: Viking Press, 1984 (A21).

J130 ——. "Editor's Introduction." *Diversity and Depth in Fiction: Selected Critical Writings of Angus Wilson,* pp. ix-xvi (J129).

J131 Malin, Irving. "Metaphors of Enclosure: Angus Wilson's *The Old Men at the Zoo* (1961)." *Old Lines, New Forces: Essays on the Contemporary British Novel, 1960-1970.* Ed. Robert K. Morris. London: Associated University Presses; Rutherford, NJ: Fairleigh Dickinson University Press, 1976, pp. 1-11.

Reprinted: *Critical Essays on Angus Wilson,* ed. Jay L. Halio, pp. 115-122 (J86).

J132 Mander, John. "A House Divided: The Short Stories of Angus Wilson." *The Writer and Commitment.* London: Secker & Warburg, 1961, pp. 111-138.

J133 Manners, Penelope J., ed. "Angus Wilson (b. 1913)." *Novels of Today: Extracts from Contemporary English Novels.* London: University of London Press, 1967, pp. 84-85. *See also* B29.

J134 Marković, Vida E. "Angas Vilson [Angus Wilson]." *Engleski Roman XX Veka* [Vol. I]. Belgrade: Naucna Knjiga, 1965, pp. 172-183, 254-255.

J135 Mayne, Richard. "The Mantle of Swift: A Note on Angus Wilson." *Cambridge Anthology.* Ed. Peter Townsend. London: Hogarth, 1952, pp. 13-22.

J136 Minnen, C.L. van. "Angus Wilson en de utopie." *Wildgroei* (Leiden), 6 (maart/april 1984), 2-17.

J137 Monod, Sylvère. *Histoire de la littérature anglaise de Victoria à Elisabeth II.* Paris: Librarie Armand Colin, 1970, pp. 364-366.

J138 ——. "A Bit Off the Darling Set: The World of Sir Angus Wilson's Short Stories." *Les Cahiers de la nouvelle/Journal of the Short Story in English* (Angers), 1 (1983), 91-101.

J139   Nielsen, Johs. "Den engelske romans nye haab [The English Novel's New Hope]." *Berlingske Aftenavis* (Copenhagen), 22 May 1953.

J140   Oakland, John. "Angus Wilson and Evil in the English Novel." *Renascence: Essays on Values in Literature* (Milwaukee), 26 (Autumn 1973), 24-36.

J141   O'Connor, William Van. "Two Types of 'Heroes' in Post-War British Fiction." *Publications of the Modern Language Association of America* (New York), 77 (1962), 168-174.

J142   Oka, Teruo. *Angus Wilson*. Tokyo: Kenkyusha, 1970. [In Japanese.]

J143   Ollier, Jean-Claude. "Derrière la façade." *Cahiers des Saisons* (Paris), 40 (hiver 1965), 525-527.

J144   O'Shea, Michael. "Sources and Analogues in Angus Wilson's *Setting the World on Fire*." *Critical Essays on Angus Wilson*. Ed. Jay L. Halio. Boston: Hall, 1985, pp. 203-217.

J145   Pritchett, V.S. "London Literary Letter: A Report on Writers and Writing." *New York Times Book Review*, 11 May 1958, p. 18.

J146   ———. "Angus Wilson: Going Downhill." *The Tale Bearers: Literary Essays*. New York: Random House, pp. 104-114.

J147   Quinton, Anthony. "The New Novelists: An Enquiry." *London Magazine*, 5 no. 11 (November 1958), 13-17 (13, 15-16).

J148   Raban, Jonathan. *The Technique of Modern Fiction: Essays in Practical Criticism*. London: Arnold, 1968; Notre Dame, IN: University of Notre Dame Press, 1969, pp. 37-44, 140, 142-143.

J149   ———. "Profile 1: Angus Wilson." *New Review*, 1 (April 1974), 16-24.

J150   Rabinovitz, Rubin. "Angus Wilson." *The Reaction Against Experiment in the English Novel, 1950-1960*. New York and London: Columbia University Press, 1967, pp. 64-96. *See also* K19.

J151   Rauter, Herbert. " 'Raspberry Jam.' " *Die Englischekurzgeschichte*. Ed. Karl H. Göller and Gerhardt Hoffman. Dusseldorf: Bagel, 1973, pp. 308-316.

J152   ——. "Angus Wilson, *As If By Magic.*" *Englische Literatur der Gegenwart, 1971-1975.* Ed. Rainer Lengeler. Dusseldorf: Bagel, 1977, pp. 191-201.

J153   Rebelo, Luis de Sousa. "Angus Wilson e a reacção realista no moderno romance inglês." *Vertice: Revista de cultura e critica* (Lisbon), no. 210 (March 1961), 208-210. Extract (censored form) of introduction to Portugese translation of *Hemlock and After* (D92).

J154   Reve, G.K. van het. "Engelse roman: *Anglosaxon Attitudes*: Angus Wilson kent zijn grenzen." *Vrij Nederland* (Amsterdam), 10 augustus 1957, p. 6.

       Reprinted: *Schoon Schip, 1945-1984.* Amsterdam: Manteau, 1984, pp. 67-69.

J155   Rhode, Eric. "The Novelist and the Theatre." *Novelists' Theatre.* Harmondsworth: Penguin Books, 1966, pp. 7-19 (13-15).

J156   Riddell, Edwin. "The Humanist Character in Angus Wilson." *English* (Oxford), 21 (Summer 1972), 45-53.

J157   Rippier, Joseph S. "Angus Wilson." *Some Postwar English Novelists.* Frankfurt: Diesterweg, 1965, pp. 19-45.

J158   Sadkowski, Wacław. "Poza anglosaskie pozy [Beyond Anglo-Saxon attitudes]." *Drogi i rożdroża literatury Zachodu.* Warsaw: Książka i Wiedza, 1968, pp. 195-205 (195-197).

J159   Sage, Lorna. "Taking Risks." *Twentieth Century Literature* (Hempstead, NY), 29 (Summer 1983), 190-194.

J160   Scheer-Schlazler, Brigitte. "Angus Wilson." *Englische Literatur der Gegenwart.* Stuttgart: Alfred Kroner Verlag, 1970, pp. 104-132.

J161   Schlüter, Kurt. "Angus Wilson." *Englische Dichter der Moderne. Ihr Leben und Werk. Unter Mitarbeit Zahlreicher Fachgelehrter.* Ed. Rudolf Suhnel and Dieter Riesner. Berlin: Erich Schmidt, 1971, pp. 536-545.

J162   ——. "Angus Wilson: *The Middle Age of Mrs Eliot.*" *Der moderne englische Roman: Interpretationen.* Ed. Horst Oppel. Berlin: Erich Schmidt, 2nd rev. edn. 1971, pp. 361-376.

J163   ——. *Kuriose Welt im modernen englischen Roman: Dargestellt an ausgewählten Werken von Evelyn Waugh und Angus Wilson.* Berlin: Erich Schmidt, 1969, pp. 126-133.

J164 Schwarzbach, F.S. "A Portrait of the Artist as Householder." *Twentieth Century Literature* (Hempstead, NY), 29 (Summer 1983), 162-169.

J165 Schultze, Bruno. "Das Bild der Wirklichkeit in den Romanen Angus Wilsons." *Die Neueren Sprachen* (Frankfurt-am-Main), 22 (1973), 210-220.

J166 Scott-Kilvert, Ian. "Angus Wilson." *Review of English Literature* (London), 1 no. 2 (April 1960), 42-53.

Reprinted: *Critical Essays on Angus Wilson*, ed. Jay L. Halio, pp. 73-81 (J86).

J167 Servotte, Herman. "Experiment en traditie: Angus Wilson's *No Laughing Matter.*" *Dietsche Warande en Belfort* (Antwerp), 113 (1968), 324-335.

J168 ——. "A Note on the Formal Characteristics of Angus Wilson's *No Laughing Matter.*" *English Studies* (Lisse), 50 (February 1969), 58-64.

J169 Sharma, V.P. "Novelist-Figures in Angus Wilson's Fiction." *AIETC PUNE 84: Abstracts.* Ed. Prashant K. Sinha and Rajeev S. Patke. Abstracts of the All-India Teachers' Conference, 1-3 December 1984. Poona: Department of English, University of Poona, 1984, p. 34.

J170 Shaw, Valerie. "*The Middle Age of Mrs Eliot and Late Call*: Angus Wilson's Traditionalism." *Critical Quarterly* (Hull), 12 (Spring 1970), 9-27.

Reprinted: *Critical Essays on Angus Wilson*, ed. Jay L. Halio, pp. 98-115 (J86).

J171 Sinha, Krishna Kant. *Angus Wilson and the Modern World.* Patna—Ranchi—Varanasi: Jyoti, 1985. *See also* K21.

J172 Smith, William James. "Angus Wilson's England: The Novelist as Social Historian." *Commonweal* (New York), 82 no. 1 (26 March 1965), 18-21.

J173 Snow, C.P. "The English Realistic Novel, 1957." *Moderna Sprak* (Stockholm), 51 (1957), 265-270 (268).

J174 Spiel, Hilde. *Welt im Widerschein*. Munich: Beck, 1960, pp. 75-81.

J175 Stefanović, Aleksandar V. "Angas Vilson—svedok našeg vremana [Angus Wilson—Witness of Our Time]." *Savremenik* (Belgrade), 10 (1964), 578-598.

J176 Stinson, John J. "The English Short Story, 1945-1950." *The English Short Story 1945-1980: A Critical History*. Ed. Dennis Vannatta. Boston: Twayne, 1985, pp. 10-15.

J177 Sudrann, Jean. "The Lion and the Unicorn: Angus Wilson's Triumphant Tragedy." *Studies in the Novel* (Denton, TX), 3 (Winter 1971), 390-400.

Reprinted: *Critical Essays on Angus Wilson*, ed. Jay L. Halio, pp. 130-139 (J86).

J178 Swinden, Patrick. *The English Novel of History and Society, 1940-80: Richard Hughes, Henry Green, Anthony Powell, Angus Wilson, Kingsley Amis, V.S. Naipaul*. London: Macmillan, 1984, pp. 130-179.

J179 Szabó-Pap, Judit. "The Lonely Man in Angus Wilson's Fiction." *Hungarian Studies in English* (Debrecen), 9 (1975), 87-101.

J180 Turnell, Martin. "Zola et l'angleterre." *Presence de Zola*. Ed. Marc Bernard. Paris: Fasquelle, 1953, pp. 13-16 (15). On *Emile Zola*.

J181 Vallette, Jacques. "Lettres anglo-saxonnes: Angus Wilson un peu par lui-même." *Mercure de France* (Paris), 332 (octobre 1958), 313-316.

J182 Vansittart, Peter. "Angus Wilson: The Garden As Metaphor." *London Magazine*, ns 23 no. 4 (July 1983), pp. 21-27.

J183 Walker, D.P. et al. "Talking About Angus Wilson." *Twentieth Century Literature* (Hempstead, NY), 29 (Summer 1983), 115-141. Including reminiscences by Hortense Calisher, Nadine Gordimer, James Purdy, Patrick White and others.

J184 Warburg, Frederic. *All Authors Are Equal: The Publishing Life of Frederic Warburg, 1936-1971*. London: Hutchinson, 1973, pp. 273-281.

J185 Wardle, Irving. *The Theatres of George Devine*. London: Cape, 1978, pp. 175-178. On the Royal Court production of *The Mulberry Bush*.

J186    Wilcock, J. Rodolfo. "Il monologo interiore: nota sull' evoluzione del romanzo." *Il Tempo Presente* (Rome), 4 (1959), 208-213.

J187    Williams, Raymond. "Realism and the Contemporary Novel." *Partisan Review* (New York), 26 (Spring 1959), 200-213.

Reprinted: *The Long Revolution*. London: Chatto & Windus, 1961, Chapter 7.

J188    Williamson, Audrey and Charles Landstone. *The Bristol Old Vic: The First Ten Years*. London: J. Garnet Miller, 1957, pp. 161-163. On *The Mulberry Bush*.

J189    Wilson, Edmund. "An Interview with Edmund Wilson." *New Yorker*, 2 June 1962, pp. 118-128 (120).

J190    Wogatzky, Karin. *Angus Wilson: Hemlock and After, A Study in Ambiguity*. Schweizer anglistische Arbeiten, Band 62. Berne: Francke Verlag, 1971. *See also* K27.

J191    Yuill, W.E. "Tradition and Nightmare: Some Reflections on the Postwar Novel in England and Germany." *Affinities: Essays in German and English Literature*. Ed. R.W. Last. London: Oswald Wolff, 1971, pp. 154-167 (158-159).

# K. THESES AND DISSERTATIONS

K1    Albertyn, D.S. "The Satirical Element in the Novels of Angus Wilson." DLitt thesis. University of the Orange Free State, 1978.

K2    Arnold, Gloria Cockerell. "An Analysis of Angus Wilson's *No Laughing Matter.*" MA thesis. North Texas State University, 1975.

K3    Blanc, Jessica. "Les Modes de l'ironie dans l'oêuvre romanesque d'Angus Wilson." Thèse de doctorat 3e cycle. Université de Provence (Aix-Marseille I), 1982.

K4    Bontaleb-Follé, H. "A la recherche d'un sens de la vie: une vision réaliste des relations humaines et sociales dans les romans d'Angus Wilson." Thèse de doctorat 3e cycle. Université de Provence (Aix-Marseille), 1977.

K5    Carton, Jeanne-Marie. "The Hero in Four Novels by Angus Wilson." Thesis, Université de Grenoble, 1980-81.

K6    Conrad, Leroy A. "Angus Wilson: His Art and His Critics." MA thesis. University of Iowa, 1960.

K7    Edelstein, Arthur. "Realism and Beyond: Essays on Twentieth-Century Fiction." PhD dissertation. Stanford University, 1977. [Abstract: *DA*, 38 (1977), 1377-1378A.] *See also* J57.

K8    Enkemann, Jurgen. "Die satirische darstellunggesellschaftlicher Disintegration bei Aldous Huxley, Evelyn Waugh und Angus Wilson: Untersucht am Motiv der Party und an ahnlichen Grup-

172

pensituationen." PhD thesis. Technische Universität, Berlin, 1970.

K9    Escudié, Danielle. "Deux aspects de l'aliénation dans le roman anglais contemporain, 1945-1965: Angus Wilson et William Golding." Doctorat d'Etat thesis. Université de Nice, 1974. *See also* J60.

K10   Harris, Marilyn Riley. "Self-Awareness and Family Influence in the Works of Angus Wilson." PhD dissertation. Georgia State University, 1974. [Abstract: *DA*, 35 (1975), 4523-4524A.]

K11   Hasan, R.A. "A Linguistic Study of Contrasting Features in the Style of Two Contemporary English Prose Writers: William Golding and Angus Wilson." PhD thesis. University of Edinburgh, 1963-64.

K12   Hazell, S. "Alternatives to Social Realism: A Study of Angus Wilson's Fiction." PhD thesis. University College, London, 1981. [D70777/82]

K13   Hovet, Grace O'Neill. "The *Bildungsroman* of the Middle-Aged Woman: Her Emergence as Heroine in British Fiction Since 1920." PhD dissertation. University of Kansas, 1976. [Abstract: *DA*, 37 (1976), 5142A.]

K14   Jaidev. "A Study of Angus Wilson's Writings." PhD thesis. Meerut University, 1977.

K15   Keesom, C.H.A. "Sir Angus Wilson: Mimic of the Mind and of Fiction." MA thesis. Amsterdam University, 1983.

K16   Larrière, Claire. "Un étape dans le développement de la nouvelle anglaise, 1945-1974." Doctorat d'Etat thesis, Université de Paris III (Sorbonne Nouvelle), 1981.

K17   Oakland, J.G. "An Examination of the Word 'Satire' When Applied to the Writings of Angus Wilson." MPhil thesis. Leeds University, 1970-71.

K18   Rabinovitz, Rubin. "The Reaction Against Experiment: A Study of the English Novel, 1950-1960." PhD dissertation. Columbia University, 1966. *See also* J150.

K19   Sewell, Michael Walker. "Parent and Child in the Garden: The

Early Novels of Angus Wilson." PhD dissertation. University of Iowa, 1974. [Abstract: *DA*, 35 (1975), 4556-4557A.]

K20　Sinha, Krishna Kant. "The Theme of Wasted Life in Angus Wilson's Novels." PhD thesis, University of Patna, 1980. *See also* J171.

K21　Smith, Catherine Simmons. "The Other Angus Wilson: Fantasy in His Fiction." PhD dissertation. Georgia State University, 1980. [Abstract: *DAI*, 41 (1980), 683A.]

K22　Spann, Ekkehard. " 'Problemkinder' " in der englischen Erzahlkunst der Gegenwart: Greene, A. Wilson, Wain, Amis, Murdoch, Golding, Braine, Sillitoe." PhD thesis. University of Tubingen, 1970.

K23　Thomas, Anne N. "In Search of Self: Art as Awareness in the Later Novels of Angus Wilson." PhD dissertation. Drew University, 1984. [Abstract: *DAI*, 45 (May 1985), 3355A.]

K24　Weil, Nicole. "A Critical Study of Mr Angus Wilson's *Anglo-Saxon Attitudes*." Thesis, Université de Paris, April 1964.

K25　Wight, Marjorie. "An Analysis of Selected British Novelists between 1945 and 1966, and Their Critics." PhD dissertation. University of Southern California, 1968. [Abstract: *DA* 28 (1968), 4651-4652A.]

K26　Wogatzky, Karin. "Angus Wilson: *Hemlock and After*, A Study in Ambiguity." PhD thesis, Universität Zurich, 1971. [Abstract: *DAI-C*, 43 (Spring 1982), 7/75c.] *See also* J190.

K27　Zimmerman, Muriel. "The Fiction of Angus Wilson." PhD dissertation. Temple University, 1967. [Abstract: *DA*, 28 (1968), 4195-4196A.]

# L. Reviews

Place of publication of English newspapers is London unless otherwise indicated.

## THE WRONG SET AND OTHER STORIES

L1   Anon. *Times Literary Supplement*, 26 March 1949, p. 197.

L2   ——. *Kirkus Reviews*, 18 (15 January 1950), 33.

L3   ——. *Wisconsin Library Bulletin*, 46 (April 1950), 19.

L4   ——. "Surprise Around the Corner." *Time*, 10 April 1950, pp. 96, 98-99.

L5   Barry, Iris. "With All the Awful Reality of Life." *New York Herald Tribune Book Review*, 19 March 1950, p. 4.

L6   Benét, Rosemary Carr. "On the Way Up or Down." *Saturday Review of Literature*, 18 March 1950, p. 15.

L7   Bowen, Elizabeth. *Tatler and Bystander*, 6 April 1949, pp. 24-25 (25).

Reprinted: *The Mulberry Tree: Writings of Elizabeth Bowen*. Ed. Hermione Lee. London: Virago, 1986, pp. 171-172.

L8   Cooper, Lettice. "Short Stories." *Time and Tide*, 30 (4 June 1949), 572, 574 (574).

L9          Croft-Cooke, Rupert. "Our Bookshelf." *Sketch*, 8 June 1949,
            p. 400.

L10         Davis, Robert Gorham. "Fiction Chronicle." *Partisan Review*, 17
            (May-June 1950), 519-523 (523).

L11         Engle, Paul. "Delightful, Disturbing Short Tales." *Chicago Sun-
            day Tribune*, 19 March 1950, Pt. 4, p. 6.

L12         Evans, Webster. "Short Stories Grave and Gay." *John
            O'London's Weekly*, 8 July 1949, p. 437.

L13         Fishback, Henry. *Tribune*, 22 April 1949, p. 21.

L14         George, Daniel. *Bookman*, April 1949, p. 8.

L15         Jones, Ernest. "From the Head." *Nation*, 170 (1 April 1950),
            302-303.

L16         Miles, George. *Commonweal*, 51 (31 March 1950), 659-660.

L17         O'Faoláin, Seán. "New Novels." *Listener*, 41 (7 April 1949),
            594.

L18         Pickrel, Paul. "Outstanding Novels." *Yale Review*, ns 39 (Sum-
            mer 1950), 765-768 (767-768).

L19         Putt, S. Gorley. "Story-Tellers." *Observer*, 29 May 1949, p. 7.

L20         Rofe, L.G. "Etched in Acid." *New York Times Book Review*,
            21 May 1950, p. 26.

L21         Scott, J.D. "Short Stories." *New Statesman and Nation*, ns 37
            (30 April 1949), 452.

L22         Straus, Ralph. "Dissatisfactions." *Sunday Times*, 27 March 1949,
            p. 3.

L23         Toynbee, Philip. *Horizon*, 19 no. 113 (May 1949), 372-373.

L24         W., W.R. *San Francisco Chronicle*, 30 April 1950, *This World*,
            p. 28.

L25         Willis, Katherine T. *Library Journal*, 75 (15 March 1950),
            492-493.

L26 Wilson, Edmund. "Bankrupt Britons and Voyaging Romantics." *New Yorker*, 15 April 1950, pp. 128-129.

Reprinted as: "Emergence of Angus Wilson." *The Bit Between My Teeth: A Literary Chronicle of 1950-1965.* New York: Farrar, Straus & Giroux, 1966, pp. 270-273.

Reprinted: *Critical Essays on Angus Wilson*, ed. Jay L. Halio, pp. 23-24 (J86).

## SUCH DARLING DODOS AND OTHER STORIES

L27 Anon. "North Oxford to China." *Times Literary Supplement*, 28 July 1950, p. 465.

L28 ———. *Kirkus Reviews*, 18 (1 November 1950), 661.

L29 ———. "Briefly Noted." *New Yorker*, 6 January 1951, pp. 85-86.

L30 ———. *Booklist*, 47 (15 February 1951), 220.

L31 ———. *"Potpourri." Atlantic Monthly*, March 1951, p. 86.

L32 ———. "Romanciers témoins." *Roman* (St-Paul, Alpes Maritimes), no. 4 (septembre 1951), 381-384 (382).

L33 Blakeston, Oswell. "Lovable Nasties." *Public Opinion*, 1 September 1950, p. 18.

L34 Bond, Alice Dixon. "A Writer of Stature." *Boston Herald*, 11 February 1951, p. B2.

L35 Boyle, F. A. *Library Journal*, 76 (1 January 1951), 41.

L36 Croft-Cooke, Rupert. "Our Bookshelf." *Sketch*, 16 August 1950, p. 152.

L37 Evans, Webster. "Such Charming People." *John O'London's Weekly*, 18 August 1950, p. 512.

L38 Johnson, Pamela Hansford. "Readability a Virtue." *Daily Telegraph*, 4 August 1950, p. 6.

L39 Jones, Ernest. "Moments of Vision." *Nation*, 172 (17 February 1951), 158-159.

L40    Kennedy, Milward. "Novels." *National and English Review*, September 1950, pp. 308-311 (308).

L41    Kupferberg, Herbert. "Names Writ in Vitriol." *New York Herald Tribune Book Review*, 14 January 1951, p. 8.

L42    Laski, Marghanita. "Fiction." *Spectator*, 184 (28 July 1950), 126, 128 (128).

L43    Lewis, Frederick. "Dreadful People." *News Chronicle*, 24 July 1950, p. 4.

L44    Lewis, Naomi. "Disturbing People." *Observer*, 13 August 1950, p. 7.

L45    Mallet, Isabelle. "Genteelness and Humbug." *New York Times Book Review*, 14 January 1951, p. 5.

L46    Painter, George D. "New Novels." *Listener*, 44 (3 August 1950), 174.

L47    Peden, William. "Extreme Personalities." *New Republic*, 124 (26 March 1951), 20.

L48    Pickrel, Paul. "Outstanding Novels." *Yale Review*, ns 40 (March 1951), 573-576 (576).

L49    Poster, William S. "Antipodal Fiction." *Partisan Review*, 18 (May-June 1951), 353-357 (356-357).

L50    Pritchett, V.S. *Bookman*, July/August 1950, pp. 8-9 (9).

L51    Richardson, John. "New Short Stories." *New Statesman and Nation*, ns 40 (12 August 1950), 181-182.

       Reprinted: *Critical Essays on Angus Wilson*, ed. Jay L. Halio, pp. 25-26 (J86).

L52    Ross, Alan. "The Wrong Dodos." *Tribune*, 11 August 1950, p. 20.

L53    Shand, P. Morton. "Short Stories." *Time and Tide*, 31 (12 August 1950), 810.

L54    Snow, C.P. "A Remarkable Novel." *Sunday Times*, 23 July 1950, p. 3.

L55     Thomson, George Malcolm. *Evening Standard,* 25 July 1950, p. 9.

L56     W., B. "Recent Fiction." *Irish Times,* 5 August 1950, p. 6.

L57     West, Ray B., Jr. "Two Way Irony." *Saturday Review of Literature,* 20 January 1951, pp. 11-12.

# EMILE ZOLA: AN INTRODUCTORY STUDY OF HIS NOVELS

L58     Anon. "Emile Zola: A Neglected Novelist." *Times,* 23 February 1952, p. 8.

L59     ——. "Critic of Society." *Times Literary Supplement,* 16 May 1952, p. 330.

L60     ——. *Booklist,* 48 (15 June 1952), 338.

L61     ——. "Popular Pessimist." *Time,* 30 June 1952, pp. 84, 86.

L62     ——. *New Yorker,* 23 August 1952, p. 86.

L63     [Booth, Bradford A.] "Current Books." *Nineteenth-Century Fiction,* 7 (December 1952), 231-235 (234-235).

L64     Burns, Colin. *Montjoie,* 1 no. 2 (Autumn 1953), 35-37.

L65     Charques, R.D. "Zola Reconsidered." *Spectator,* 188 (29 February 1952), 268, 270.

L66     Cocking, John. *World Review,* ns 38 (April 1952), 67.

L67     Connolly, Cyril. "A Manet of Despair." *Sunday Times,* 17 February 1952, p. 3.

L68     Davis, Joe Lee. "Books in Brief." *New Republic,* 127 (21 July 1952), 22-23.

L69     H., L. "Two Frenchmen." *Irish Times,* 8 March 1952, p. 6.

L70     Korg, Jacob. "An Englishman on Zola." *Nation,* 174 (21 June 1952), 607.

L71     LeSage, L. *Saturday Review*, 2 August 1952, p. 34.

L72     Nairne, Campbell. "Zola's Stormy Career." *John O'London's Weekly*, 7 March 1952, p. 221.

L73     Peyre, Henri. "Zola's Obsessions." *New York Times Book Review*, 18 May 1952, p. 5.

L74     Pritchett, V.S. "Zola." *New Statesman and Nation*, ns 43 (29 March 1952), 377-378.

L75     Salvan, Albert J. *Thought*, 29 (Summer 1954), 301-302.

L76     Spagnoli, John J. *French Review*, 26 (February 1953), 313-314.

L77     Stonier, G.W. "Zolaesque." *Observer*, 2 March 1952, p. 7.

L78     T., E.N. "En bok om Zola." *Samtid och Framtid* (Stockholm), May 1952, p. 318.

L79     Trilling, Lionel. "Zola's Quality." *Griffin*, 2 (1952), 4-11 (5-7, 10).

        Reprinted as: "In Defense of Zola." *A Gathering of Fugitives*. Boston: Beacon Press, 1956; London: Secker & Warburg, 1957; New York: Harcourt, Brace, Jovanovich, 1978, pp. 12-19.

L80     Trower, Philip. "Zola's Return." *Time and Tide*, 33 (8 March 1952), 233.

L81     Vallette, Jacques. "Lettres anglo-saxonnes." *Mercure de France* (Paris), 315 (août 1952), 717-724 (722).

L82     Walbridge, Earle F. *Library Journal*, 77 (15 May 1952), 893.


# HEMLOCK AND AFTER

L83     Anon. *Kirkus Reviews*, 20 (15 July 1952), 429.

L84     ——. "New Books." *Queen*, 30 July 1952, p. 38.

L85     ——. "Unpleasant People in Brilliant Novel." *Eastern Province Herald* (Port Elizabeth, S. Afr.), 6 August 1952, p. 4.

L86     ——. "Corruption Rife." *Times Literary Supplement*, 8 August 1952, p. 516.

L87     ——. "Among the New Books." *Walthamstow Post*, 14 August 1952, p. 2. [Syndicated.]

L88     ——. "Defeat of a Humanist Is Well Told." *Pretoria News*, 18 August 1952, p. 3.

L89     ——. "Shorter Notes." *Punch*, 27 August 1952, p. 298.

L90     ——. "Uncommitted Talents." *Times Literary Supplement*, 29 August 1952, p. iii.

L91     ——. "New Books." *Western Morning News* (Plymouth), 24 September 1952, p. 4.

L92     ——. "The Lower Depths." *Time*, 29 September 1952, pp. 97-98.

L93     ——. "A Liberal Humanist." *Glasgow Herald*, 16 October 1952, p. 3.

L94     ——. "Young Writers Lacking in Universality of Approach." *Sunday News*, 2 November 1952, p. 6.

L95     ——. "Twee satirici over vrijheid en gezag." *Nieuwe Rotterdamse Courant*, 11 april 1953, *Wekelijks bijvoegsel*, p. 2.

L96     Betjeman, John. "A Novelist with an Acute Sense of Observation." *Daily Telegraph*, 18 July 1952, p. 6.

L97     Breen, Melwyn. "Greek Love and Loss." *Saturday Night* (Toronto), 68 (25 October 1952), 39.

L98     Brooke, Jocelyn. "Desert Rose." *Time and Tide*, 33 (18 July 1952), 819-820.

L99     Butcher, Maryvonne. "Worlds Apart." *Tablet*, 16 August 1952, p. 132.

L100    Calder-Marshall, Arthur. "New Novels." *Listener*, 48 (24 July 1952), 155.

L101    Connell, John. "Waugh and Hemlock." *Evening News*, 26 July 1952, p. 4.

L102    Evans, Brian. *Western Mail* (Cardiff), 23 July 1952, p. 4.

L103    Fane, Vernon. "The World of Books.' *Sphere*, 210 (9 August 1952), p. 214.

L104    Flint, F. Cudworth. "Fiction Chronicle." *Sewanee Review*, 62 (1954), 166-180 (170-172).

L105    Hayman, Ronald. "Le roman anglais d'après-guerre." *La Revue des lettres modernes*, 1 no. 3 (avril 1954), 17-32 (31-32).

L106    Hilton, James. "A Scintillating Novel of a Seamy London Wasteland." *New York Herald Tribune Book Review*, 5 October 1952, p. 3.

L107    Jenkins, Elizabeth. "New Fiction." *Manchester Guardian*, 18 July 1952, p. 4.

        Reprinted: *Manchester Guardian Weekly*, 31 July 1952, p. 12.

L108    Johnson, Pamela Hansford. "The Scale of Novels." *John O'London's Weekly*, 61 (18 July 1952), 695.

L109    Jones, Ernest. "Contemporary Fable." *Nation*, 175 (11 October 1952), 331.

L110    Kerr, Walter. "A Cold Eye on the Best People." *Commonweal*, 57 (24 October 1952), 72-73.

L111    Lambert, J.W. "The Bad and the Mad." *Sunday Times* 20 July 1952, p. 5.

        Reprinted as: "London's Squalid Side." *Straits Times* (Singapore), 4 August 1952, p. 8.

L112    Laws, Frederick. "The Pitiless Mr Wilson." *News Chronicle*, 18 July 1952, p. 4.

L113    McGloin, J.T. *Extension* (Chicago), 47 no. 9 (February 1953), p. 33.

L114    Manousos, Demetrius. "Confused and Confusing Modern Men of Letters." *Books on Trial* (Chicago), November 1952, p. 56.

L115    Maynell, Laurence. "Distaste for Humanity." *Express & Star* (Wolverhampton), 28 July 1952, p. 4.

L116   Meewis, Wim. *Nieuw Vlaams Tijdschrift* (Antwerp), 12 (1958), 888-891.

L117   Muir, Edwin. "The Damned." *Observer*, 13 July 1952, p. 7.

L118   Parrish, Philip. "New Novels." *Tribune*, 22 August 1952, pp. 14-15 (15).

L119   Paul, David. "It Could Have Been Otherwise." *Twentieth Century*, 152 (October 1952), 355-361 (356-359).

L120   Peden, William. "The Traitorous Leader." *Saturday Review*, 4 October 1952, p. 35.

L121   Pickrel, Paul. "Outstanding Novels." *Yale Review*, ns 42 (Winter 1953), vi-xviii (xiv).

L122   P[ritchett]., V.S. *Bookman*, June 1952, pp. 7-8.

L123   Rolo, Charles J. "Reader's Choice." *Atlantic Monthly*, November 1952, pp. 104-111 (110).

L124   Schwartz, Delmore. "Long After Eden." *Partisan Review*, 19 (November-December 1952), 701-706 (704-706).

L125   Scott, J.D. "New Novels." *New Statesman and Nation*, ns 44 (2 August 1952), 142.

L126   Sheldon, G.A. "New Novels." *Birmingham Post*, 22 July 1952, p. 3.

L127   Smith, Stevie. "Succès de Scandale." *World Review*, ns 44 (October 1952), 72.

L128   Spain, Nancy. "Without Charity." *Daily Express*, 17 July 1952, p. 4.

   Reprinted: *Auckland Star*, 23 August 1952, p. 8.

L129   Strong, L.A.G. "Fiction." *Spectator*, 189 (18 July 1952), 110.

   Reprinted: *Critical Essays on Angus Wilson*, ed. Jay L. Halio, pp. 26-27 (J86).

L130   Symons, Julian. "Satire—With a Bite and a Grin . . ." *Manchester Evening News*, 17 July 1952, p. 2.

L131   Thomson, George Malcolm. "So Clever . . . So Unpleasant." *Evening Standard*, 21 July 1952, p. 9.

L132   Veen, Adriaan van der. "Het kleine en het grote kwaad." *Haagse Post* (The Hague), 4 april 1953.

L133   Wagenknecht, Edward. *Chicago Sunday Tribune*, 12 October 1952, p. 7.

L134   Walbridge, Earle F. *Library Journal*, 77 (15 September 1952), 1507.

L135   Waugh, Evelyn. "A Clean Sweep." *Month*, ns 8 (1952), 238-240.

Reprinted: *Evelyn Waugh—A Little Order: A Selection from his Journalism*. Ed. Donat Gallagher. London: Eyre Methuen, 1981; Boston: Little, Brown, 1981, pp. 92-94.

Reprinted: *The Essays, Articles and Reviews of Evelyn Waugh*. Ed. Donat Gallagher, London: Methuen, 1983; Boston: Little, Brown, 1984, pp. 421-423.

L136   Weaver, William F. "Bernard's Dilemma." *New York Times Book Review*, 28 September 1952, p. 4.

L137   Weir, Andrew. "Pictures of a Society." *Yorkshire Post* (Leeds), 18 July 1952, p. 2.

L138   West, Anthony. "Decline and Fall." *New Yorker*, 27 September 1952, pp. 113-115.

L139   Whately, Rosaleen. "We're Frightened to Enjoy Our Reading." *Liverpool Daily Post*, 22 July 1952, p. 3.

## FOR WHOM THE CLOCHE TOLLS
## A SCRAP-BOOK OF THE TWENTIES

L140   Adams, Phoebe. *Atlantic*, February 1974, p. 96.

L141   Anon. *Publishers Weekly*, 202 (11 December 1972), 37.

L142   ——."Shorter Reviews." *Choice*, 11 (April 1974), 263.

L143   ——.*Queen's Quarterly*, 81 (Summer 1974), 323.

L144    Beaton, Cecil. "Bright Old Things." *Observer*, 28 June 1953, p. 10.

L145    Betjeman, John. "A Subtle Picture of the Nineteen-Twenties." *Daily Telegraph*, 19 June 1953, p. 8.

L146    Blakeston, Oswell. *Books and Bookmen*, 19 no. 1 (October 1973), 105.

L147    Broberg, Jan. *Vasabladet* (Vaasa), 2 April 1974.

L148    Conrad, Peter. "In Search of an Author." *Spectator*, 237 (11 September 1976), 23-24.

L149    Davenport, Guy. "Maisie Markham Dreamed Her Life Like a Lucky Emma Bovary." *New York Times Book Review*, 15 April 1973, p. 5.

        Reprinted: *International Herald Tribune* (Paris), 23 April 1973, p. 10.

L150    Hill, William B. *Best Sellers*, 34 (1 April 1974), 9.

L151    Kinross [Patrick Balfour]. "Madly Ungay?" *Time and Tide*, 34 (25 July 1953), 996-997.

L152    K[istrup], J[ens]. "Tilbageblik paa tyverne." *Berlingske Tidende* (Copenhagen), 18 July 1953, p. 6.

L153    K[nudsen], M[ogens]. "Hvem ringer klokkehatten for?" *Information* (Copenhagen), 4 August 1953, p. 2.

L154    Lång, Carl-Olof. *Göteborgs-Tidningen*, 16 August 1953.

L155    McLellan, Joseph. "Briefly Noted." *Washington Post*, 17 February 1974, *Book World*, p. 4.

L156    N[eiiendam), H[enrik]. *Ekstra Bladet* (Copenhagen), 23 July 1953.

L157    Palmer, Tony. "All in Favour." *Spectator*, 231 (4 August 1973), 157-158 (158).

L158    Raven, Simon. "The Famous 'Twenties." *Listener*, 49 (25 June 1953), 1073.

L159    Sjögren, Margaretha. *Expressen* (Stockholm), 27 July 1953.

L160    Stanford, Derek. "Confused Loyalty." *Scotsman* (Edinburgh), 25 August 1973, *Week-End Scotsman*, p. 3.

L161    Stokoe, Denis. "Maisie Dotes on Many Men." *Journal* (Newcastle), 28 July 1973, p. 7.

L162    Stonier, G.W. "What They Saw in Maisie." *New Statesman and Nation*, ns 45 (20 June 1953), 752-753.

## THE MULBERRY BUSH

For reviews of performances, *see* L. Miscellaneous Reviews.

L163    Anon. "Dramatic Themes." *Times Literary Supplement*, 10 February 1956, p. 82.

L164    Bonnerot, L.F. *Etudes anglaises* (Paris), 10 (octobre-décembre 1957), 456-457.

L165    Broncel, Zdzisław. "Angielski asmodeusz." *Wiadomości* (London), 27 May 1956, p. 3. [In Polish.]

L166    Granger, Derek. "Themes for New Voices." *London Magazine*, 3 no. 12 (December 1956), 41-47 (41, 44, 47).

L167    Hope-Wallace, Phillip. *Time and Tide*, 37 (7 April 1956), 387.

L168    Inglis, Brian. *Spectator*, 196 (23 March 1956), 386.

L169    K., E.O.D. *Punch*, 2 May 1956, p. 533.

L170    Levin, Bernard. "Three Plays." *Truth*, 156 (24 February 1956), 224-225 (224).

L171    Selander, Sten. "Angus Wilson som dramatiker." *Svenska Dagbladet* (Stockholm), 7 May 1956, p. 13.

## ANGLO-SAXON ATTITUDES

L172    Amis, Kingsley. "Dodos Less Darling." *Spectator*, 196 (1 June 1956), 764-765.

Reprinted: *New Republic*, 135 (15 October 1956), 27-28.

L173    Anon."New Fiction." *Times*, 17 May 1956, p. 13.

L174    ——. "On the Wide Screen." *Glasgow Herald*, 17 May 1956, p. 3.

L175    ——. "Professional and Personal." *Scotsman* (Edinburgh), 17 May 1956, p. 15.

L176    ——. "Mourning Becomes Elvira." *Times Literary Supplement*, 18 May 1956, p. 296.

L177    ——. "Briljante satire in dienst van waarheidsdrift." *Nieuwe Rotterdamse Courant*, 26 mei 1956, *Wekelijks bijvoegsel*, p. 2.

L178    ——. *Kirkus Reviews*, 24 (15 August 1956), 591.

L179    ——. "*Anglo-Saxon Attitudes*, A Novel." *Booklist*, 53 (15 September 1956), 36.

L180    ——. *Tamarack Review*, 1 (Autumn 1956), 94.

L181    ——. "The Diabolical 'Joke.' " *Newsweek*, 8 October 1956, p. 95.

L182    ——. "A Carnival of Humbug." *Time*, 29 October 1956, p. 108.

L183    ——. *Bookmark*, 16 (November 1956), 37.

L184    ——. "Brief Notices." *Chicago Review*, 10 no. 4 (Winter 1957), 98-101 (100).

L185    Antonini, Giacomo. "Laurea con lode per i romanziere Angus Wilson." *La Fiera letteraria* (Rome), 1 luglio 1956, p. 6.

L186    Bittner, William. "Hemlock and Piltdown." *Nation*, 183 (13 October 1956), 311-312.

L187    Bowen, Elizabeth. "Master of the Sardonic." *Tatler*, 30 May 1956, p. 484.

Reprinted: *The Mulberry Tree: Writings of Elizabeth Bowen*. Ed. Hermione Lee. London: Virago: 1986, pp. 179-181.

L188    Brunius, Teddy. "Engelsk nutidsroman." *Stockholms-Tidningen*, 15 June 1956, p. 4.

L189    Cass, Cashenden. "New Novels." *Time and Tide*, 37 (19 May 1956), 595-596.

L190    Church, Richard. *Bookman*, April 1956, pp. 1-3.

L191    Connell, John. "A Pagan Relic in a Bishop's Tomb." *Evening News*, 12 May 1956, p. 4.

L192    ———. "There Is Still Hope for the British Novel." *Evening Dispatch* (Edinburgh), 18 May 1956, p. 12.

L193    Connolly, Cyril. "Time the Present." *Sunday Times*, 13 May 1956, p. 5.

L194    Cooper, Lettice. "A Choice of New Novels." *Yorkshire Post* (Leeds), 18 May 1956, p. 4.

L195    Corke, Hilary. "Lack of Confidence." *Encounter*, 7 (July 1956), 75-78.

L196    Cosman, Max. *New Mexico Quarterly*, 27 (April 1957), 131-133.

L197    Cournos, John. *Commonweal*, 65 (7 December 1956), 257.

L198    Cranston, Maurice. "Mr Wilson's Comic Saga." *Manchester Guardian*, 15 May 1956, p. 4.

Reprinted as: "Satirist's Saga." *Manchester Guardian Weekly*, 24 May 1956, p. 10.

L199    Daiches, David. "Human Relations." *New York Times Book Review*, 7 October 1956, p. 5.

L200    Davenport, John. "New Novels." *Observer*, 13 May 1956, p. 12.

L201    Davies, Robertson. "That Dares Not Speak Its Name." *Saturday Night* (Toronto), 71 (1 September 1956), 16-17.

L202    DeMott, Benjamin. "Agonists, Agonizers, and a Utopian." *Hudson Review*, 10 (Spring 1957), 140-146 (142-144).

L203    D[urston], J.H. "Bookshelf: Abroad with Some Not-So-Innocents." *House and Garden* (New York), November 1956, pp. 36-37 (37).

L204    Ekman, Ulf. *Information* (Copenhagen), 17 August 1956.

L205    Elgström. A.L. "Anglosaxiska attityder." *Sydsvenska Dagbladet Snällposten* (Malmö), 23 August 1956, p. 4. [Also on *Hemlock and After*.]

L206    Fiedler, Leslie. "British Fiction." *Commentary*, 23 (March 1957), 294, 296-298 (296-298).

L207    Flint, R.W. "The Undying Apocalypse." *Partisan Review*, 24 no. 1 (Winter 1957), 139-145 (139-142).

L208    Fuller, Edmund. "Substantial Novel That May Not Be Your Dish." *Chicago Sunday Tribune*, 21 October 1956, Pt. 4, p. 4.

L209    Gill, Brendan. "New Old Ways." *New Yorker*, 6 October 1956, pp. 176, 178.

L210    Göransson, Bengt. *Kvällsposten* (Malmö), 3 October 1956.

L211    Gray, James. *Saturday Review*, 6 October 1956, p. 22.

L212    Hobson, Harold. "English View of 'Attitudes.' " *Christian Science Monitor*, 5 July 1956, p. 13.

L213    Holmqvist, Bengt. "Angus Wilsons England." *Dagens Nyheter* (Stockholm), 13 May 1956, p. 4.

L214    Holzhauer, Jean. "Through the Foggy Social Sounds of England Today." *Commonweal*, 65 (19 October 1956), 76-77.

L215    Hughes, Riley. "New Books." *Catholic World*, 184 (January 1957), 309-312 (311).

L216    Kehler, Henning. *Berlingske Aftenavis* (Copenhagen), 15 August 1956.

L217    Laski, Marghanita. "A Major Work of Fiction." *Daily Telegraph*, 18 May 1956, p. 8.

L218    Levidova, I. "O pozak i positsiak." *Inostrannia literatura* (Moscow), 1957, pp. 265-266.

L219    Lindblom, Paul. *Morgon-Tidningen* (Stockholm), 18 June 1956.

L220    McLaughlin, Richard. *Springfield Republican* (MA), 18 November 1956, p. 10C.

L221 Neiiendam, Henrik. *Ekstra Bladet* (Copenhagen), 16 June 1956.

L222 Oesterreicher, Arthur. "Paganism and Piety." *New Leader*, 39 no. 46 (12 November 1956), 27-28.

L223 Ohlon, Sonja. "Angus Wilsons första roman." *Göteborgs-Posten*, 4 July 1956, p. 2.

L224 O'Rourke, Elizabeth. *Best Sellers*, 16 (1 December 1956), 306-307.

L225 Perlström, Åke. "Böcker och författare." *Göteborgs-Posten*, 13 October 1956, p. 2.

L226 Poore, Charles. "Books of The Times." *New York Times*, 4 October 1956, p. 31.

L227 Praz, Mario. "Atteggiamenti Anglosassoni." *L'Italia che scrive* (Rome), febbraio 1957, pp. 29-30.

Reprinted: *Cronache letterarie anglosassoni* [Vol. 4]. Rome: Edizioni di storia e letteratura, 1966, pp. 113-120.

L228 Price, R.G.G. "Hemlock and After and After." *Punch*, 27 June 1956, pp. 775-776.

L229 Pritchett, V.S. "The World of Angus Wilson." *New Statesman and Nation*, 51 (12 May 1956), 533-534.

Reprinted: *Critical Essays on Angus Wilson*, ed. Jay L. Halio, pp. 27-29 (J86).

L230 ——. "Review of Anglo-Saxon Attitudes." *Griffin*, October 1956, pp. 15-19.

L231 Quennell, Peter. "When a Rich Man Lives a Lie . . ." *Daily Mail*, 17 May 1956, p. 4.

L232 Rajecki, Jan. "Anglosasi Angusa Wilsona." *Wiadomości* (London), 12 August 1956, p. 5. [In Polish.]

L233 Raymond, John. "The Blistering Penetration of Angus Wilson." *News Chronicle*, 17 May 1956, p. 8.

L234 Rhodes, Anthony. "New Novels." *Listener*, 17 May 1956, p. 655.

L235    Rolo, Charles J. "Scandal in a Coffin." *Atlantic Monthly*, October 1956, pp. 105-106.

L236    Söderhjelm, Henning. *Arbetarbladet* (Malmö), 31 May 1956.

L237    S-m., H. [Söderhjelm, Henning]. "Ironisk tidsspegel." *Göteborgs Handels-och Sjöfarts-tidning*, 8 May 1956, p. 3.

L238    Spain, Nancy. "Oh, No . . . Angus Wilson's Gone Serious." *Daily Express*, 12 May 1956, p. 8.

L239    Stallings, Sylvia. "Angus Wilson's Finely Plotted, Absorbing Novel of English Life." *New York Herald Tribune Book Review*, 7 October 1956, pp. 1, 8.

L240    Taylor, Griffin. " 'What Doth it Profit a Man . . .?' Three British Views of the Null and the Void." *Sewanee Review*, 66 (1958), 132-146 (141-146).

L241    Thompson, John. "Farewell to Bloomsbury." *Truth*, 156 (18 May 1956), 580-581.

L242    Thomson, George Malcolm. "Mr Wilson Joins the Chamber of Horrors. . ." *Evening Standard*, 15 May 1956, p. 18.

L243    Triomphe, M. *Etudes anglaises* (Paris), 10 (octobre-décembre 1957), 457.

L244    V., J. *San Francisco Chronicle*, 25 November 1956, *Christmas Book Section*, pp. 17, 20.

L245    Van Ghent, Dorothy. "Recent Fiction: The Race, the Moment, and the Milieu." *Yale Review*, ns 46 (Winter 1956), 274-288 (285-286).

L246    [Veen, Adriaan van der.] "Briljante satire in dienst van waarheidsdrift." *Nieuwe Rotterdamse Courant*, 26 mei 1956, Supplement, p. 2.

L247    Walker, Peregrine. "Unearthing the Will." *Tablet*, 207 (26 May 1956), 500.

L248    Willis, Katherine T. *Library Journal*, 81 (1 October 1956), 2255.

L249    Woods, George A. *America*, 96 (3 November 1956), 134-135.

L250    Wyndham, Francis. *London Magazine*, 3 no. 7 (July 1956), 81-83.


# A BIT OFF THE MAP AND OTHER STORIES

L251    Amis, Kingsley. "Dodos on the Wing." *Spectator*, 199 (18 October 1957), 521.

Reprinted: *Critical Essays on Angus Wilson*, ed. Jay L. Halio, p. 30 (J86).

L252    Anon. *Kirkus Reviews*, 25 (1 August 1957), 554.

L253    ———. "Strijd tegen de schone schijn." *Nieuwe Rotterdamse Courant*, 5 oktober 1957, *Wekelijks bijvoegsel*, p. 2.

L254    ———. "Teddy Boy's Anthropologist." *Times*, 17 October 1957, p. 13.

L255    ———. "Human Frailty." *Times Literary Supplement*, 18 October 1957, p. 621.

L256    ———. "Brilliant Gossip." *Time*, 25 November 1957, pp. 126, 129.

L257    ———. *Booklist*, 54 (1 December 1957), 202.

L258    Arnold, James W. *Best Sellers*, 17 (1 February 1958), 368.

L259    Bäckström, Lars. *Uppsala Nya Tidning*, 13 March 1958.

L260    Bacon, Martha. "More Than a Dash of Bitters." *New York Herald Tribune Book Review*, 17 November 1957, p. 6.

L261    Bengtson, Göran. "Samhällo skartografen." *Sydsvenska Dagbladet Snällposten* (Malmö), 12 December 1957, p. 15.

L262    Brooke, Jocelyn. "Soho and Subtopia." *Time and Tide*, 38 (19 October 1957), 1305-1306.

L263    Brunius, Teddy. "Angus Wilson en intelligensmaskin." *Stockholms-Tidningen*, 11 November 1957, p. 6.

L264    Clay, George R. "The Case Against Boredom." *Reporter*, 17 (26 December 1957), 38-40 (38-39).

L265    Corke, Hilary. "New Novels." *Listener*, 58 (24 October 1957), 667.

L266    Davenport, John. "Micro-Master." *Observer*, 13 October 1957, p. 19.

L267    Dolbier, Maurice. "Book Review." *New York Herald Tribune*, 16 November 1957, p. 8.

L268    Fonsmark, Henning. *Berlingske Aftenavis* (Copenhagen), 7 January 1958.

L269    Forster, Peter. "Short Stories." *Truth*, 157 (1 November 1957), 1251.

L270    Fuller, Edmund. "Satirical Collection Is Work of Quality." *Chicago Sunday Tribune*, 22 December 1957, Pt. 4, p. 3.

L271    Fuller, Roy. *London Magazine*, 4 no. 12 (December 1957), 60-62, 65 (60-61).

L272    Green, Martin. "Artist Astray." *Chicago Review*, 12 (Autumn 1958), 76-79.

L273    Habich, William. "Subtle, Amusing and Bitter." *Courier-Journal* (Louisville, KY), 1 December 1957, Sect. 4, p. 6.

L274    Harley, John. *Library Journal*, 82 (15 September 1957), 2144.

L275    Hughes, Riley. "New Books." *Catholic World*, 186 (February 1958), 387-389 (387-388).

L276    John, K. "Notes for the Novel-Reader." *Illustrated London News*, 7 December 1957, p. 1000.

L277    Maclaren-Ross, J. "Up to the Moment." *Punch*, 6 November 1957, pp. 550-551.

L278    Millgate, Michael. "Angus Wilson's Guide to Modern England." *New Republic*, 137 (25 November 1957), 17-18.

L279    Mohn, Bent. "To engelske fakkelbaerere: Nyt fra "De Vrede.' " *Information* (Copenhagen), 23 July 1958, p. 4.

L280    Moore, Harry T. "Teddy Boys and Genteel Madmen." *New York Times Book Review*, 17 November 1957. p. 4.

L281    Mudrick, Marvin. "Is Fiction Human?" *Hudson Review*, 11 (Summer 1958), 294-301 (298-299).

L282    Peden, William. "Eight from Britain—London 'Crowd.' " *Saturday Review*, 30 November 1957, pp. 15-17, 31-32 (16).

L283    Perlström, Åke. *Göteborgs-Posten*, 21 November 1957.

L284    Peters, W. *Streven* (Leuven), 11 no. 1 (januari 1958), 395.

L285    Raymond, John. "Mid-Century Blues." *New Statesman*, 54 (12 October 1957), 464, 466.

L286    Shrapnel, Norman. "Dodos and Teddy-Thinkers." *Manchester Guardian*, 15 October 1957, p. 6.

        Reprinted as: "Short Stories and Novels: English and American." *Manchester Guardian Weekly*, 31 October 1957, p. 11.

L287    S-m., H. [Söderhjelm, Henning]. "Fräna noveller." *Göteborgs Handels-och Sjöfarts-tidning*, 30 September 1957, p. 3.

L288    Stanley, Donald. "What Is the Truth Really Like?" *San Francisco Examiner*, 2 February 1958, *Modern Living*, p. 12.

L289    Sudrann, Jean. "The Necessary Illusion: A Letter from London." *Antioch Review*, 18 (Summer 1958), 236-244 (237-238).

L290    Wakefield, Dan. "Post-Post-Kipling." *Commonweal*, 67 (13 December 1957), 293-294.

L291    Webster, Harvey Curtis. "Four Interesting British Novelists." *New Leader*, 41 no. 21 (26 May 1958), 26-27 (27).

L292    Weightman, J.G. "The Month: A Personal Diary." *Twentieth Century*, 163 (January 1958), 70-77 (73).

L293    Young, Kenneth. "Angus Wilson's Incredible Young Men." *Daily Telegraph*, 11 October 1957, p. 13.


## THE MIDDLE AGE OF MRS ELIOT

L294    Anon."Angus Wilson's New Novel." *Scotsman* (Edinburgh), 20 November 1958, p. 8.

L295    ——. "Vitality of Angus Wilson." *Times*, 20 November 1958, p. 15.

L296    ——. "A Rather Different Mr Wilson." *Birmingham Mail*, 27 November 1958, p. 10.

L297    ——. "Angus Wilsons portret van Mrs Eliot." *Nieuwe Rotterdamse Courant*, 3 januari 1959, *Wekelijks bijvoegsel*, p. 2.

L298    ——. "A Portrait of Loneliness." *The Friend* (Bloemfontein, S. Afr.), 8 January 1959, p. 4.

L299    ——. *Kirkus Reviews*, 27 (15 January 1959), 59.

L300    ——. *Booklist*, 55 (1 February 1959), 277.

L301    ——. "Storyteller at His Best." *Newsweek*, 23 March 1959, p. 108.

L302    ——. "The Widow Britannia." *Time*, 30 March 1959, pp. 91-92.

L303    ——. *Bookmark*, 18 (April 1959), 175.

L304    ——. "Wilson's New Novel." *Weekly Mail* (Madras), 5 April 1959, p. 11.

L305    Bäckström, Lars. *Uppsala Nya Tidning*, 30 April 1959.

L306    Beddoes, John. "Mr Wilson Sounds the Retreat." *Tribune*, 12 December 1958, p. 10.

L307    Bengston, Göran. "Angus Wilson och moralen." *Sydsvenska Dagbladet* (Malmö), 10 February 1959, p. 4.

L308    Bloom, Beryl. "New Fiction." *Cape Times* (Cape Town), 31 December 1958, p. 8.

L309    Boyd, John D. "She Looked for a Happy Ending." *America*, 101 (2 May 1959), 281.

L310    Budtz-Jørgensen, Jørgen. "Kvindeportraetter." *Berlingske Tidende* (Copenhagen), 10 January 1959, p. 6.

L311    Caliri, Fortunata. *Sign* (Union City, NJ), 38 no. 10 (May 1959), 73.

L312 Campbell, Ross. "The Weird English Mob." *Daily Telegraph* (Sydney), 21 March 1959, p. 22.

L313 Churchill, R.C. "New Novels." *Birmingham Post*, 2 December 1958, p. 3.

L314 Connell, John. "I Think This Is a Miracle." *Evening News*, 27 November 1958, p. 4.

L315 ———. "Three Novels To Remember." *Evening Dispatch* (Edinburgh), 29 November 1958, p. 8.

L316 Cooper, William. "The Milder Age of Mr Wilson." *News Chronicle*, 19 November 1958, p. 6.

L317 Cosman, Max. "Coming to Terms with Life." *New Leader*, 42 no. 15 (13 April 1959), 26-27.

L318 Cruttwell, Patrick. "Fiction Chronicle." *Hudson Review*, 12 (Summer 1959), 286-295 (290-291).

L319 Curran, Charles. "Room at the Bottom." *New Republic*, 140 (1 June 1959), 18-19.

L320 D., D.J.N. "Catastrophe." *Weekly Scotsman* (Edinburgh), 8 January 1959, p. 5.

L321 Derrick, Christopher. "Contra Mundum." *Tablet*, 212 (29 November 1958), 483-484.

L322 Edinburgh, Arnold. "Life without Purpose." *Saturday Night* (Toronto), 74 (14 February 1959), 31-32.

L323 E[nehjelm], H[elen] af. "Wilson och Murdoch." *Hufvudstadsbladet* (Helsinki), 1 February 1959, p. 9.

L324 Engle, Paul. "Author's Fine Talent Lost in Novel's Length." *Chicago Sunday Tribune*, 29 March 1959, Pt. 4, p. 4.

L325 Fane, Vernon. "Bonanza Queen." *Sphere*, 235 (6 December 1958), 394.

L326 Farrell, Kathleen. "Reading for Pleasure." *Nursing Times* (London), 2 January 1959, pp. 7-8 (8).

L327    Fremantle, Anne. "Prism of Relations." *Commonweal*, 70 (8 May 1959), 160-161.

L328    Fröier, Lennart. "Han är inte tråkig." *Arbetarbladet* (Malmö), 22 December 1958.

L329    G., R. "Wilson's Way." *Irish Times*, 20 December 1958, p. 6.

L330    George, Daniel. *Bookman Annual*, December 1958, pp. 11-12.

L331    Gilliatt, Penelope. "Books for Christmas." *Vogue*, 114 no. 13 (December 1983), p. 92.

L332    Glanville, Brian. "Mrs Eliot Develops Middle-Age Spread." *Reynolds News & Sunday Citizen*, 23 November 1958, p. 6.

L333    Grady, R.F. *Best Sellers*, 19 (1 April 1959), 7.

L334    Grut, Mario. "Medelålderns Vändkors." *Aftonbladet* (Stockholm), 4 November 1958, p. 2.

L335    Guiton, Helen. "The Modern Sophisticate." *Montreal Gazette*, 13 December 1958, p. 42.

L336    H., J.E. "Troubled Years." *Edmonton Journal* (Alberta), 3 January 1959, p. 19.

L337    H., O. *The Sun* (Sydney), 8 April 1959, p. 30.

L338    Hancox, Ralph. "Middle Age and Sweet Pubescence." *Peterborough Examiner* (Ontario), 17 January 1959, p. 4.

L339    Hicks, Granville. "The Importance of People." *Saturday Review*, 21 March 1959, p. 22.

L340    Hogan, William. "Portrait of a Lady in the Role of a Widow." *San Francisco Chronicle*, 16 April 1959, p. 43.

L341    Hoggart, Richard. "Some Kinds of Isolation." *Manchester Guardian*, 28 November 1958, p. 6.

        Reprinted as: "Explorations of Loneliness." *Manchester Guardian Weekly*, 4 December 1958, p. 10.

L342    Holmqvist, Bengt. "Världen och stillheten." *Dagens Nyheter* (Stockholm), 6 April 1959, p. 4.

L343    Hughes, Isabelle. "Woman's Rather Pointless Life." *Globe and Mail* (Toronto), 17 January 1959, p. 16.

L344    Hughes, Riley. "New Books." *Catholic World*, 189 (July 1959), 322-327 (322).

L345    Hugh-Jones, Siriol. "Books I Am Reading." *Tatler*, 10 December 1958, p. 676.

L346    Johnson, Pamela Hansford. "Three-Legged Race." *New Statesman*, 56 (22 November 1958), 732.

L347    K., F.J. "The Case of Mr Angus Wilson." *Irish Independent*, 14 February 1959, p. 8.

L348    K., N. "An Angus Wilson Novel." *Bulletin* (Sydney), 18 March 1959, pp. 66-67.

L349    Kaufmann, R.J. "Uses of the Past: Angus Wilson." *Nation*, 188 (23 May 1959), 478-480.

L350    Kelly, Clive. "Widow's Efforts to Come to Terms with Life." *Advertiser* (Adelaide), 31 January 1959, p. 12.

L351    Kermode, Frank. "Mr Wilson's People." *Spectator*, 201 (21 November 1958), 705-706.

        Reprinted: *Puzzles and Epiphanies: Essays and Reviews 1958-1961.* New York: Chilmark Press, 1962, pp. 193-197.

        Reprinted: *Critical Essays on Angus Wilson*, ed. Jay L. Halio, pp. 30-33 (J86).

L352    Laker, J.H.C. "Family Bookshelf." *Southport Journal*, 2 January 1959, p. 2. [Syndicated.]

L353    Lapicque, F. *Etudes anglaises* (Paris), 14 (juillet-septembre 1961), 261.

L354    Lister, Richard. "Mrs Eliot Makes Her Decision." *Evening Standard*, 18 November 1958, p. 12.

L355    Lucas, Barbara. *Twentieth Century*, 165 (January 1959), 96-98.

L356    M., G. "Great Novel of a Widow's Battle Against Loneliness." *Sunday Tribune* (Johannesburg), 25 January 1959.

L357    McCormack, Robert. "Will Meg Adjust To Her New Life? Will Angus Turn to Soap Opera?" *Toronto Daily Star*, 13 December 1958, p. 28.

L358    Metcalf, John. "Portrait of a Woman." *Sunday Times* 16 November 1958, p. 18.

L359    Meynell, Laurence, "A Sensitive Writer's Best Book to Date." *Express & Star* (Wolverhampton), 24 November 1958, p. 5.

L360    Millar, Ruby. "Novels." *National and English Review*, February 1959, pp. 72-74 (72-73).

L361    Miller, George. "End of the Trip." *Daily Express*, 20 November 1958, p. 6.

L362    Milne, Angela. "It's Only a Game." *Sketch*, 17 December 1958, pp. 590-591 (591).

L363    Mooney, Harry, Jr. "Wilson Adroit, Subtle." *Pittsburgh Press*, 22 March 1959, Sect. 5, p. 8.

L364    Moore, Harry T. "Warm Friends Grew Cold." *New York Times Book Review*, 22 March 1959, pp. 5, 30.

L365    Nicholls, Alan. "When Middle Age Meets Crisis." *Age* (Melbourne), 14 February 1959, p. 18.

L366    Nyren, Karl. *Library Journal*, 84 (1 April 1959), 1154.

L367    Österling, Anders. "Engelska romaner-berättarkonstens triumf." *Stockholms-Tidningen* (Stockholm), 30 November 1958, p. 4.

L368    Parisis, Jean-Marc. "Angus Wilson et l'agonie du pudding." *Libération* (Paris), 9 août 1983, p. 20. [On the Folio Gallimard edition.]

L369    Peterson, Virgilia. "Angus Wilson's Novel of a Woman's Violent Awakening to Reality." *New York Herald Tribune Book Review*, 22 March 1959, p. 1.

L370    Powell, Dawn. "Meet Mrs Eliot." *New York Post*, 22 March 1959, p. M11.

L371    Price, Martin. "Intelligence and Fiction: Some New Novels." *Yale Review*, ns 48 (Spring 1959), 451-464 (458-460).

L372　　Price, R.G.G. *Punch*, 3 December 1958, p. 738.

Reprinted as: "Novel of Middle Age Shows Harsh Charity." *Vancouver Sun*, 3 January 1959, p. 5.

L373　　Puffmore, Henry. "Under Review." *Bookseller*, 22 November 1958, pp. 2042-2043 (2042).

L374　　Quigley, Isabel. "The Dying Novel?" *Encounter*, 12 (January 1959), 84-86 (85).

L375　　Quinton, Anthony. "Away from the Dodos." *Observer*, 16 November 1958, p. 21.

L376　　R., G. "Angus Wilson's Achievement." *Eastern Daily Press* (Norwich), 18 November 1958, *Christmas Book Supplement*, p. IX.

L377　　Raymond, John. "Meg Eliot Surprised." *Times Literary Supplement*, 21 November 1958, p. 672.

Reprinted: *The Doge of Dover and Other Essays*. London: Macgibbon & Kee, 1960, pp. 170-178.

L378　　Rees, Goronwy. "New Novels." *Listener*, 60 (27 November 1958), 892.

L379　　Rolo, Charles J. "Portrait of a Woman." *Atlantic Monthly*, April 1959, pp. 138-139.

L380　　Scott, Margerie. "A Study in Loneliness for Women Past 40." *Windsor Daily Star* (Ontario), 3 January 1959, p. 35.

L381　　Sherman, Thomas B. "A Woman Unprepared for the Reversal of Fortune." *St Louis Post-Dispatch*, 15 March 1959, p. 4B.

L382　　Simon, Clare. "Satire Is Angus Wilson's Undoing." *Catholic Herald*, 26 December 1958.

L383　　Simon, Irene. "Some Recent English Novels." *La Revue des Langues Vivantes* (Brussels), 25 (1959), 219-230 (227-229).

L384　　Singleton, Frank. "Notable Novel of Our Day: Mr Angus Wilson's Achievement." *Bolton Evening News*, 10 February 1959, p. 2.

L385　　Söderhjelm, Henning. "Sympati för de rotlösa." *Göteborgs Handels-och Sjöfarts-tidning*, 18 November 1958, p. 3.

L386     Spring, Howard. "Private Thoughts of a Best Seller." *Country Life*, 15 January 1959, pp. 127, 129 (129).

L387     Stephane, Nelly. "Romans anglais." *Europe*, 417-418 (janvier-février 1964), 282-288 (287-288).

L388     Thomas, Keith. "Angus Wilson Gone Solemn." *Nation* (Sydney), 11 April 1959, p. 22.

L389     Urquhart, Fred. "New Novels." *Time and Tide*, 40 (3 January 1959), 17.

L390     Wain, John. "Books: Comment on Widowhood." *New Yorker*, 11 April 1959, pp. 164-166.

L391     Wallace, Martin. "Cronin, Angus Wilson and Collette." *Belfast Telegraph*, 3 January 1959, p. 4.

L392     Watling, E.F. "Failure To Find Place in Life." *Sheffield Telegraph*, 3 January 1959, p. 3.

L393     Watson, Colin. "Life Collapses." *Journal* (Newcastle), 20 December 1958, p. 4.

L394     Whately, Rosaleen. "Widow Works Out Her Salvation." *Liverpool Daily Post*, 3 December 1958, p. 9.

L395     Wood, Frederick T. "Current Literature, 1958." *English Studies*, 41 (1960), 48-58 (48).

L396     Wyndham, Francis. *London Magazine*, 6 no. 2 (February 1959), 64-66 (64-65).

L397     Young, Kenneth. "Angus Wilson's Great Creation." *Daily Telegraph*, 21 November 1958, p. 15.

L398     Young, Phyllis. "Choice of Novels." *Yorkshire Post* (Leeds), 20 November 1958, p. 5.

## THE OLD MEN AT THE ZOO

L399     Adams, Phoebe. "War in Fantasy." *Atlantic*, November 1961, p. 191.

L400     Anon. *Kirkus Reviews*, 29 (15 August 1961), 747.

L401     ———. "New Fiction." *Times*, 28 September 1961, p. 15.

L402     ———. "Beyond the Fringe." *Times Literary Supplement*, 29 September 1961, p. 641.

L403     ———. "Angus Wilson's Moral Fable." *Scotsman* (Edinburgh), 30 September 1961, *Week-End Scotsman*, p. 3.

L404     ———. "Animal Chaos." *Eastern Daily Press* (Norwich), 6 October 1961, p. 11.

L405     ———. *Bookmark*, 21 (November 1961), 39.

L406     ———. "Animal Crackers." *Time*, 3 November 1961, p. 86.

L407     ———. "Caged." *Newsweek*, 6 November 1961, p. 104.

L408     ———. *Booklist*, 58 (1 February 1962), 342-343.

L409     Aldiss, Brian W. "Puzzles and Farce at the Zoo." *Oxford Mail*, 28 September 1961, p. 8.

L410     Berezowski, M. "Niepokój angielskiego liberala." *Trybuna Ludu* (Warsaw), 16 November 1961, p. 6.

L411     Bishop, Dorothy. "A Novel of the Week." *Ottawa Journal*, 2 December 1961, p. 39.

L412     Bowen, John. "Wish Fulfilment." *Punch*, 4 October 1961, p. 515.

L413     Bowen, Robert O. "Variations on a Palling Theme." *National Review*, 12 (16 January 1962), 29-30.

L414     Burgess, Anthony. "Angus Wilson's Best." *Yorkshire Post* (Leeds), 5 October 1961, p. 4.

L415     Church, Richard. "A Novel Rich in Realism." *Country Life*, 5 October 1961, pp. 785-786.

L416     Cox, C.B. *Critical Quarterly*, 3 (Winter 1961), 369-370.

L417     Davis, Robert Gorham. "The Caged and Uncaged." *New York Times Book Review*, 29 October 1961, pp. 4-5.

L418     Dennis, Nigel. "Keeping the Beasts in Their Place." *Sunday Telegraph*, 24 September 1961, p. 7.

L419    Derrick, Christopher. "Uphill." *Tablet*, 215 (7 October 1961), 954.

L420    Edinga, H. "Bizar boek van Wilson." *Elseviers Weekblad* (Amsterdam), 14 november 1961.

L421    Enehjelm, Helen af. "Engelsk romankost." *Hufvudstadsbladet* (Helsinki), 24 January 1962, p. 7.

L422    Engle, Paul. "A Tart View of England in the 1970s." *Chicago Sunday Tribune*, 5 November 1961, Pt. 4, p. 6.

L423    Eriksson, Göran [R.] *Västerbottens-Kuriren* (Umeå), 1 November 1961.

L424    Fadiman, Clifton. *Book-of-the-Month-Club News*, November 1961, p. 7.

L425    Forrest, Alan. "Inside the Zoo with Wilson the Wasp." *Reynolds News & Sunday Citizen*, 24 September 1961, p. 10.

L426    Fuller, John. "Two New Novels." *Listener*, 66 (5 October 1961), 527.

L427    Furbank, P.N. "Moments of Awful Truth." *John O'London's*, 5 (28 September 1961), 359.

L428    Gardiner, John. "Crisis at the Zoo." *Windsor Daily Star* (Ontario), 2 December 1961, p. 40.

L429    George, Daniel. "Angus Wilson's Wild Animals." *Daily Telegraph*, 29 September 1961, p. 19.

L430    Golding, William. *Bookman*, October 1961, p. 43.

L431    Griffin, Lloyd W. *Library Journal*, 86 (15 October 1961), 3494.

L432    Gross, John. "Elephants and Blind Men." *Commentary*, 33 (March 1962), 265-267.

L433    Grut, Mario. *Aftonbladet* (Stockholm), 12 March 1962.

L434    Halio, Jay L. "Response vs. Responsibility." *Critique: Studies in Modern Fiction*, 5 (Spring-Summer 1962), 77-82.

Reprinted: *Angus Wilson*, Writers and Critics Series, pp. 84-92 (J84).

L435    Harvey, Elizabeth. "After 'Hemlock and After.'" *Birmingham Post*, 26 September 1961, p. 3.

L436    Heje, Johan. "Den usandsynlige fremtid." *Information* (Copenhagen), 6 August 1962, p. 4.

L437    Hemmel, Jan. *Kvällsposten* (Malmö), 4 January 1962.

L438    Hicks, Granville. "Politics on an Animal Farm." *Saturday Review*, 21 October 1961, p. 22.

L439    Hope, Francis. "Novels." *Encounter*, 17 (November 1961), 77, 79, 81 (77, 79).

L440    Hobsbaum, Philip. "Jungle Warfare at All Levels." *Western Daily Press and Time & Mirror* (Bristol), 20 November 1961, p. 8.

L441    Huygens, G.W. "Het kwaad breekt los in Wilsons dierentuin." *Nieuwe Rotterdamse Courant*, 7 oktober 1961, *Wekelijks bijvoegsel*, p. 2.

L442    Jeffries, Barbara. "Macabre Entertainment." *Sydney Morning Herald*, 3 February 1962, p. 12.

L443    Johnson, Lucy. "High Polish." *Progressive*, 26 (January 1962), 49-50.

L444    K., F.J. "Human Selfishness in the Zoo." *Irish Independent*, 11 November 1961, p. 10.

L445    K., P.A. "From Leaden Feet into Flights of Pure Fantasy." *Pretoria News*, 4 January 1961, p. 10.

L446    Lång, Carl-Olof. *Göteborgs-Posten*, 2 December 1961.

L447    Laws, Frederick. "Comedy of Terrors." *Daily Herald*, 25 September 1961, p. 9.

L448    Lid, Richard W. "Micawber Figures People Wilson's Zoo." *San Francisco Chronicle*, 5 November 1961, *This World*, p. 29.

L449    Lorentzen, Ragnhild. "I zoologisk hage—et fremtidsperspektiv." *Verdens Gang* (Oslo), 25 November 1961, p. 3.

L450    Lundberg, Bengt. *Östgöta Correspondenten* (Linköping), 17 November 1961.

L451    M., K.M. "Ten Years from Now." *Daily Dispatch* (East London, S. Afr.), 17 November 1961, p. 14.

L452    McDowell, Frederick P.W. " 'The Devious Involutions of Human Character and Emotions': Reflections on Some Recent British Novels." *Wisconsin Studies in Contemporary Literature*, 4 (Autumn 1963), 339-366 (359-362).

L453    MacGillivray, Arthur. *Best Sellers*, 21 (1 December 1961), 361.

L454    McGuinness, Frank. *London Magazine*, ns 1 no. 10 (January 1962), 92-95.

L455    McLaughlin, Richard. *Springfield Sunday Republican* (MA), 31 December 1961, p. 4D.

L456    Marra, Nelson. "Alegoría contemporánea: Angus Wilson y su metáfora zoomórfica." *El Pais* (Madrid), 16 October 1986. [On the Alfaguara edition.]

L457    Mitgang, Herbert. "Books of The Times." *New York Times*, 2 December 1961, p. 21.

L458    Montagnes, Anne. "Angus Wilson Turns to the Zoo." *Globe and Mail* (Toronto), 6 January 1962, p. 10.

L459    Mortimer, John. "A Fatal Giraffe." *Spectator*, 207 (29 September 1961), 431.

L460    Mortimer, Penelope. "Will the Future Really Be Like This, Mr Wilson?" *Evening Standard*, 26 September 1961, p. 21.

L461    Mortimer, Raymond. "Only Man Is Vile." *Sunday Times*, 24 September 1961, p. 30.

L462    Nielsen, Johs. "Om dyr og mennesker." *Jyllands-Posten* (Aarhus), 12 March 1962.

L463    Norrie, Ian. "On the Wilson Wavelength." *Hampstead & Highgate Express*, 29 September 1961, p. 6.

L464    ——. "The New Angus Wilson." *Books and Bookmen*, 7 no. 2 (November 1961), 38.

L465   O'Brien, E.D. "A Literary Lounger." *Illustrated London News*, 14 October 1961, p. 641.

L466   Perlström, Åke. *Göteborgs-Posten*, 2 December 1961.

L467   Pickrel, Paul. "The Other Wilson." *Harper's*, November 1961, pp. 110, 114.

L468   Pitman, Robert. "From the Pen of Mr Wilson a Tale of Terror." *Sunday Express*, 24 September 1961, p. 6.

L469   Porter, Frederick. "Conflict at the Zoo." *Glasgow Herald*, 28 September 1961, p. 6.

L470   Pritchett, V.S. "Bad-Hearted Britain." *New Statesman*, 62 (29 September 1961), 429-430.

L471   Pryce-Jones, David. "Wilsonian Attitudes." *Financial Times*, 25 September 1961, p. 14.

L472   Pugh, Griffith T. "From the Recent Books." *English Journal*, 51 (May 1962), 374-377 (375).

L473   Raphael, Frederic. "Animal Crackers." *Time and Tide*, 26 October 1961, p. 1804.

L474   Ross, Mary Lowrey. "Further Anglo-Saxon Attitudes." *Saturday Night* (Toronto), 76 (9 December 1961), 41.

L475   Rubin, Louis D., Jr. "Six Novels and S. Levin." *Sewanee Review*, 70 (Summer 1962), 504-514 (506-508).

L476   Sale, Roger. "Novels, and Being a Novelist." *Hudson Review*, 15 (Spring 1962), 134-142 (136-137).

L477   Share, Bernard. "These Animals Bite." *Irish Times*, 7 October 1961, p. 8.

L478   Smith, Vivian B. "Don't Feed the Vultures." *Bulletin* (Sydney), 27 January 1962, pp. 48-49.

L479   Spector, Robert D. "The Way It Was in 1970-1973." *New York Herald Tribune Books*, 29 October 1961, p. 4.

L480   Symons, Julian. "Politics and the Novel." *Twentieth Century*, 170 (Winter 1962), 147-154 (151-153).

L481    T., I.R. "Moments of Awful Truth." *Eastern Province Herald* (Port Elizabeth, S. Afr.), 29 November 1961, p. 17.

L482    Thomas, Keith. "In London Cages." *Nation* (Sydney), 10 February 1962, p. 23.

L483    W., N. "Bloodless in the Zoo." *Freedom* (Cape Town), 20 January 1962.

L484    Wain, John. "Angus Wilson Takes Off into the Future." *Observer*, 24 September 1961, p. 30.

L485    Wilding, Michael. "Recent Fiction." *Isis* (Oxford), 25 October 1961, p. 20.

L486    Williams, Owen. "A Too-Mellow Angus Wilson." *Cape Times* (Cape Town), 8 November 1961, p. 12.

L487    Williams, Raymond. "The End of a Mimic." *Manchester Guardian*, 29 September 1961, p. 7.

      Reprinted: *Manchester Guardian Weekly*, 5 October 1961, p. 11.

L488    Wylder, D.E. *New Mexico Quarterly*, 33 (Autumn 1963), 357-359.

# THE WILD GARDEN
# OR SPEAKING OF WRITING

L489    Anon. "Getting Stockport Right." *New Statesman*, 66 (15 November 1963), 706.

L490    ——. "Getting Themselves Taped." *Times Literary Supplement*, 21 November 1963, p. 948.

L491    ——. "The Three-Legged Race." *Times Literary Supplement*, 21 November 1963, p. 947.

L492    ——. "Angus Wilson en zijn tuinen." *Nieuwe Rotterdamse Courant*, 14 maart 1964, *Wekelijks bijvoegsel*, p. 2.

L493    ——. *Choice*, 1 (June 1964), 136.

L494    Arblaster, Anthony. "The Men Who Fought the Poetic Revolution." *Tribune*, 13 December 1963, p. 13.

L495    [Beebe, Maurice.] "Modern Fiction Newsletter." *Modern Fiction Studies*, 11 (Summer 1964), 182-218 (196).

L496    Bowen, John. "Literary Letter from London." *New York Times Book Review*, 24 November 1963, pp. 66-67.

L497    ——. "A Quartet of Self-Examinations." *Punch*, 11 December 1963, p. 866.

L498    Bradbury, Malcolm. *Listener*, 70 (28 November 1963), 893, 895.

L499    Budtz-Jørgensen, Jørgen. "Liv og digtning." *Berlingske Tidende* (Copenhagen), 18 February 1964, p. 19.

L500    Churchill, R.C. "Novelists on Novels." *Birmingham Post*, 12 November 1963, p. 4.

L501    Davis, Robert Gorham. "The Roots of the Story." *New York Times Book Review*, 16 February 1964, pp. 22, 26.

L502    Duchene, Anne. "Speaking of Writing." *Guardian*, 15 November 1963, p. 9.

L503    F., X. *Anglo-Portugese News* (Lisbon), 7 December 1963, p. 14.

L504    Ghose, Zulfikar. "Artists and Entertainers." *Spectator*, 211 (13 December 1963), 798.

L505    Guirdham, Quentin. "Anatomy of an Author." *Yorkshire Post* (Leeds), 1 January 1964, p. 3.

L506    Hicks, Granville. "Talks along the Thames." *Saturday Review*, 14 December 1963, pp. 39-40.

L507    Jeffries, Terence. *Books and Bookmen*, 9 no. 4 (January 1964), 20.

L508    Johns, Richard. "Dissecting Jelly-Fish." *Western Mail* (Cardiff), 30 November 1963, p. 6.

L509    Johnson, Louis. "A Writer Reviews Himself." *Hawke's Bay Herald-Tribune* (Hastings, N.Z.), 1 February 1964, p. 6.

L510    K., P.A. "Novelist Speaks on Writing, Criticism." *Pretoria News*, 9 April 1964, p. 6.

L511    L., C.C.M. "A Writer's Guide to Himself." *Glasgow Herald*, 11 January 1964, p. 9.

L512    Lundberg, Bengt. *Östgöta Correspondenten* (Linköping), 11 November, 1963.

L513    Mardle, Jonathan. "Angus Wilson on Himself." *Eastern Daily Press* (Norwich), 21 November 1963, *Christmas Book Supplement*, p. I.

L514    Nye, Robert. "Why Speak at All?" *Scotsman* (Edinburgh), 4 January 1964, *Week-End Scotsman*, p. 3.

L515    Ohmann, Richard. "The Private Corridor of Angus Wilson's Mind." *Commonweal*, 79 (21 February 1964), 638-640.

L516    Panton, George. "What Makes a Writer Tick?" *Sunday Gleaner* (Kingston, Jam.), 12 January 1964, p. 4.

L517    Pryce-Jones, Alan. "On Explaining the Unexplainable." *Book Week*, 1 (9 February 1964), 2, 19. [Syndicated.]

L518    Pryce-Jones, David. "Do It Yourself." *Financial Times*, 28 November 1963, p. 26.

L519    Raven, Simon. "Inside Story." *Observer*, 10 November 1963, p. 25.

L520    Smith, Vivian B. "Inside the Labyrinth: The Tragic World of Angus Wilson." *Bulletin* (Sydney), 22 February 1964, pp. 40-41.

L521    Sørenson, Roald. "Angus Wilson om seg selv." *Arbeiderbladet* (Oslo), 13 January 1964, p. 8.

L522    Willis, Katherine T. *Library Journal*, 88 (1 December 1963), 4646.

L523    Zimon, H.D. "How Writers Write." *Daily Telegraph*, 15 November 1963, p. 20.

## LATE CALL

L524　Anon. "New Fiction." *Times*, 12 November 1964, p. 18.

L525　——. "Not Painted—But Made Up." *Times Literary Supplement*, 12 November 1964, p. 1013.

Reprinted: *T.L.S. Essays and Reviews from The Times Literary Supplement, 1964*. London: Oxford University Press, 1965, pp. 103-105.

L526　——. "Current Fiction." *Weekly Mail* (Madras), 9 January 1965, p. 11.

L527　——. "Among the Aspidistras." *Newsweek*, 11 January 1965, pp. 80-81.

L528　——. *Booklist*, 61 (15 January 1965), 473.

L529　——. "Briefly Noted." *New Yorker*, 16 January 1965, p. 128.

L530　——. "Anglo-Saxon Platitudes." *Time*, 22 January 1965, pp. 79-80.

L531　——. *Choice*, 2 (June 1965), 230.

L532　Arblaster, Anthony. "Principles and Sympathy." *Tribune*, 18 December 1964, p. 12.

L533　Barrett, William. "Reader's Choice." *Atlantic*, March 1965, pp. 190-191.

L534　Baumbach, Jonathan. "In Time To Save Her Soul." *Saturday Review*, 16 January 1965, p. 29.

L535　Bergonzi, Bernard. "A New Angus Wilson." *New York Review of Books*, 25 February 1965, pp. 21-23. *See also* J23, pp. 157-159.

L536　Berridge, Elizabeth. "Dissection of a New Town." *Daily Telegraph*, 12 November 1964, p. 21.

L537　Bowen, John. "What Is Sylvia?" *New York Times Book Review*, 10 January 1965, p. 5.

L538　Bradbury, Malcolm. "New Novels." *Punch*, 6 January 1965, p. 32.

L539    Brockway, James. "Angus Wilsons *Late Call.*" *Nieuwe Rotterdamse Courant*, 6 februari 1965, *Wekelijks bijvoegsel*, p. 2.

Reprinted as: "Angus Wilson: streven naar het goede." *Waar zijn de Angry Young Men gebleven?* Amsterdam/Antwerp: Uitgeverij Contact, 1965, pp. 139-143.

L540    Bronzwaer, W. "Angus Wilsons nieuwe roman *Late Call.*" *De Tijd-Maasbode* (Netherlands), 12 december 1964, pp. 11-12.

L541    Burgess, Anthony. "Powers That Be." *Encounter*, 24 no. 1 (January 1965), 71-76.

Reprinted: *Critical Essays on Angus Wilson*, ed. Jay L. Halio, pp. 34-36 (J86).

L542    Calder-Marshall, Arthur. "New Novels." *Financial Times*, 12 November 1964, p. 22.

L543    Cook, Roderick. *Harper's*, February 1965, pp. 127-128.

L544    Cummings, Elizabeth W. *Library Journal*, 90 (1 February 1965), 669-670.

L545    Curley, Daniel. "The Virtues of Service." *New Leader*, 48 (15 February 1965), 21-22 (22).

L546    Cutler, Alec. "Growing Old in a World of Change." *Cape Times* (Cape Town), 20 January 1965, p. 12.

L547    Daniel, John. "Versions of Britain in the Sixties." *Manchester Guardian*, 13 November 1964, p. 9.

Reprinted as: "Two Versions of Modern Britain." *Manchester Guardian Weekly*, 19 November 1964, p. 10.

L548    Davenport, Guy. "A Plague of Despair." *National Review*, 17 (23 February 1965), 155-156 (156).

L549    Elliott, Margaret. "Sylvia Finds Out Who She Is the Hard Way." *Life*, 19 February 1965, p. 12.

L550    Enehjelm, Helen af. Blidare med åren." *Hufvudstadsbladet* (Helsinki), 22 December 1964, p. 7.

L551    English, Isobel. "Mistaken Morals." *Catholic Herald*, 4 December 1964, p. 7.

L552    Eriksson, G[öran] [R.], *Västerbottens-Kuriren* (Umeå), 15 March 1965.

L553    Evans, Illtud. "Our World and Welcome To It." *Tablet*, 218 (21 November 1964), 1317.

L554    Green, Howard. "The Countess' Hat." *Hudson Review*, 18 (Summer 1965), 278-289 (278-279).

L555    Gross, John. "Blessed Are the Pure in Heart." *Observer*, 8 November 1964, p. 27.

Reprinted as: "Bienheureux les coeurs purs." *Cahier des Saisons* (Paris), 40 (hiver 1965), 532-534. [Translated into French by Léo Dilé.]

L556    ——. "Sylvia Is a Love, That's Who." *Book Week*, 10 January 1965, p. 5.

L557    Halio, Jay L. "A Sense of the Present." *Southern Review*, ns 2 (October 1966), 952-966 (957-959).

L558    Hamilton, Alex. *Books and Bookmen*, 10 no. 4 (January 1965), 28.

L559    Hill, William B. *Best Sellers*, 24 (15 February 1965), 446.

L560    Holloway, David. *Bookman*, November 1964, p. 31.

L561    Hope, Francis. "Grace and Favour." *New Statesman*, 68 (27 November 1964), 834, 836.

L562    Johnson, B.S. "Getting On." *Spectator*, 213 (13 November 1964), 644.

L563    Johnson, Lucy. "Two Witty Novels." *Progressive*, 29 (March 1965), 40-42.

L564    Jones, Donald D. "Sylvia Is a Great Old Girl." *Kansas City Star*, 21 February 1965, p. D5.

L565    K., P.A. "Overlong Analysis of Human Relations." *Pretoria News*, 4 March 1965, p. 6.

L566    Kennedy, Maurice. "Who Is Sylvia?" *Irish Times* (Dublin), 24 November 1964, p. 9.

L567  M., J. "Self-Saved Soul". *Scotsman* (Edinburgh), 28 November 1964, *Week-End Scotsman*, p. 2.

L568  McGuinness, Frank. *London Magazine*, ns 4 no. 10 (January 1965), 100-103 (100-102).

L569  Maddocks, Melvin. "Encore to Cleverness." *Christian Science Monitor*, 14 January 1965, p. 7.

L570  Mannheimer, Carin. "Tradition med liv." *Göteborgs Handels-och Sjöfarts-tidning*, 1 July 1965, p. 3.

L571  Maslin, Penelope. "Sympathetic Code." *Western Mail* (Cardiff), 19 November 1964, p. 6.

L572  Millgate, Jane. "Who Is Sylvia?" *Tamarack Review*, 34 (Winter 1965), 111-114.

L573  Pryce-Jones, Alan. "Angus Wilson's 5th Novel—A Memorable Creation." *New York Herald Tribune*, 14 January 1965, p. 19.

L574  Puffmore, Henry. "Under Review." *Bookseller*, 21 November 1964, pp. 2080, 2082 (2080).

L575  R., B. "The Problems of Mrs Calvert." *Eastern Province Herald* (Port Elizabeth, S. Afr.), 3 March 1965, p. 17.

L576  Raes, Hugo. "Late Roeping." *Het Laatste Nieuws* (Brussels), 19 november 1964, p. 9.

L577  Ricks, Christopher. "A Celebration of Decency." *Sunday Times*, 8 November 1964, p. 48.

L578  Smart, Elizabeth. "Mellow Wasp in Newtown." *Queen*, 2 December 1964, p. 26.

L579  Smith, Peter Douglas. "Shorter Reviews." *Saturday Night* (Toronto), 80 (August 1965), 28.

L580  Smith, Vivian B. "The Old Age of Mrs Calvert." *Bulletin* (Sydney), 6 February 1965, pp. 45-46.

L581  Spender, Stephen. "Must There Always Be a Red Brick England?" *The Great Ideas Today 1965*. Ed. Robert M. Hutchins and Mortimer J. Adler. Chicago: Encyclopaedia Britannica, 1965, pp. 176-186 (176-180).

L582    Stallings, Sylvia. "The Last of Life, for Which the First Was Made. *Houston Post*, 17 January 1965, *Spotlight*, p. 6.

L583    Stearns, Murray S. "Sylvia Adjusts." *Newark Sunday News*, 28 February 1965, p. A2.

L584    Tracy, Honor. "O Brave New Hell." *New Republic*, 152 (6 February 1965), 23-26.

L585    Wall, Stephen. "New Novels." *Listener*, 72 (19 November 1964), 806.

L586    Wood, Frederick T. "Current Literature 1964." *English Studies*, 46 (August 1965), 360-366 (361).

## NO LAUGHING MATTER

L587    Ackler, Robert. "Chronicle of Unpleasant People." *Fresno Bee* (CA), 7 January 1968, *Country Life*, p. 26F.

L588    Adams, Robert Martin. "Fiction Chronicle." *Hudson Review*, 21 (Spring 1968), 225-231 (225-226).

L589    Anon. *Publishers Weekly*, 192 (11 September 1967), 67-68.

L590    ——. *Kirkus Reviews*, 35 (15 September 1967), 1165.

L591    ——. "Playing the Game." *Times Literary Supplement*, 5 October 1967, p. 933.

Reprinted: *T.L.S. Essays and Reviews from The Times Literary Supplement, 1967*. London: Oxford University Press, 1968, pp. 201-204.

L592    ——. "Man-Sized Romp." *Cambridge News*, 7 October 1967, p. 6.

L593    ——. "Novels Shelf." *Scarborough Evening News*, 13 October 1967, p. 8.

L594    ——. *Booklist*, 64 (1 November 1967), 319-320.

L595    ——. *Long Beach Press-Telegram* (Lone Pines, CA), 15 November 1967.

L596    ——. "Novel in the Round." *Newsday*, 18 November 1967, p. 31W.

L597    ——. "The Hindsight Saga." *Time*, 1 December 1967, pp. 121-122.

L598    ——. "Books in Review." *Citizen-Advertiser* (Auburn, NY), 9 December 1967.

L599    ——. *Kenya Weekly News* (Nakuru), 22 December 1967, p. 38.

L600    ——. "Family Saga." *Advertiser* (Geelong), 23 December 1967.

L601    ——. "Eccentric Family Novel." *St Bernard News* (LA), 29 May 1968, p. 9.

L602    ——. *Choice*, 5 (September 1968), 780.

L603    Ainsworth, Tom. "A Family Placed under the Microscope." *Southern Evening Echo* (Southampton), 7 October 1967, p. 12.

L604    Antonini, Giacomo. "Sempre ironico Wilson sulla famiglia Borghese." *Il Gazzetino* (Treviso), 23 aprile 1968, p. 3.

L605    Arnold, Paula. "Puzzling Family Chronicle." *Jerusalem Post*, 5 January 1968, *Week-End Magazine*, p. 11.

L606    B., D.G. "Another Success to Angus Wilson." *Otago Daily Times* (Dunedin, N.Z.), 3 April 1968, p. 14.

L607    B., E. "Family Detachments." *Glasgow Herald*, 30 September 1967, p. 9.

L608    Bail, Jay. "About Satisfied, Weak People." *Blade* (Toledo, OH), 5 November 1967, p. G5. [Syndicated.]

L609    Baisden, Katherine. "Inside and Out." *Chattanooga Times*, 28 January 1968, p. 20.

L610    Baxter, John. "Too Much Dust for the Light To Show Through." *Bulletin* (Sydney), 16 December 1967, p. 81.

L611 Bentley, Phyllis. "Pen Dipped in Vitriol." *Yorkshire Post* (Leeds), 2 October 1967, p. 5.

L612 Bergonzi, Bernard. *London Magazine*, ns 7 (November 1967), 89-91. *See also* J23, pp. 159-161.

L613 Birns, Margaret B. "The Saga of the Family." *Sunday Press-Enterprise* (Riverside, CA), 14 January 1968, p. B-13.

L614 Bitker, Marjorie M. "With Angus Wilson as Guide, 50 English Years Unfold Again." *Milwaukee Journal*, 3 December 1967, p. 2.

L615 Boston, Richard. "Family Troubles." *New York Times Book Review*, 26 November 1967, pp. 4, 74.

L616 Brendon, Piers. "Piers Brendon on a Surgical Axe." *Books and Bookmen*, 13 no. 2 (November 1967), 42.

L617 Brien, Jeremy. "Wilson's Latest Is a Near- Masterpiece." *Evening Post* (Bristol), 19 October 1967, p. 26.

L618 Brown, Marjorie. "The Decline of a Family." *Houston Chronicle*, 26 November 1967.

L619 C., H. "Portrait of a Family." *Oxford Times*, 6 October 1967, p. 28.

L620 Cami, Ben. "Met humor maar zeer ernstig." *Het Laatste Nieuws* (Brussels), 29 februari 1968, p. 11.

L621 Carpenter, William. "Witty Novel Tells of Family Trials Over 55 Years." *Wilmington Morning News*, 13 December 1967.

L622 Carr, Leslie. "Abnormal Family Life Reported." *Evening Post* (Charleston, SC), 12 April 1968.

L623 Carroll, John M. *Library Journal*, 92 (1 October 1967), 3449.

L624 Church, Richard. "A Ferocious Family Saga." *Country Life*, 19 October 1967, p. 1015.

L625 Churchill, R.C. "Snobbery: Angus Wilson's Attitudes." *Birmingham Post*, 30 September 1967, *Midland Magazine*, p. II.

L626 Collamore, Elizabeth. "Family Chronicle Novel." *Hartford Courant* (CT), 24 December 1967, *Courant Magazine*, p. 15.

L627 Dennis, Nigel. "England and the Other Mr Wilson." *Sunday Telegraph*, 1 October 1967, p. 12.

L628 Dienstag, Eleanor. *Commonweal*, 87 (8 March 1968), 695-697.

L629 Dodwell, Arthur. "Ambition Achieved." *Scotsman* (Edinburgh), 30 September 1967, *Week-End Scotsman*, p. 5.

L630 Dolbier, Maurice. "Life Went Thataway." *Sunday Journal* (Providence, RI), 26 November 1967, p. W25.

L631 E[nehjelm], H[elen] af. "En samhällssa tiriker." *Hufvudstadsbladet* (Helsinki), 8 October 1967, pp. 9-10.

L632 Ewart, Gavin. "All About the Family." *Evening Standard*, 3 October 1967, p. 10.

L633 Eyrich, Claire. "Chronicle of Family by Wilson Excellent." *Fort Worth Star-Telegram*, 7 January 1968.

L634 Fries, Maureen. "A Family's Life Picked Apart." *Courier Express* (Buffalo, NY), 17 March 1968, p. 101.

L635 Funke-Bordewijk, Nick. "Angus Wilson schreef van spot doortrokken mini-Forsyte Saga." *Haagse Courant* (The Hague), 17 februari 1968.

L636 G., I. "Mr Wilson's England." *Kentish Gazette* (Canterbury), 26 January 1968, p. 10.

L637 Gains, Derek. "Balchin and Wilson Dominate the Scene." *Northern Despatch* (Darlington), 6 October 1967, p. 10.

L638 Gardner, Marilyn. "Family Novel on the Level of History." *Christian Science Monitor*, 7 December 1967, p. 21.

L639 Gardner, Paul. "An English Generation." *Catholic World*, 206 (February 1968), 236.

L640 Ghose, Zulfikar. "Visited Upon the Children." *Western Mail* (Cardiff), 7 October 1967, p. 8.

L641 Goolrick, Esten. "It's What the Novel Is About." *Times & World News* (Roanoke, VA), 24 March 1968.

L642 Grosvenor, Peter. "Angus Wilson 'Bites' Again." *Daily Express*, 5 October 1967, p. 8.

L643 Gurley, Mary. "They Aren't Very Nice People, but Nobody Can Call Them Dull." *Evening News* (Ada, OK), 14 January 1968, p. 7.

L644 H., C. "New Novel by Wilson Studies Era." *Star* (Anniston, AL), 19 November 1967.

L645 Halio, Jay L. "Angus Wilson's *No Laughing Matter*." *Massachusetts Review*, 10 (Spring 1969), 394-397.

L646 Hall, Anthea. "Civil War in the Family." *Journal* (Newcastle), 30 September 1967, p. 8.

L647 Hedberg, Johannes. "Inget att skratta åt." *Göteborgs Handels-och Sjöfarts-tidning*, 7 February 1968, p. 7.

L648 Hicks, Granville. "They Lived in Three Worlds." *Saturday Review*, 18 November 1967, pp. 27-28.

L649 Hodgart, Patricia. "Family Relationships." *Illustrated London News*, 21 October 1967, p. 50.

L650 Hofstra, Jan Willem. "Kunst-licht." *De Tijd* (Amsterdam), 16 december 1967, Supplement, p. 2.

L651 Hogan, William. "Angus Wilson's Family Portrait." *San Francisco Chronicle*, 20 November 1967, p. 43. [Syndicated.]

L652 Holdsworth, Peter. "Wilson in Top Form." *Telegraph & Argus* (Bradford), 2 October 1967, p. 4.

L653 Holloway, David. "Angus Wilson's Passing Show." *Daily Telegraph*, 5 October 1967, p. 21.

Reprinted as: "Aspects of English Life." *Tribune*, 15 December 1967, p. 10.

L654 Hope, Francis. "All in the Family." *Observer*, 1 October 1967, p. 27.

L655    Ingle, Agnes. "Novels of the Month." *Baptist Times*, 9 November 1967, p. 6.

L656    Jillett, Neil. "More a Way of Life." *Age* (Melbourne), 23 December 1967, p. 23.

L657    Keane, F.J. "Clambering Back on a Pedestal." *Irish Independent*, 18 November 1967, p. 16.

L658    Kitchen, Paddy. "Aspects of English Life." *Tribune*, 15 December 1967, p. 10.

L659    Kramer, Leonie. "Six Children in Search of Family Identity." *Sydney Morning Herald*, 16 December 1967, p. 20.

L660    Lang, Cynthia. "Books." *Glamour*, March 1968, pp. 60, 62.

L661    Lanier, Sterling. "Nothing To Laugh At." *Boston Sunday Globe*, 26 November 1967, p. A32.

L662    Lask, Thomas. "Ancient Warfare." *New York Times*, 23 November 1967, p. 31. [Syndicated.]

L663    Lenihan, Liam. *Nation*, 206 (15 April 1968), 512.

L664    Loprete, Nicholas J., Jr. *Best Sellers*, 27 (1 January 1968), 390.

L665    Lundgren, Caj. "Ingenting att skratta at." *Svenska Dagbladet* (Stockholm), 5 February 1968, p. 5.

L666    McGuinness, Frank. "Books." *Queen*, 27 September 1967.

L667    McNay, M.G. "Threat to Liberal England." *Oxford Mail*, 5 October 1967, p. 10.

L668    MacNevin, Gladys. "Family Panorama." *Kerryman* (Tralee), 7 October 1967, p. 12.

L669    Martins, Eivor. "Diger krönika om oanständig familj." *Göteborgs-Tidningen*, 15 October 1967.

L670    May, Derwent. "Chronorama." *Listener*, 78 (5 October 1967), 444.

L671    Mayne, Richard. "A British Museum." *Reporter*, 38 (8 February 1968), 44, 46-47.

L672    Mohn, Bent. "England igennem 60 år: Denne bogsaesons mest omtalte engelske roman." *Politiken* (Copenhagen), 13 January 1968, p. 12.

L673    Montagnes, Anne. "Anglo-Saxon Attitudes." *Saturday Night* (Toronto), 83 (May 1968), 44.

L674    Moody, Minnie Hite. "Family Novel Mirrors Generation of Change." *Dispatch* (Columbus, OH), 17 December 1967, p. 22.

L675    Murray, James G. "Above-Average Novels; Not Quite Seamless Garments." *Long Island Catholic*, 30 November 1967.

L676    Nemoianu, Virgil. "Un nou roman al lui Angus Wilson." *Calmul Valorilor* (Cluj, Dacia), 1971, pp. 188-191.

L677    Newquist, Roy. "Wilson's 'Major' Novel." *Chicago Heights Star*, 19 November 1967.

L678    Oliver, Mark. "Angus Wilson's Family Chronicle." *Eastern Daily Press* (Norwich), 2 October 1967, p. 9.

L679    O'Neill, John. "Realizing the Self with Modifications." *Atlanta Journal and Constitution*, 19 November 1967, p. 7D.

L680    Parrinder, Patrick. "Pastiche and After." *Cambridge Review*, 89A (4 November 1967), 66-67.

L681    Pitman, Robert. "Spotlight on a Most Remarkable Family." *Sunday Express*, 1 October 1967, p. 6.

L682    Price, R.G.G. "New Novels." *Punch*, 4 October 1967, p. 524.

L683    Pritchett, V.S. "Ventriloquists." *New York Review of Books*, 18 January 1968, pp. 10, 12-13.

L684    Pryce-Jones, David. "The Fiction-Making Atmosphere." *Financial Times*, 5 October 1967, p. 12.

L685    Puffmore, Henry. "Under Review." *Bookseller*, 14 October 1967, pp. 2078, 2080 (2078).

L686    Pybus, Rodney. "Recent Fiction." *Stand* (Newcastle-upon-Tyne), 9 no. 3 (1968), 54-61 (54-57).

L687    Raphael, Frederic. "Book Bazaar." *Harper's Bazaar*, February 1968, pp. 106, 108.

L688    Ratcliffe, Michael. "The Death of Privacy." *Times*, 5 October 1967, p. 8.

L689    Raven, Simon. "Angus Agonistes." *Spectator*, 219 (6 October 1967), 396-397.

L690    Raymond, John. "Critics' Choice of the Year." *Sunday Times*, 3 December 1967, p. 29.

L691    Raymond, Robert. "Family's Half Century a Social Commentary." *Staten Island Advance*, 31 December 1967.

L692    Ricks, Christopher. "A Family and Its Fortunes." *Sunday Times*, 1 October 1967, p. 57.

L693    Rogers, Eva. "Ikke noget at le af." *Kristeligt Dagblad* (Copenhagen), 2 February 1968, p. 7.

L694    Rogers, W.G. "Novel Traces Life of English Family." *Vindicator* (Youngstown, OH), 26 November 1967, p. E-6. [Syndicated.]

L695    Roos, Elisabeth de. "De listen en lagan van Angus Wilson." *Het Parool* (Amsterdam), 11 november 1967.

L696    Rush, Thomas. *Book-of-the-Month Club News*, January 1968, p. 10.

L697    Scott-James, R.A. "English Fiction: 1967." *British Book News*, 331 (March 1968), 165-169.

L698    Servotte, Herman. "Uitzonderlijkje Wilson." *De Standaard* (Brussels), 18-19 november 1967.

L699    Share, Bernard. *Dublin Magazine*, 7 (Autumn/Winter 1968), 103-104.

L700    Sokolov, Raymond A. "Six Characters in Search." *Newsweek*, 20 November 1967, 114B, 114D, 115.

L701    Sörensen, Lennart. "En bättre Forsyte-Saga." *Kvällsposten* (Malmö), 22 January 1968, p. 4.

L702    Stanley, Donald. "Looking in on British." *San Francisco Examiner*, 16 November 1967, p. 37.

L703    Steiner, George. "Good Night, Ladies." *New Statesman,* 74 (6 October 1967), 436-437.

L704    Stella, Charles. "Angus Wilson Creates Masterwork." *Cleveland Press*, 8 December 1967, p. 17.

L705    Strating, J.J. *Literair Paspoort* (Amsterdam), December 1967, pp. 261-262.

L706    Thompson, John. "Old Friends." *Commentary*, 45 (January 1968), 65-69 (67-68).

L707    Thornton, Eugenia. "Six Children Worth Meeting." *Plain Dealer* (Cleveland), 10 December 1967, p. 6H.

L708    Thorpe, Michael. "Current Literature 1967." *English Studies*, 49 (1968), 269-281 (269).

L709    Trainor, Marian. "One Family's Struggle with the 20th Century." *Daily Express* (Detroit), 14 January 1968.

L710    Tuohy, Frank. "Anglo-Saxon Charades." *Manchester Guardian*, 6 October 1967, p. 9.

        Reprinted as: "The Master of Mimicry." *Manchester Guardian Weekly*, 12 October 1967, p. 11.

L711    Trickett, Rachel. "Recent Novels: Craftsmanship in Violence and Sex." *Yale Review*, ns 57 (March 1968), 438-452 (446-448).

L712    Waldron, Ann. "Reverse Spock." *Houston Post*, 12 November 1967.

L713    Weigel, John A. "Wilson Utilizes Tradition Rather Than Rejecting It." *Cincinnati Enquirer*, 1 December 1967.

L714    Wellejus, Ed. *Times-News* (Erie, PA), 4 February, 1968.

L715    Whately, Rosaleen. "Family of Our Century." *Liverpool Daily Post*, 11 October 1967, p. 5.

L716    Williamson, Bruce. "Unhappy Family." *Irish Times*, 30 September 1967, p. 8.

L717    Woods, Eddie. "The World's a Stage." *Morning Star*, 26 October 1967, p. 4.

## DEATH DANCE

L718    Anon. *Publishers Weekly*, 195 (10 March 1969), 70.

L719    ——. "Clue Works." *Best Sellers*, 29 (1 September 1969).

L720    Baldeshwiler, Eileen. *Studies in Short Fiction*, 8 (Summer 1971), 477-478.

L721    Barkham, John. "Master Craftsmen Leave Their Mark." *Grand Rapids Press*, 1 June 1969, p. 2-G.

L722    Brackley, Gene. "Wilson's *Death Dance*: Glee Glosses Horror." *Boston Globe*, 6 March 1970.

L723    Brady, Charles A. "Three Short-Story Collections Brim with Vitality, Insight." *Buffalo Evening News*, 3 May 1969, p. B12.

L724    Carroll, John M. *Library Journal*, 94 (1 June 1969), 2252.

L725    Cassill, R.V. "Tales of an Old World and a New One." *Washington Post*, 25 May 1969, *Book World*, p. 4.

L726    Hogan, William. "Collected Writings of Greene, Wilson." *San Francisco Chronicle*, 5 June 1969, p. 5.

L727    Kirsch, Robert. "*Death Dance*: 25 Stories Designed To Be Dipped Into." *Los Angeles Times*, 25 August 1969, Pt. IV, p. 8.

L728    Meyer, Gerald. "Short Stories." *Des Moines Sunday Register*, 15 June 1969, p. 7-T.

L729    Oates, Joyce Carol. *Saturday Review*, 5 July 1969, pp. 33-34.

L730    Sisson, Gertrude. "Gets Under Your Skin." *Sunday Telegram* (Worcester, MA), 25 May 1969.

L731    Smith, Jeanne. "*Death Dance* Makes Class Distinctions." *Oklahoma Journal Fun Guide*, 25 May 1969, p. 10.

L732    Vernon, Donald. "As For Fiction . . ." *Augusta Chronicle* (GA), 30 July 1970, p. 6C.

# THE WORLD OF CHARLES DICKENS

L733 Adell, Alberton. "El Shakespeare de la Novela." *Insula* (Madrid), 27 (enero 1972), 13.

L734 Allen, Trevor. "Books in Brief." *Books and Bookmen*, 18 no. 1 (January 1973), 124.

L735 ———. "Dickens in the Underworld." *Books and Bookmen*, 18 no. 1 (March 1973), *Paperback Supplement*, II-IV (III-IV).

L736 Anon. "Angus Wilson würdigte Charles Dickens." *Tages-Anzeiger* (Zurich), 13 May 1970, p. 20.

L737 ———. "Dickens' Centenary Volume." *Coventry Evening Telegraph*, 28 May 1970, p. 6.

L738 ———. "Showcase." *Books and Bookmen*, 15 no. 9 (June 1970), 40-41.

L739 ———. "Dickens: 1812-1870." *Times Literary Supplement*, 4 June 1970, pp. 597-598.

Reprinted: *TLS: Essays and Reviews from The Times Literary Supplement, 1970*. London: Oxford University Press, 1971, pp. 1-7.

L740 ———. "Mr Wilson (Angus, We Mean) Is on a Winner." *Bury Free Press* (Bury St Edmunds), 5 June 1970, p. 12.

L741 ———. "Sight and Smell: *The World of Charles Dickens*." *Economist*, 235 (20 June 1970), 54.

L742 ———. *Publishers Weekly*, 197 (22 June 1970), 59.

L743 ———. *British Book News*, July 1970, p. 560.

L744 ———. "Charles Dickens: Man for All Seasons." *Argus* (Cape Town), 1 July 1970, *Literary Review*, p. 10.

L745 ———. "Fertile but Fickle World of Dickens." *Guardian Journal* (Nottingham), 1 July 1970, p. 4.

L746 ———. "Het leven als een harde strafschop: De briljante analyse van Dickens' leven en werken door Angus Wilson." *Nieuwe Rotterdamse Courant*, 11 juli 1970, *Wekelijks bijvoegsel*, p. 2.

L747     ——. "And What a Gallery of Them He Created!" *Grand Rapids Press*, 30 August 1970, p. 2E.

L748     ——. *Best Sellers*, 30 (15 September 1970), 236-237.

L749     ——. "Briefly Noted." *New Yorker*, 19 September 1970, p. 137.

L750     ——. "1970 Books—A Spot Review." *Christian Science Monitor*, 27 November 1970, p. B4.

L751     ——. "Maga's Reviews." *Blackwood's Magazine*, 308 (December 1970), 569-574 (569).

L752     ——. *Choice*, 7 (December 1970), 1378.

L753     B., J. "Dickens' Appeal Is Everlasting." *Vindicator* (Youngstown, OH), 30 August 1970, p. B-14.

L754     B., Y.J. "Timely Work on Life of Dickens." *Eastern Province Herald* (Port Elizabeth, S. Afr.), 25 May 1970, p. 18.

L755     Bailey, Paul. "A Simple-Minded Writer of Genius." *Nova*, July 1970, pp. 14, 17, 19.

L756     Bayley, John. "Irresistible Dickens." *New York Review of Books*, 8 October 1970, pp. 8, 10, 12 (8, 10).

L757     Bell, Adrian. "Demonic 'Little Dickens All Painted in Black and Red . . .' " *Eastern Daily Press* (Norwich), 29 May 1970, p. 14.

L758     Bell, Pearl K. "A Curious Grudgery." *New Leader*, 54 (25 January 1971), 15-16.

L759     Bowen, Elizabeth. "Dickens and the Demon Toy Box." *Spectator*, 224 (30 May 1970), 713.

L760     Brown, Adger. "Another Dickens Biography." *State* (Columbia, SC), 16 August 1970, p. 5-E.

L761     Budtz-Jørgensen, Jørgan. "Ingen har glem ham." *Berlingske Tidende* (Copenhagen), 9 June 1970, p. 20.

L762     Carey, John. "When Dickens Starts Laughing." *Listener*, 83 (28 May 1970), 724-725 (724).

L763     Carlisle, Richard. "Dickens of a Centennial." *Patriot Ledger* (Quincy, MA), 16 September 1970.

L764     Comerford, Anthony. "Charles Dickens." *Socialist Commentary*, July 1970, pp. 19-20.

L765     Cosgrave, Mary Silva. *Horn Book Magazine*, 47 (February 1971), 73-74.

L766     Czubakowski, Janusz. "Book Making: Charles Dickens." *Women's Wear Daily*, 12 August 1970, p. 14.

L767     D., R.D. "The Tree of Dickens." *Glasgow Herald*, 30 May 1970, p. 5.

L768     Dickens, Monica. "Here's Richness!" *Sunday Telegraph*, 24 May 1970, p. 11.

L769     Donoghue, Denis. "Reviews." *Nineteenth-Century Fiction*, 27 (September 1972), 216-218.

L770     Enehjelm, Helen af. "Charles Dickens värld." *Hufvudstadsbladet* (Helsinki), 7 June 1970, p. 7.

L771     Evans, Ifor. "The Selfish Male. Angus Wilson Casts New Light on Dickens." *Birmingham Post*, 30 May 1970, *Saturday Magazine*, p. II.

L772     Fens, K. "Terzijde: Dickens en Multatuli." *Streven* (Antwerp), 24 (October 1970), 54-57.

L773     Fido, M.A. *Victorian Studies*, 15 (September 1971), 101-102.

L774     Fielding, K.J. *Dickensian*, 66 (September 1970), 248.

L775     ——. "The Novelist as Sun, The Novels as Planets Revolving around Him." *New York Times Book Review*, 13 September 1970, p. 7.

L776     Foot, Michael. "Dickens's Trouble with Women." *Evening Standard*, 2 June 1970, p. 21.

L777     Fowles, John. "Guide to a Man-Made Planet." *Life*, 4 September 1970, pp. 8-9.

L778    Frazier, Harriet C. "Dickens's Life Shapes His Books." *Kansas City Star*, 20 September 1970, p. 3D.

L779    Frykmann, Erik. "Och nu, Mr Dickens . . ." *Svenska Dagbladet* (Stockholm), 14 September 1970, p. 4.

L780    Galvin, Thomas J. *Library Journal*, 95 (15 September 1970), 2920.

L781    Gross, John. "Tale of Two Dickenses." *Observer*, 24 May 1970, p. 30.

L782    Hardwick, Michael and Mollie. "Beginning the Long Dickensian Haul." *Kent Messenger* (Ashford), 22 May 1970, p. 8.

L783    Hartley, Alec. "Dickens and His Deepest Beliefs." *Morning Telegraph* (Sheffield), 6 June 1970, p. 14.

L784    Hibbert, Christopher. "A Failure to Judge Women." *Washington Post*, 13 September 1970, *Book World*, p. 5.

Reprinted: *International Herald Tribune* (Paris), 22 September 1970, p. 14.

L785    Hogan, William. *San Francisco Chronicle*, 11 December 1970, p. 51.

L786    Holloway, John. "Dickens' Word-World." *Encounter*, 34 (June 1970), 63-68 (63).

L787    Hoyt, Charles A. "Angus Wilson: Looking at Dickens 100 Years Later." *Courier-Journal* (Louisville, KY), 6 September 1970, p. H5.

L788    Hutchens, John K. "One Thing and Another." *Saturday Review*, 19 December 1970, p. 30.

L789    Ikeler, A. Abbott. "Dickens Studies Since 1970." *British Studies Monitor*, 9 no. 3 (Winter 1980), 26-48 (33).

L790    Jankowska, Hilda. "Ksiazka Angusa Wilsona—Dickens aktorem." *Zycie Literackie* (Cracow), 20 no. 30 (1970), 15.

L791    Jeffares, A. Norman. "From Opium to Asprin." *Yorkshire Post* (Leeds), 7 May 1970, p. 8.

L792    Katona, Anna. *Helikon* (Budapest), 17 (1971), 503-504.

L793    Keister, Don A. "Dickens the Durable." *Plain Dealer* (Cleveland), 20 December 1970, p. 7-F.

L794    Kirstein, Lincoln. *Nation*, 211 (21 December 1970), 666.

L795    Lalley, J.M. "The Topography of Genius." *Modern Age*, 15 (Spring 1971), 185-190.

L796    Lane, Lauriat, Jr. "Satire, Society, and Symbol in Recent Dickens Criticism." *Studies in the Novel*, 5 (Spring 1973), 125-138 (131, 133-134).

L797    Lloyd, Eric. "Mr. Dickens: Some Great Expectations Fulfilled." *Wall Street Journal*, 21 August 1970, p. 6.

L798    Lundberg, Bengt. "Charles Dickens och hans värld." *Östgöta Correspondenten* (Linköping), 30 May 1970.

L799    Lundqvist, °Akë. "Lättläst och livfullt om Charles Dickens liv." *Dagens Nyheter* (Stockholm), 21 August 1977, p. 6.

L800    McIlwraith, John. "Exposing the Horrors." *News* (Perth), 11 July 1970, p. 12.

L801    Macneil, Alan. "Genial Genius." *Times-Reporter* (Bellows Falls, VT), 15 September 1970.

L802    Metcalfe, James. "The Key to Dickens's Greatness." *Press & Journal* (Aberdeen), 13 June 1970, p. 8.

L803    Millar, Neil. "The Inimitable Boz." *Christian Science Monitor*, 1 October 1970, Sect. 2, p. 11.

L804    Mittet, Hans. "Dickens' verden." *Verdens Gang* (Oslo), 1 July 1970, p. 24.

L805    Monod, Sylvère. *Dickens Studies Newsletter*, 2 (May 1971), 39-42.

L806    Murray, Isobel. "The Best of Dickens." *Scotsman* (Edinburgh), 27 June 1970, *Week-End Scotsman*, p. 3.

L807    Murray, James G. "Hats Off to the Scribes!" *Long Island Catholic*, 27 August 1970.

L808   Napper, Gillian. "An Age of Contrasts." *Evening Post* (Bristol) 4 June 1970, p. 13.

L809   Neiiendam, Henrik. *Berlingske Aftenavis* (Copenhagen), 11 July 1970.

L810   P., W.E. "Five More Salute Dickens. 'Diamond Sharp' Wilson." *Methodist Recorder*, 11 June 1970, p. 15.

L811   Pick, John. "Dickens 100 Years Later." *Journal* (Milwaukee), 20 September 1970, Pt. 5, p. 4.

L812   Porterfield, Christopher. "Boz Will Be Boz." *Time*, 28 December 1970, pp. 59-60.

L813   Praz, Mario. "I passi di Dickens." *Il Tempo* (Rome), 28 April 1970, p. 3.

       Reprinted as: "Dickens cent' anni dalla morte." *Studi e svaghi inglesi* [Vol. 2]. Milan: Garzanti, 1983, pp. 231-235.

L814   Price, Martin. "Taking Dickens Seriously." *Yale Review*, ns 61 (December 1971), 271-279 (278-279).

L815   Pritchett, V.S. "A Visionary Society." *New Statesman*, 79 (5 June 1970), 807-808.

L816   Reid, Margaret W. "Dickens—A Reappraisal." *Wichita Falls Times*, 11 October 1970, *Features Magazine*, p. 3.

L817   Ricks, Christopher. "The Great Perceiver." *Sunday Times*, 31 May 1970, p. 31.

L818   Robert-Blunn, John. "All This and Dickens, Too." *Manchester Evening News*, 1 December 1970, p. 8.

L819   Roberts, Roger L. "Dickensiana." *Church Times*, 5 June 1970, p. 6.

L820   Russ, Margaret C. "Two Authors Succeed in Capturing Dickens." *Courier Express* (Buffalo), 24 January 1971.

L821   Saiijo, Takao. *Hiroshima Studies in English Language and Literature*, 17 (1970), 72-78. [In Japanese.]

229

L822    Shaw, Mildred Hart. "Return to Dickens." *Daily Sentinel* (Grand Junction, CO), 11 October 1970.

L823    Shroyer, Frederick. "A Guide for Old Movie Buffs." *Los Angeles Herald-Examiner*, 23 August 1970, p. D10.

L824    Small, Rosemary. "Dickens—An Inexhaustible Life." *Morning Star*, 11 June 1970, p. 4.

L825    Snow, C.P. "Salute to Dickens." *Financial Times*, 4 June 1970, p. 12.

L826    ——. "Books To Give." *Financial Times*, 26 November 1970, p. 33.

L827    Sörensen, Lennart. "Bra för fattare upptäckt: Charles Dickens, 100." *Kvällsposten* (Malmö), 29 May 1970.

L828    Soule, George. "A Rich Legacy: Dickens Left Us His World." *Minneapolis Tribune*, 27 September 1970, pp. 8-9.

L829    Starkmann, Alfred. "Charles Dickens: Stratege des Herzens." *Die Welt der Literatur*, 28 May 1970, p. 4.

L830    Sucksmith, Harvey Peter. "Revaluations of Dickens." *Southern Review* (Adelaide), 5 (March 1972), 68-77 (75-76).

L831    Swahn, Sven Christer. "Charles Dickens värld." *Sydsvenska Dagbladet Snällposten* (Malmö), 9 June 1970, p. 4.

L832    Tiger, Virginia. "Celebrating Dickens." *Washington Post*, 30 December 1970, p. B4. [Syndicated.]

L833    Townend, Marion. "Dickens: Contradictions Fed His Novels." *Observer* (Charlotte, NC), 13 September 1970, p. 5F.

L834    Veen, Adriaan van der. "Angus Wilson over Dickens: briljant analyse van leven en werk." *Nieuwe Rotterdamse Courant*, 11 July 1970, p. 32.

L835    Vintner, Maurice. "The Riches of Dickens." *Age* (Melbourne), 15 August 1970.

L836    W., D.A. "Sympathetic Picture Biography of Dickens." *Columbus Dispatch* (OH), 15 November 1970, p. 17.

L837     W., M. *Northern Echo* (Darlington), 29 May 1970, p. 6.

L838     Wall, Stephen. "Dickens in 1970." *Essays in Criticism*, 21 (July 1971), 261-280 (276).

L839     Weintraub, Stanley. "Master of Comic Invention." *Sunday Bulletin* (Philadelphia), 13 September 1970, Sect. 2, p. 3.

L840     Weisman, John. "Please, Sirs, We've Had Enough Dickens!" *Los Angeles Times*, 24 January 1971, pp. 4, 15 (4).

L841     White, Terence de Vere. "A Century of Dickens." *Irish Times*, 6 June 1970, p. 7.

L842     Williams, Raymond. "Dickens Celebrations." *Guardian*, 28 May 1970, p. 15.

         Reprinted as: "The Dickens Celebration." *Guardian Weekly*, 6 June 1970, p. 18.

L843     Wing, George. "Some Recent Dickens Criticism and Scholarship." *Ariel*, 1 (October 1970), 56-66 (59-60).

L844     Wolff, Geoffrey. "Man Mountain." *Newsweek*, 31 August 1970, pp. 73-74.

L845     Yglesias, Helen. "Monsters, Bores, Clowns, Idiots." *Nation*, 211 (23 November 1970), 540-541.


# AS IF BY MAGIC

L846     Adams, Phoebe. "Short Reviews: Books." *Atlantic*, November 1973, p. 128.

L847     Allen, Bruce. "Two Searchers for Beauty and Magic." *Chicago Sun-Times*, 2 December 1973, *Showcase*, p. 15.

L848     Amis, Martin. "Kith of Death." *New Statesman*, 85 (1 June 1973), 811-812.

L849     Anon. "Showcase." *Books and Bookmen*, 18 no. 4 (January 1973), 40-41.

L850     ——. "Novel Notes." *Irish Press*, 21 July 1973, p. 10.

L851      ——. *British Book News*, August 1973, p. 558.

L852      ——. *Kirkus Reviews*, 41 (1 August 1973), 837.

L853      ——. "The Green and Brown Revolution." *Times Literary Supplement*, 1 June 1973, p. 605.

Reprinted: *T.L.S. Twelve: Essays and Reviews from The Times Literary Supplement 1973*. London: Oxford University Press, 1974, pp. 60-64.

L854      ——. *Publishers Weekly*, 204 (10 September 1973), 41.

L855      ——. *National Observer*, 10 November 1973, p. 23.

L856      ——. "Third-World Follies." *Newsweek*, 26 November 1973, p. 108.

L857      ——. "1973: A Selection of Noteworthy Titles. Fiction." *New York Times Book Review*, 2 December 1973, p. 76.

L858      ——. *Choice*, 11 (April 1974), 263.

L859      ——. *Virginia Quarterly Review*, 50 (Summer 1974), lxxxii.

L860      Bayley, John. "The Trends That Fail." *Manchester Guardian*, 31 May 1973, p. 14.

Reprinted: *Manchester Guardian Weekly*, 9 June 1973, p. 24.

L861      Beach, G.C.W. "Abra Cadabra Ca-Thud." *The Sun* (Baltimore), 2 December 1973, p. D5.

L862      Bell, Pearl K. "Masterful Music and Muddled Magic." *New Leader*, 56 (26 November 1973), 14-15.

L863      Blakeston, Oswell. "Accusations and Charades." *Tribune*, 1 June 1973, p. 7.

L864      Brace, Keith. "The End of an Illusion." *Birmingham Post*, 26 May 1973, *Saturday Magazine*, p. 2.

L865      Bridges, Linda. "Books in Brief." *National Review*, 26 (13 September 1974), 1055.

L866      Brown, Adger. " 'Magic' Expands His Reputation." *State* (Columbia, SC), 13 November 1973, p. 8.

L867    C., W.N.W. *Methodist Recorder*, 18 October 1973, p. 13.

L868    Carter, Harriet R. "A Creative Literary Work." *Sunday Telegram* (Worcester, MA), 23 December 1973, p. 8E.

L869    Cheney, Eleanor G. "Elusive Search." *Hartford Courant* (CT), 2 December 1973, p. 10F.

L870    Crawley, Philip. "Long Way To No Exit." *Journal* (Newcastle), 2 June 1973, p. 13.

L871    Dalbey, Alice. "The Magic Fails; So Does Novel." *Independent-Journal* (San Rafael, CA), November 1973.

L872    DeFeo, Ronald. 'Fiction Chronicle." *Hudson Review*, 26 (Winter 1973-74), 773-785 (780-781).

L873    Drabble, Margaret. "Occult Is No Panacea, but Magic Rice Alone Can't Feed the World." *National Observer*, 10 November 1973, p. 23.

L874    Duffy, Dennis. "Dickens and Borges: An Earthy Grasp That Sex, Power and Money Are the Real Magics." *Globe and Mail* (Toronto), 16 June 1973, p. 33.

L875    Eriksson, G[öran] R. *Västerbottens-Kuriren* (Umeå), 21 December 1973.

L876    Evans, William R. *Best Sellers*, 33 (15 January 1974), 470-471.

L877    Feinstein, Elaine. "Sweetmeats." *London Magazine*, ns 13 no. 3 (August-September 1973), 148-150.

L878    Flora, Joseph M. "Step on a Crack: Recent Fiction." *Michigan Quarterly Review*, 14 (Winter 1975), 101-107 (103).

L879    Glendinning, Victoria. "Magic Moments." *Irish Times*, 2 June 1973, p. 10.

L880    Goldstein, S. Laine. "Magical Solutions." *Staten Island Sunday Advance*, 6 January 1974, p. E4.

L881    Gottlieb, Augusta. *St Louis Post-Dispatch*, 27 December 1973, p. 3B.

L882    Hardy, Barbara. "Book Reviews." *Dickensian*, 69 (September 1973), 182-183.

L883    Harris, Marilyn. "Action Wins Over Magic." *Atlanta Journal and Constitution*, 13 January 1974, p. 6-C.

L884    Hartley, Lodwick. "What's Become of Angus? Wilson's Mod *As If By Magic*." *News & Observer* (Raleigh, NC), 23 December 1973.

L885    Hartridge, Jon. "Wilson's Eccentrics." *Oxford Mail*, 31 May 1973, p. 6.

L886    Heidenry, John. "Wilson Spoofs Radical Left." *St Louis Globe Democrat*, 24-25 November 1973, p. 6C.

L887    Holloway, David. "The Danger of Illusion." *Daily Telegraph*, 31 May 1973, p. 10.

L888    Hope, Francis. "Busting Out All Over." *Observer*, 27 May 1973, p. 36.

L889    Hunter, Alan. "Angus Wilson's New Novel: Rice and Sensuality." *Eastern Daily Press* (Norwich), 28 May 1973, p. 9.

L890    Jones, D.A.N. "Magic and Trickery." *Listener*, 89 (31 May 1973), 726.

L891    Krzeczkowski, Henryk. *Literatura na Swiecie* (Warsaw), 3 (1974), 355-358.

L892    L., R.L. *Connecticut Fireside and Review of Books* (Hamden), June 1974, p. 60.

L893    Lewis, Peter. "Well, How Many Novels Are More Nourishing Than a Pound of Good Steak?" *Daily Mail*, 31 May 1973, p. 7.

L894    Lundgren, Caj. "Trolleri i vår tid." *Svenska Dagbladet* (Stockholm), 30 May 1973, p. 5.

L895    McSweeney, Kerry. "The Editor's Column." *Queen's Quarterly*, 81 (Spring 1974), 165-168.

L896    Maddocks, Melvin. "Vile Bodies Revisited." *Time*, 3 December 1973, pp. 107-108.

L897   Mannheimer, Monica. "Engelsk prosa om nutidsmänniskor."
       *Göteborgs-Posten*, 5 February 1974, p. 2.

L898   Marion, John. "Wilson Novel Is Sophisticated." *State*
       (Columbia, SC), 3 February 1974, p. 4E.

L899   Maslin, Penelope. "A Modern Morality Tale." *Western Mail*
       (Cardiff), 2 June 1973, p. 9.

L900   Mohn, Bent. "Kan vi hjoelpe den tredie verden?" *Politiken*
       (Copenhagen), 21 July 1973, p. 4.

L901   Moorcock, Michael. "Angus Wilson's Magic." *Books and
       Bookmen*, 18 no. 10 (July 1973), 32-35.

L902   Nesbitt, W.J. "Complex Magic." *Northern Echo* (Darlington),
       1 June 1973, p. 6.

L903   Oates, Quentin. "Critics Crowner." *Bookseller*, 2 June 1973,
       pp. 2674, 2676-2677 (2676).

L904   O'Flaherty, Lucy. "Wilson's 'Albatross' Gone." *Winston-Salem
       Journal & Sentinel* (NC), 13 January 1974, p. C4.

L905   Palmer, Tony. "The Wayward Wilson." *Spectator*, 230 (2 June
       1973), 685-686.

L906   Powers, Ed. "The Magic Has Gone out of Magic." *Cleveland
       Press*, 7 December 1973, *Showtime*, p. 18.

L907   Price, Martin. "The Stuff of Fiction: Some Recent Novels." *Yale
       Review*, ns 63 (June 1974), 554-566 (563-566).

L908   Raban, Jonathan. "Global Charades." *Encounter*, 41 (July 1973),
       78-81.

L909   Ratcliffe, Michael. "The Natural Noise of the World." *Times*,
       31 May 1973, p. 10.

L910   S., C. "New Novels: Anti-Magician." *Glasgow Herald*, 2 June
       1973, Supplement, p. II.

L911   Scholes, Marthe. *Library Journal*, 98 (August 1973), 2339.

L912   Scott, Paul. "Beyond All Men." *Country Life*, 31 May 1973,
       pp. 1572-1573 (1573).

L913    Sörensen, Lennart. "Förlorade illusioner." *Sydsvenska Dagbladet Snällposten* (Malmö), 15 June 1973, p. 5.

L914    Stanford, Derek. "Over Clothed Satire." *Scotsman*, (Edinburgh), 16 June 1973, *Week-End Scotsman*, p. 3.

L915    Symons, Julian. "Magic and the Real World." *Sunday Times*, 27 May 1973, p. 41.

L916    ———. *Washington Post*, 11 November 1973, *Book World*, p. 13.

L917    Taylor, James L. *Oxford Literary Review*, Trinity Term 1973, pp. 11-12.

L918    Thornton, Eugenia. "A Big Bite by Angus Wilson." *Plain Dealer* (Cleveland), 25 November 1973, p. 16H.

L919    Toft, John. "For Far East Fans." *Evening Despatch* (Darlington), 18 June 1973, p. 3.

L920    Waugh, Auberon. "The Professor and a Cast of Thousands." *Evening Standard*, 29 May 1973, p. 27.

        Reprinted as: "Vengeance . . .!" *Liverpool Daily Post*, 1 June 1973, p. 4.

L921    Weigel, John A. "Without Past or Future." *Cincinnati Enquirer*, 20 December 1973, p. 42.

L922    White, Edmund. *New York Times Book Review*, 14 October 1973, p. 7.

L923    Williamson, David. "No New Tricks." *Winnipeg Free Press*, 22 September 1973, *Leisure Magazine*, p. 13.

L924    Wood, Michael. "It's Later Than You Think." *New York Review of Books*, 1 November 1973, pp. 20-21 (20).

L925    Woods, Eddie. "Telling It Straight." *Morning Star*, 14 June 1973, p. 4.

L926    Worsley, T.C. "Angus All Over." *Financial Times*, 1 June 1973, p. 16.

# THE STRANGE RIDE OF RUDYARD KIPLING
# HIS LIFE AND WORKS

L927    Anon. "Greatness Mishandled." *Economist*, 265 (12 November 1977), 101-102.

L928    ——. *Booklist*, 74 (15 November 1977), 520.

L929    ——. "Rudyard Kipling—A New Look." *Surrey Mirror* (Redhill & Reigate), 9 December 1977, p. 17. [Syndicated.]

L930    ——. *Kirkus Reviews*, 46 (1 January 1978), 43.

L931    ——. "PW Forecasts. Nonfiction." *Publishers Weekly*, 102 (2 January 1978), 60.

L932    ——. "The Poetic Spirit and Its Echo." *Cultural Information Services* (New York), 3 April 1978, p. 9.

L933    ——. "Short Reviews." *Atlantic*, May 1978, pp. 92-93.

L934    ——. *Choice*, 15 (September 1978), 876.

L935    ——. *Journal of Modern Literature*, 7 (1979), 755.

L936    Andrews, Peter. "Just So." *Saturday Review*, 4 March 1978, pp. 24-25.

L937    Barnes, Julian. "Seeing Kipling Through Writer's Eyes." *Oxford Mail*, 24 November 1977, p. 4.

L938    Bauer, Malcolm. "Biographer Shows Kipling's Magic World." *Sunday Oregonian* (Portland), 26 March 1978, p. B4.

L939    Beachey, R.W. *Four Decades of Poetry 1890-1930*, 2 (July 1979), 227-229.

L940    Beasley, Rex. *Dallas Times Herald*, 19 March 1978, p. 4-H.

L941    Beatty, Jack. "Pre-Imperial Kipling Was a Writer of Magic." *Boston Sunday Globe*, 2 April 1978, p. A13.

L942    Bell, J. Leslie. "Study of Rudyard Kipling." *Calgary Herald*, 16 December 1978, p. F12.

L943 Bready, Richard. "The Poet-Laureate of Imperialism." *Sunday Sun* (Baltimore), 2 April 1978, p. D3.

L944 Burgess, Anthony. "White Man's Burden." *Observer*, 6 November 1977, p. 29.

Reprinted as: "Questioning Kipling." *Homage to Qwert Yuiop: Essays by Anthony Burgess.* London: Hutchinson, 1986; *But Do Blondes Prefer Gentlemen? Homage to Qwert Yuiop and Other Writings.* New York: McGraw-Hill, 1986, pp. 320-323.

L945 Campbell, Ross. "A Good Book About a Strange Man." *Bulletin* (Sydney), 24 January 1978, pp. 39-40.

L946 Carey, John. "Kipling's Jungle: Red in Tooth and Claw." *Sunday Times*, 6 November 1977, p. 41.

L947 Carrington, C.E. "Something of Himself." *New Review*, 4 (November 1977), 47-49.

L948 Clark, Jeff. "Wilson's *Rudyard Kipling* A Strange, Splendid Ride." *Daily Bruin* (University of California, Los Angeles), 17 April 1978.

L949 Clemons, Walter. "Lest We Forget." *Newsweek*, 27 March 1978, pp. 92-93.

L950 Clew, William J. "Kipling Revisited." *Hartford Courant* (CT), 2 April 1978, p. 8G.

L951 Cooper, Douglas W. "Book Review. Literature." *Library Journal*, 102 (15 November 1977), 2349.

L952 ———. *Bookviews*, December 1977, p. 58.

L953 Cross, Jack. "Gentle-Violent Man." *Times Educational Supplement*, 25 November 1977, p. 24.

L954 Cuffe, E.D. "On Kipling." *America*, 139 (1 July 1978), 18-19.

L955 Culler, A. Dwight. "Kipling, Forster, and the Anglo-Indian Dilemma." *Yale Review*, 68 (Autumn 1978), 110-113 (110-112).

L956 Dennis, Nigel. "Perchance To Dream." *Sunday Telegraph*, 6 November 1977, p. 16.

L957    Dhar, Tej Nath. *Hindustan Times* (New Delhi), 4 May 1980, Magazine section, p. iv.

L958    Dolbier, Maurice. "The Man Who Was Kipling: A New Critical Study." *Providence Sunday Journal* (RI), 19 March 1978, *Arts and Travel*, p. H-14.

L959    Duhamel, Albert. *Boston Herald American*, 26 March 1978, p. D10.

L960    Dunlevy, Maurice. "Was Kipling Banished to a Kind of Living Death?" *Canberra Times*, 11 February 1978, p. 16.

L961    Evans, Ifor. "Kipling's Roots in the Secret World of Kim." *Birmingham Post*, 5 November 1977, p. 2.

L962    Farquharson, Janice. "Not Enough Rudyard." *Pretoria News*, 9 June 1978, p. 10.

L963    Finlayson, Iain. "The Strength of Kipling." *Hampstead & Highgate Express*, 25 November 1977, p. 46.

L964    Foote, Timothy. "O Kipling, My Kipling." *Harper's*, March 1978, pp. 125-127.

L965    Forster, Margaret. "Lost in the Kipling Jungle." *Evening Standard*, 29 November 1977, p. 18.

L966    Fremont-Smith, Eliot. "The Good, the Bad, and the Strange." *Village Voice*, 3 April 1978, pp. 69-70.

L967    Gays, Donna. "Bookshelf." *Asia Mail*, September 1978, p. 15.

L968    Gould, Tony. "World of Action." *New Society*, 42 (10 November 1977), 314.

L969    Green, Benny. "Tensions." *Spectator*, 239 (19 November 1977), 25.

L970    Green, Martin. "The Sun Never Sets on Rudyard Kipling." *Washington Post*, 26 March 1978, *Book World*, pp. G1, 3.

L971    Green, Roger Lancelyn. "News and Notes. A New Book on Kipling." *Kipling Journal*, 44 (December 1977), 4.

L972    ———. "News and Notes." *Kipling Journal*, 45 (March 1978), 2-4.

L973    Grigson, Geoffrey. "A Contradictory Genius." *Country Life*, 12 January 1978, p. 111.

L974    Halperin, John. *Modern Fiction Studies*, 25 (Summer 1979), 300-303 (300-302).

L975    Hanauer, Joan. "The Man Who Would Be Kipling." *Cleveland Press*, 30 March 1979, p. D17. [Syndicated.]

L976    Hibbert, Dorothy. "Kipling Attempted To Show Complex Fabric of Conflicts." *Atlanta Journal and Constitution*, 3 December 1978, p. 4-E.

L977    Hillman, Serrell. *Sunday Press-Enterprise* (Riverside, CA), 23 April 1978, p. C-10.

L978    Howard, Michael. "Voice of an Age." *Books and Bookmen*, 23 no. 6 (March 1978), 33-34.

L979    Howes, Victor. "Two Kiplings Appear in This New Biography." *Christian Science Monitor*, 12 April 1978, p. 27.

L980    Ingham, Gordon. "In Kipling Country." *Auckland Star*, 25 February 1978, p. 8.

L981    Jeffares, A. Norman. "Writing Star of an Empire." *Yorkshire Post* (Leeds), 10 November 1977, p. 9.

L982    Keating, Peter. *British Book News*, March 1978, p. 245.

L983    Keister, Don A. "Rudyard Kipling's 'Ride' from India." *Sunday Plain Dealer* (Cleveland), 2 April 1978, Sect. 7, p. 17.

L984    Kelly, Gordon. *Phaedrus: An International Journal of Children's Literature Research*, 6 no. 2 (Summer 1979), pp. 39-40.

L985    Kettle, Arnold. "Dr Rudyard and Mr Kipling." *Morning Star*, 17 November 1977, p. 4.

L986    Kiely, Benedict. "Chronicles of Empire." *Irish Times*, 26 November 1977, p. 13.

L987    Kirkaldy, John. "Rudyard Kipling and Angus." *Weekend Australian Magazine* (Melbourne), 18 February 1978, p. 9.

L988 Kirsch, Robert. "Quest for the Authentic Kipling." *Los Angeles Times*, 29 March 1978, Pt. IV, p. 6.

L989 Kroeber, Karl. "Recent Studies in the Nineteenth Century." *Studies in English Literature, 1500-1900*, 19 (Autumn 1979), 721-755 (739).

L990 Laski, Marghanita. "He-Who-Has-Got-To-Be-Read." *Listener*, 98 (17 November 1977), 659-660.

L991 Lawson, Edward. "When Genius Alone Wasn't Quite Enough." *Philadelphia Inquirer*, 23 April 1978, p. 13-M.

L992 Lehmann-Haupt, Christopher. "Books of The Times." *New York Times*, 16 March 1978, p. C21.

L993 Levine, Martin. "On Rudyard Kipling at His Best . . . and His Worst." *Newsday*, 12 March 1978, p. 16.

L994 Lilienfeld, Jane. "Missing the Mystique." *Worcester Telegram* (MA), 14 May 1978, p. 10E.

L995 Lintas, Lalu. *Asia*, September/October 1978, p. 39.

L996 Lotan, Yael. "Old Imperialist." *Jerusalem Post*, 10 March 1978, *Week-End Magazine*, p. 13.

L997 Lund, Donna. "Book Puts New Light on Life of Kipling." *Pittsburgh Press*, 9 April 1978, p. K-7.

L998 Malouf, David. "Back from Mandalay." *Nation Review* (Melbourne), 2 February 1978, p. 16.

L999 Mathewson, Ruth. "The Kipling Debate." *New Leader*, 61 (27 March 1978), 18-19.

L1000 Medlin, John. "Rudyard Kipling: Imperialist, Pessimist and Artist." *Tribune*, 30 December 1977, p. 11.

L1001 Middleton, Harry. "Every Book a Room." *Figaro*, 10 May 1978, Sect. 2, p. 8.

L1002 Modert, Jo. "Adding a Dimension to Kipling." *St Louis Post-Dispatch*, 25 February 1979, p. 4C.

L1003 Nye, Robert. "Ruddy Rudyard Rides Again." *Scotsman* (Edinburgh), 26 November 1977, p. 2.

L1004 Panter-Downs, Mollie. "Kipling." *New Yorker*, 3 April 1978, pp. 121-125.

L1005 Petrie, Sir Charles. "The Mystery of Rudyard Kipling." *Illustrated London News*, January 1978, p. 56.

L1006 Pickering, Sam. "Kipling's Dominion." *Sewanee Review*, 87 (Winter 1979), 165-169.

L1007 Potter, Dennis. "Kipling, Man and Boy." *Guardian Weekly*, 25 December 1977, p. 22.

L1008 Powell, Anthony. "Behind the Kipling Myth." *Daily Telegraph*, 10 November 1977, p. 14.

L1009 Praz, Mario. "L'India è sogno. Kipling nella biografia di Angus Wilson." *Giornale Nuovo* (Milan), 28 April 1978.

Reprinted as: "Fortuna postuma di Kipling." *Studi e svaghi inglesi* [Vol. 2]. Milan: Garzanti, 1983, pp. 311-314.

L1010 Price, K. McCormick. "A New View of Rudyard Kipling." *Denver Post*, 22 May 1978, p. 19.

L1011 Pritchett, V.S. "A Gentle-Violent Man." *New York Review of Books*, 9 March 1978, pp. 3-4.

L1012 ——— ."Rudyard Kipling: A Pre-Raphaelite's Son." *The Tale Bearers: Literary Essays*. New York: Random House, 1980, pp. 31-42.

L1013 Raine, Craig. "Double Thunder." *New Statesman*, 94 (11 November 1977), 657-658.

L1014 Ratcliffe, Michael. "Kipling Redux." *Times*, 7 November 1977, p. 10.

L1015 Reed, John R. "A Personal View of Kipling." *Michigan Quarterly Review*, 18 (Fall 1979), 658-660.

L1016 Reeves, Walter J. "From New Delhi to New York via Phraxos, with Kipling, Fran, and Fowles." *Books in Canada*, 7 (October 1978), 34-35.

L1017   Reid, Margaret W. "Kipling Lifted Out of Limbo." *Wichita Falls Times* (TX), 2 April 1978, *Sunday Magazine*, p. 22.

L1018   Rhodes, Gordon. "Nuances of the Raj." *Eastern Daily Press* (Norwich), 21 November 1977, *Christmas Books in Review*, p. I.

L1019   Rowberry, Michael. "Giving Kipling His Due." *Coventry Evening Telegraph*, 9 February 1978, p. 8.

L1020   Rowse, A.L. "Kipling: A New Appreciation." *Blackwood's Magazine*, June 1978, pp. 468-474.

L1021   Salmon, Mary. "Life from the Nursery Window." *Irish Independent*, 3 December 1977, p. 6.

L1022   Savage, D.S. "The Flaw of Hatred." *Glasgow Herald*, 1 December 1977, p. 15.

L1023   Schønnemann, Annelise. "Haevnen og latteren." *Politiken* (Copenhagen), 17 May 1978, Sect. 2, p. 7.

L1024   Scott, Otto J. "Kipling Image Remains Firm." *San Diego Union*, 13 April 1978, p. A-20.

L1025   Seiler-Franklin, Andreas. "Nicht bloss Barde des Imperiums." *Neue Zürcher Zeitung* (Zurich), 14-15 January 1978, p. 57.

L1026   Sheppard, R.Z. "The Demon and The Muse." *Time*, 13 March 1978, pp. 73-74.

L1027   Snow, C.P. "Triumph or Despair." *Financial Times*, 10 November 1977, p. 28.

L1028   Stokes, Eric. "Magician of the Grand Trunk Road." *Times Literary Supplement*, 23 December 1977, p. 1449.

L1029   Stover, Candice. "New Biography Leaves Kipling in Shadows." *Winston-Salem Journal* (NC), 21 May 1978, p. C4.

L1030   Swallow, D.A. *Modern Asian Studies*, 13 (October 1979), 702-703.

L1031   Taylor, Doris. "Kipling Book Meticulously Documented." *Sunday Oklahoman* (Oklahoma City), 2 July 1978, p. 27.

L1032   Theroux, Paul. "Puzzling Kipling." *New York Times Book Review*, 12 March 1978, pp. 1, 20, 22.

L1033   Way, Ernest. "Imperialist and Artist." *Month*, 2nd ns 11 (February 1978), 70-71.

L1034   Wald, Richard. "The Writer Who Would Be a King." *Chicago Tribune*, 19 March 1978, *Book World*.

L1035   Walker, Dale L. *El Paso Times*, 2 April 1978, *Sunday Magazine*, p. 28.

L1036   Wellejus, Ed. "Literary Biographies." *Erie Times* (PA), 1 June 1978.

L1037   West, Woody. "In Search of Kipling: New Dimensions for an Artist with 'Elusive Magic.' " *Washington Star*, 12 March 1978, p. H-20.

L1038   White, Bruce. "Kipling Rediscovered: Wilson's Biography Delves into Magic." *Burlington County Times* (NJ), 2 April 1978, p. C-4.

L1039   Wiggs, Margaret E. "Briton Steeped in Kipling's Work." *Fort Wayne News-Sentinel* (IN), 8 April 1978, p. 14W.

L1040   Williams, David. "Best of a Good Lot." *Punch*, 31 October 1979, pp. 806-807 (807).

L1041   Wilson, Colin. "Kipling . . . and the Secret That Remains So Elusive." *Evening News*, 7 November 1977, p. 7.

L1042   Woodrow, Robert. *Savannah News-Press* (GA), 16 April 1978, *Sunday Magazine*, p. 5F.

## SETTING THE WORLD ON FIRE

L1043   Anon. "Holiday Reading." *Observer*, 13 July 1980, p. 29.

L1044   ——. *The Lady*, 31 July 1980, p. 178.

L1045   ——. *Kirkus Reviews*, 48 (15 August 1980), 1113-1114.

L1046   ——. "Fiction." *Publishers Weekly*, 218 (5 September 1980), 64-65.

L1047   ——. "Rewarding Reading." *Sunday Gleaner* (Kingston, Jam.), 14 September 1980, Magazine section, p. vi.

L1048     ———. "Short Reviews." *Atlantic*, October 1980, p. 99.

L1049     ———. "Fantasy within a Novel." *Sunday Mirror* (Redhill & Banstead), 5 December 1980, p. 24; *Caterham Times and Weekly Press*, 5 December 1980.

L1050     ———. *Erie Times* (PA), 11 January 1981.

L1051     ———. "Doing It Better Than Phaeton." *Saturday Evening Mercury* (Hobart, Austral.), 17 January 1981, p. 29.

L1052     Abelman, Paul. "Class List." *Spectator*, 245 (12 July 1980), 22-23.

L1053     Baum, Carolyn. "Wilson: A House and Two Brothers." *Houston Chronicle*, 9 November 1980.

L1054     Bergonzi, Bernard. "Chariot Wheels of Fortune." *Times Literary Supplement*, 11 July 1980, p. 773.

L1055     Bering-Jensen, Henrik. *Jyllands-Posten* (Aarhus), 23 September 1980.

L1056     Blakeston, Oswell. "Untypical Triviality." *Tribune*, 27 June 1980, p. 9.

L1057     Blishen, Edward. *Freethinker*, December 1980, pp. 186-187.

L1058     Blom, J.M. and L.R. Leavis. "Current Literature 1980." *English Studies*, 62 (1981), 442-464 (445-446).

L1059     Boston, Richard. "A Knight's Tale." *Punch*, 9 July 1980, p. 70.

L1060     Brevitz, Ruth Ann. "No Virtue in Poison Penmanship." *Grand Rapids Magazine*, January 1981.

L1061     Brockway, James. "Sir Angus Wilson wordt irritant." *Het Vaderland* (The Hague), 11 October 1980, p. 21.

L1062     Broyard, Anatole. "At the Core of England." *New York Times*, 18 October 1980, p. 16.

L1063     Burgess, Anthony. "The Fire Next Time." *Observer*, 6 July 1980, p. 28.

          Reprinted as: "Fire and Order." *Homage to Qwert Yuiop: Essays by*

*Anthony Burgess*. London: Hutchinson, 1986; *But Do Blondes Prefer Gentlemen? Homage to Qwert Yuiop and Other Writings*. New York: McGraw-Hill, 1986, pp. 509-511.

L1064   Byatt, A.S. "The Middle Age of Mr Wilson." *Times Educational Supplement*, 11 July 1980, p. 22.

L1065   Carlson, Jerry W. "Angus Wilson's Style: Not Just Grand Opera." *Chicago Sun-Times*, 30 November 1980, *Show*, p. 11.

L1066   Carter, Angela. "Illusory Flames." *Guardian Weekly*, 10 July 1980, p. 22.

L1067   Cavaliero, Glen. "Longing for the Master's Voice." *Eastern Daily Press* (Norwich), 16 June 1980, p. 11.

L1068   Clark, Tom. "Armageddon for the Aristocracy." *Santa Barbara News & Review*, 6 November 1980, p. 22.

L1069   Coldswell, Stephen. *Huddersfield Daily Examiner*, 17 July 1980, p. 4.

L1070   Cook, Carole. "Book Briefs: Fiction." *Saturday Review*, October 1980, p. 86.

L1071   deJongh, Nicholas. "A Novel View Through a Child's Eye." *Guardian*, 28 June 1980, p. 11.

L1072   Devlin, Polly. "The House That Wilson Built." *Vogue*, June 1980, p. 21.

L1073   Dintenfass, Mark. "By, Of Angus Wilson." *Milwaukee Journal*, 28 December 1980, p. 7H.

L1074   Dolbier, Maurice. "Wilson Book Blend of Satire, Sympathy." *Providence Sunday Journal* (RI), 2 November 1980, p. H-13.

L1075   Donoghue, Denis. "You Better Believe It." *New York Review of Books*, 20 November 1980, pp. 20-22.

L1076   Drabble, Margaret. "Are the Social Graces Suspect? Is Art Itself Suspect?" *Listener*, 104 (10 July 1980), 51-52.

L1077   Drabelle, Dennis. "Angus Wilson and the Pleasures of the

English Novel." *Washington Post*, 2 November 1980, *Book World*, p. 4.

L1078 Duhamel, Albert. "I've Been Reading." *Boston Herald American*, 26 October 1980, p. C3.

L1079 Finlayson, Iain. "Order and Anarchy Finely Balanced." *Glasgow Herald*, 2 August 1980, p. 7.

L1080 Flower, Dean. "Fiction Chronicle." *Hudson Review*, 34 no. 1, (Spring 1981), 105-116 (114-115).

L1081 Forbes, Bryan. "What a Damp Squib." *Evening News*, 7 July 1980, p. 7.

L1082 Fuente, Patricia de la. "Mythical Flight, Fall Recreated." *Monitor* (McAllen, TX), 8 March 1981.

L1083 Gardam, Jane. "A Knightly Box of Fireworks." *Now!*, 4 July 1980, p. 71.

L1084 Garebian, Keith. "Symbolic Thesis Never Lights Up." *Montreal Gazette*, 18 April 1981, p. 20.

L1085 Garner, Lesley. "Good Books." *Good Housekeeping*, September 1980, p. 153.

L1086 Hackney, Leah M. "The English Life We Love Is But a Myth Now." *Tampa Tribune-Times*, 8 February 1981, p. 5-C.

L1087 Halio, Jay L. "Contemplation, Fiction, and the Writer's Sensibility." *Southern Review*, 19 (Winter 1983), 203-218 (208).

L1088 Hamill, Dorothy. "Angus Wilson's 'Tragicomic Parable.' " *Johnson City Press-Chronicle* (TN), 28 February 1981.

L1089 Harris, Roger. "Sir Angus Proffers Perfect Prose of 'Crusty' Villains." *Star-Ledger* (Newark, NJ), 14 December 1980, Sect. 4, p. 22.

L1090 Harvey, Elizabeth. "Angus Wilson on a House Divided." *Birmingham Post*, 17 July 1980, p. 4.

L1091 Hayes, E. Nelson. "Bookcast." *Boston Ledger*, 2 January 1981, p. 34.

L1092    Higgins, Alison. "Angus Wilson: Here's A Novelist to Be Savored." *Sacramento Bee* (CA), 30 November 1980, *Forum*, p. 4.

L1093    Higgins, Fitzgerald. "Youth, Glory—and a Bad Scorching." *Grand Rapids Press*, 28 December 1980, p. 7H.

L1094    Hinde, Thomas. "Thin Crust." *Sunday Telegraph*, 6 July 1980, p. 14.

L1095    Hiscock, Eric. "Personally Speaking." *Bookseller*, 12 April 1980, pp. 1660-1663 (1660).

L1096    Holloway, David. "While Phaethon Drove." *Daily Telegraph*, 10 July 1980, p. 12.

L1097    Horder, Mervyn. "Sir Angus." *Bookseller*, 26 July 1980, p. 381.

L1098    Houston, Levin. "Angus Wilson Novel Has Multi-Level Plot." *Free Lance-Star* (Fredericksburg, VA), 1 November 1980.

L1099    Jillett, Neil. "A Pain Too Intense for Frivolity." *Age* (Melbourne), 4 October 1980, p. 32.

L1100    Juhasz, Suzanne. *Library Journal*, 105 (15 October 1980), 2235-2236.

L1101    Kersey, Alan. "Acid Humour from Angus." *Cambridge Evening News*, 31 July 1980, p. 15.

L1102    Kiely, Robert. "An English Novelist." *New York Times Book Review*, 16 November 1980, pp. 1, 39, 40.

L1103    King, Nina. "Just Try To Live in Wilson's House.' *Vancouver Sun*, 17 October 1980, p. L45. [Syndicated.]

L1104    Krueger, Herbert L. "A Novel for Erudite Readers." *Sunday Telegram* (Worcester, MA), 28 December 1980.

L1105    Kuin, Johan. "Het complexe leven van rijke britten." *De Volkskrant* (Amsterdam), 17 January 1981, p. 35.

L1106    Kupfer, Steven. "Embrace of Indecision." *Hampstead & Highgate Express*, 4 July 1980, p. 56.

L1107   Laine, William G. "Angus Wilson Is Analyzed—and Speaks for Himself." *Minneapolis Tribune*, 14 December 1980, p. 13G.

L1108   Laski, Marghanita. "The Patterns of Disorder." *Country Life*, 17 July 1980, pp. 241, 243.

L1109   Levin, Bernard. "A House Divided." *Sunday Times*, 6 July 1980, p. 43.

L1110   Lively, Penelope. "Lifescapes—New Novels." *Encounter*, 55 (November 1980), 59-60.

L1111   Lodge, David. "Pratt & Van." *New Statesman*, 100 (18 July 1980), 26.

L1112   Luxemburg, Jan van. "Signalementen." *Literair Paspoort* (Amsterdam), May-June 1981, pp. 758-759.

L1113   McCarty, Robert E. *America*, 144 (11 April 1981), 303-304.

L1114   Malin, Irving. "The Middle Ground." *Virginia Quarterly Review*, 57 (Summer 1981), 566-568 (567-568).

L1115   Marker, Forrest M., Jr. "Charming Buildings Figure in Two Novels." *Nashville Banner*, 21 February 1981.

L1116   Massie, Alan. "Sir Angus: An Artist of Vision." *Scotsman* (Edinburgh), 19 July 1980, *Week-End Scotsman*, p. 3.

L1117   Meehan, Margaret M. *Best Sellers*, January 1981, pp. 359-360.

L1118   Mellors, John. "Mythmaking." *London Magazine*, ns 20 (January 1981), 81-84 (81-83).

L1119   Merkin, Daphne. "Myths and Mazola." *New Leader*, 63 (17 November 1980), 12-13 (13).

L1120   Monod, Sylvère. *Etudes anglaises* (Paris), 34 (1981), 488-489.

L1121   Moore, Jim. "Angus Wilson's Latest a Time Bomb." *Los Angeles Times Book Review*, 14 December 1980, p. 4.

L1122   Murray, Isobel. "Unruly Jades." *Financial Times*, 5 July 1980, p. 20.

L1123 Nesbitt, W.J. "Two Sides of a Coin." *Northern Echo* (Darlington), 11 July 1980, p. 16.

L1124 Oates, Quentin. "Critics Crowner." *Bookseller*, 19 July 1980, pp. 285-287.

L1125 Ostermann, Robert. "The Oblique Approach." *Detroit News*, 30 November 1980, p. 2-D.

L1126 Peereboom, J.J. "Nieuwe roman van Angus Wilson: Twee uitstekende jongens." *NRC Handelsblad* (Rotterdam), 8 augustus 1980, *Cultureel Supplement*, p. 4.

L1127 Price, K. McCormick. "Greek Myth Inspires Tale of Two Brothers." *Sunday Denver Post*, 24 November 1980, p. 23.

L1128 Pryce-Jones, David. "Books." *Harpers & Queen*, July 1980, p. 158.

L1129 Ragland, Martha. "Pastiche of Symbolism Is Difficult." *Richmond Times-Dispatch* (VA), 7 June 1981, p. G5.

L1130 Ratcliffe, Michael. *Times*, 7 July 1980, p. 13.

L1131 Rathbone, Julian. "Playing the Giddy Ox." *Literary Review*, 20 (11 July 1980), 6-7.

L1132 Ricks, Christopher. "A House and Its Heads." *London Review of Books*, 7 August 1980, pp. 4-5.

L1133 Riddell, Elizabeth. "An Amusing If Not Lovable Lot." *Bulletin* (Sydney), 28 October 1980, p. 84.

L1134 Schieder, Rupert. "Gunpowder, Treason, and Excessive Plot." *Books in Canada*, 9 (November 1980), 13-15.

L1135 Schott, Webster. "Angus Wilson Falls Off His Chair." *Plain Dealer* (Cleveland), 16 November 1980, p. 17-C.

L1136 Scott-Kilvert, Ian. *British Book News*, October 1980, p. 630.

L1137 Servotte, Herman. "Een kasteel in Londen." *De Standaard* (Brussels), 29 augustus 1980, p. 14.

L1138 Seymour-Smith, Martin. "The British Novel 1976-1980." *British Book News*, June 1981, pp. 325-328 (325).

L1139   Skierski, Marcus, Jr. "A Passionate Novel from Angus Wilson."
        *Dallas Morning News*, 25 January 1981, p. 5G.

L1140   Smith, Susan Harris. "Fire Myth Ablaze Again." *Pittsburgh
        Press*, 22 March 1981.

L1141   Stewart, Ian. "Recent Fiction." *Illustrated London News*, August
        1980, p. 89.

L1142   Taub, K. Deborah. " 'Setting the World on Fire' Just Sits There
        and Simmers." *The Sun* (Baltimore), 14 December 1980, p. D4.

L1143   Thompson, Don. "Fraternal Differences Reflected in English Art
        and Architecture." *Cedar Rapids Gazette* (IA), 2 November 1980,
        p. 5E.

L1144   Tyler, Anne. "The Tenants of Tothill House." *New Republic*,
        183 (8 November 1980), 33-34.

L1145   W., C. "Fascinating Phantasmagoria." *Natal Witness* (Pieter-
        maritzburg, S. Afr.), 29 August 1980, p. 8.

L1146   Waugh, Auberon. "The Old Wizard Misfires." *Evening Stand-
        ard*, 8 July 1980, p. 19.

## DIVERSITY AND DEPTH IN FICTION
## SELECTED CRITICAL WRITINGS OF ANGUS WILSON

L1147   Amis, Martin. "Before Taste Was Outlawed." *Atlantic*, May
        1984, pp. 112, 114, 115.

L1148   Anon. *Books and Bookmen*, 28 no. 3 (December 1983), 26.

L1149   ———. *London Review of Books*, 5 (1 December 1983), 17.

L1150   ———. *Kirkus Reviews*, 52 (1 March 1984), 255.

L1151   ———. *Booklist*, 80 (15 May 1984), 1290.

L1152   Atlas, James. "All Aboard for the Literary Enterprise." *New York
        Times Book Review*, 19 August 1984, p. 22.

L1153   Bayley, John. "Life-Enhancing World-Views." *Times Literary
        Supplement*, 16 September 1983, p. 978.

L1154   Bergonzi, Bernard. "Experts and Reader: Recent Literary Criticism." *Encounter*, 63 no. 2 (July-August 1984), 46-51 (46-47).

L1155   Collins, Van. "The Ageless Sir Angus." *Norwich Mercury*, 26 August 1983.

L1156   Conradi, Peter. "Three Critics and the Sublime." *Critical Quarterly*, 27 no. 1 (Spring 1985), 25-42 (37-41).

L1157   French, Sean. "Wilson's Choice." *Sunday Times*, 11 September 1983, p. 46.

L1158   Jaidev. "Writers as Critics." *Indian Express* (Bombay), 24 March 1985, Magazine section, p. 5.

L1159   ———. "Some Recent Fiction." *New Quest* (Bombay), 52 (July-August 1985), 241-246 (241-242).

L1160   Kearney, John. "England's Catcher in the Wry." *Irish Independent*, 28 August 1983, p. 14.

L1161   [Miller, Nolan.] *Antioch Review*, 42 (Summer 1984), 385.

L1162   Moore, Michael. "Writing To Learn, Writing To Teach." *English Journal*, 72 (September 1983), 34.

L1163   Montrose, David. *New Statesman*, 106 (9 September 1983), 26.

L1164   Nye, Robert. "Seventy Candles for Angus Wilson." *Scotsman* (Edinburgh), 3 September 1983, *Week-End Scotsman*, p. 5.

L1165   Pasles, Chris. *Los Angeles Times Book Review*, 29 July 1984, p. 8.

L1166   Sage, Lorna. "Keeping One Jump Ahead." *Observer*, 28 August 1983, p. 24.

L1167   Seabrook, John. "Angus Wilson's Anglo-Saxon Attitudes." *Washington Post*, 10 June 1984, *Book World*, p. 3.

L1168   Stape, J.H. *University of Toronto Quarterly*, 53 (Summer 1984), 435-437.

L1169   Stewart, J.I.M. "Blood Relations." *London Review of Books*, 1-21 December 1983, p. 17.

L1170 Stuttaford, Genevieve. *Publishers Weekly*, 225 (9 March 1984), 104.

L1171 Tuohy, Frank. "Sticking Clost to the Novels." *Guardian*, 1 September 1983, p. 8.

L1172 Vogel, Carl. *Library Journal*, 109 (June 1984), 1130.

L1173 Wilson, A.N. "Novelist as Critic." *Times*, 1 September 1983, p. 9.


## REFLECTIONS IN A WRITER'S EYE
## TRAVEL PIECES BY ANGUS WILSON

L1174 Annan, Gabriele. "Connaisseur of Snobs." *Sunday Telegraph*, 22 January 1986.

L1175 Anon. *Publishers Weekly*, 230 (8 August 1986), 61-62.

L1176 Bailey, Paul. "Wanderings of Angus." *Observer*, 26 January 1986, p. 51.

L1177 Bold, Alan. "Englishman Abroad." *Scotsman*, 1 March 1986, *Week-End Scotsman*, p. 3.

L1178 Binding, Paul. *New Statesman*, 7 February 1986, p. 31.

L1179 Fenton, James. "Writer Round the World." *Times*, 30 January 1986, p. 11.

L1180 Forman, Joan. "Life and Sir Angus." *Eastern Daily Press* (Norwich), 27 February 1986.

L1181 Holloway, Amanda. "On and Off the Beaten Track." *Bookseller*, 8 March 1986, pp. 973-979 (977-978).

L1182 Kincaid, Paul. *British Book News*, March 1986, p. 186.

L1183 King, Francis. "World-Wide Courtesies." *Times Literary Supplement*, 7 February 1986, p. 147.

L1184 Lesserday, Lynton. "Look Back in Angus." *Punch*, 19 February 1986.

L1185   Lewis, Roger. "Globe-trotter." *Financial Times*, 8 February 1986, p. XX.

L1186   Lloyd, Lucy-Jean. "Would You Like To See My Holiday Photos?" *Catholic Herald*, 7 February 1986.

L1187   Massie, Alan. "Winters Abroad." *Literary Review*, February 1986, pp. 10-11.

L1188   Pocock, Tom. "Angus Peeps." *Evening Standard*, 29 January 1986, p. 19.

L1189   Ross, Alan. "A Touch of the Sun." *Manchester Guardian Weekly*, 9 February 1986, p. 21.

L1190   Walsh, John. "Trivial Travel." *Books and Bookmen*, 31 no. 4 (January 1986), 27-28.

L1191   Wexler, Merin. *New York Times Book Review*, 7 September 1986, p. 23.

L1192   White, Terence de Vere. "Yesterday's Flowers." *Irish Times*, 8 February 1986, p. 13.


# MISCELLANEOUS REVIEWS

L1193   Allen, Bruce. "Dickens in Brief—for People Who've Found Him Unreadable." *Christian Science Monitor*, 9 January 1984, p. 21. Review of *The Portable Dickens* (B57).

L1194   Anon. *Dickens Studies Newsletter*, 3 (December 1972), 109-110. Review of Charles Dickens Today (C467).

L1195   Aury, Dominique. *La Nouvelle Revue Française* (Paris), no. 88 (avril 1960), 772-773. Review of translation of *The Middle Age of Mrs Eliot*. [In French.]

L1196   Dickinson, Peter. *Punch*, 23 November 1966, p. 791. Review of *A Maugham Twelve* (B31).

L1197   Drabble, Margaret. "Plain and Fancy Jane." *Manchester Guard-*

*ian Weekly,* 5 December 1968, p. 15. Review of *Critical Essays on Jane Austen* (B34).

L1198 Jaidev. "A Portable Offering." *Indian Express* (New Delhi), 5 February 1984, p. 6. Review of *The Portable Dickens* (B57).

L1199 Johnson, E.D.H. "Reviews." *Dickens Studies Newsletter,* 1 (September 1970), 5-6. Review of *Dickens 1970: Centenary Essays* (B36).

L1200 Stewart, J.I.M. *Dickensian,* 70 (September 1974), 211-212. Review of *The Mystery of Edwin Drood,* introduction by Angus Wilson (B42).

L1201 Taubman, Robert. "Military Idiot." *New Statesman,* 72 (21 October 1966), 595-596 (596). Review of *A Maugham Twelve* (B31).


*East Anglia in Verse and Prose*

L1202 Anon."Last Minute List." *Guardian,* 23 December 1982, p. 8.

L1203 ———. *Books and Bookmen,* 28 no. 5 (February 1983), 28.

L1204 B., M.L. *Industrial Archaeology Book Reviews,* 16 (1982), 375.

L1205 Booth, Martin. "Anthology Time." *Tribune,* 7 January 1983.

L1206 Forman, Joan. "A Palpable Poetry Hit." *Eastern Daily Press* (Norwich), 3 January 1983, p. 2.

L1207 Hill, Rosemary. *Country Life,* 20 January 1983, pp. 172-173 (173).

L1208 Rumens, Carol. "Scissors-and-Paste Jobs." *Observer,* 5 December 1982, p. 34.

L1209 S., M. "Books." *East Anglian Daily Times* (Ipswich), 19 February 1983, Supplement, p. 1.

L1210 Wright, Charles. "Mixed Metres." *Hampstead & Highgate Express,* 10 December 1982, p. 65.

*England*

L1211    Anon. *Publishers Weekly*, 199 (8 February 1971), 72.

L1212    ——. "This England." *Cleveland Press*, 26 March 1971, p. 19.

L1213    ——. "Quick Guide." *Times*, 8 April 1971, p. 11.

L1214    ——. *New Yorker*, 15 May 1971, p. 148.

L1215    Abel, Barbara. "England: The Power and the Gory." *Milwaukee Journal*, 13 June 1971, Pt. 5, p. 4.

L1216    Brennan, Dan. "The Book Shelf." *Minneapolis Sunday Tribune*, 12 April 1972, p. 15.

L1217    G., R.F. *Best Sellers*, 31 (15 April 1971), 45.

L1218    Kahn, E.H. "Twenty-Four Titles for the World Traveler's Book Bag." *New York Times Book Review*, 19 December 1971, p. 24.

L1219    Keown, Don. "Pleasing Portfolio for the Anglophile." *Independent-Journal* (San Rafael, CA), 17 April 1971, p. M19.

L1220    Murray, Joan. "Two Travel Books." *Artweek* (Oakland, CA), 24 July 1971.

L1221    Reid, Margaret W. "This Sceptred Isle." *Wichita Falls Times*, 18 April 1971, *Features Magazine*, p. 4.

L1222    Ripley, Warren. "Portrait of England Tourists Seldom See." *Charleston Evening Post* (SC), 26 March 1971.


*The Mulberry Bush*, Reviews of Performances

L1223    Anon. "Theatre Royal Bristol: *The Mulberry Bush.*" *Times*, 28 September 1955, p. 3. Review of performance at Bristol.

L1224    ——. "Dehydrated Shakespeare." *Liverpool Daily Post*, 7 April 1956, p. 6. Review of performance at Royal Court Theatre.

L1225    Dent, Alan. "A Dramatist in Need of Lessons." *News Chronicle*, 3 April 1956, p. 3. Review of performance at Royal Court Theatre.

L1226    Findlater, Richard. "A Play That's Fit for Adults." *Tribune*, 7 October 1955, p. 8. Review of performance at Bristol.

L1227    ——. "At Last: A Theatre for New Plays!" *Tribune*, 13 April 1956, p. 8. Review of performance at Royal Court Theatre.

L1228    Hobson, Harold. "The End Crowns All." *Sunday Times*, 8 April 1956, p. 13. Review of performance at Royal Court Theatre.

L1229    Hughes-Hallett, Lucy. "Dodos and After." *Spectator*, 196 (6 April 1956), 442. Review of performance at Royal Court Theatre.

L1230    Inglis, Brian. "The Theatre." *Spectator*, 195 (7 October 1955), 450. Review of performance at Bristol.

L1231    S[tephens], F[rances]. *Theatre World*, 42 (May 1956), p. 6. Review of performance at Royal Court Theatre.

L1232    Tynan, Kenneth. "Angus Aweigh." *Observer*, 2 October 1955, p. 9. Review of performance at Bristol.

L1233    Wilson, Cecil. "This Bad Play Is Good at Heart." *Daily Mail*, 3 April 1956, p. 3.

L1234    Worsley, T.C. "A New Voice." *New Statesman and Nation*, ns 50 (1 October 1955), 395. Review of performance at Bristol.

*The Naughty Nineties*

L1235    Jones, D.A.N. "Art Workers." *Listener*, 96 (29 July 1976), 126.

L1236    Keating, Peter. "Opulence and Its Illusions." *Times Literary Supplement*, 5 November 1976, p. 1392.

L1237    Roberts, Cecil. *Books and Bookmen*, 22 no. 1 (October 1976), 62.

L1238    Shone, Richard. "Blithe Spirits." *Spectator*, 237 (24 July 1976), 22-23.

L1239    Tindall, Gillian. "Such Darling Dodos." *New Statesman*, 92 (13 August 1976), 213.

*The Seven Deadly Sins*

L1240   Anon. "Those Fine Old Deadly Sins." *Time*, 23 November 1962, pp. 65-66.

L1241   ——. "Pride and Pasta." *Newsweek*, 3 December 1962, pp. 106-107.

L1242   ——. *New Yorker*, 29 December 1962, p. 78.

L1243   ——. *Publishers Weekly*, 191 (6 February 1967), 77.

L1244   DeMott, Benjamin. "Too Much In-Touch." *Harper's*, 226 (January 1963), 91-93 (92-93).

L1245   Dolbier, Maurice. "Tenderly Treating the Sins of Old." *New York Herald Tribune Books*, 25 November 1962, p. 3.

L1246   Elmen, P. *Christian Scholar*, Spring 1964, p. 81.

L1247   Mayhew, Leonard F.X. "Genial Hosts to Pride and Company." *Commonweal*, 77 (28 December 1962), 369.

L1248   Willis, Katherine T. *Library Journal*, 87 (1 December 1962), 441.


*Television Drama and Productions*

L1249   Anon. "After the Show." *Times*, 21 September 1959, p. 5. Review of television drama, *After the Show* (G41).

L1250   ——. "Mr Angus Wilson's *The Stranger.*" *Times*, 21 November 1960, p. 16. Review of television drama, *The Stranger* (G42).

L1251   ——. "Shrewd Playing of Double Game." *Times*, 1 April 1963, p. 14. Review of television drama, *The Invasion* (G63).

L1252   Banks-Smith, Nancy. "The People's Speakeasy." *Guardian*, 1 March 1984, p. 10. Review of *The Other Half* (G157).

L1253   Hughes-Hallett, Lucy. "Last Night's View." *Standard*, 1 March 1984, p. 27. Review of *The Other Half* (G157).

L1254   Leslie, Cecile. "Playbill." *TV Times*, 20-26 September 1959, pp. 16-17. On the television adaptation of *After the Show* (G41).

L1255 Paton, Maureen. "The Odd Couple? Not That Odd, Really." *Daily Express*, 1 March 1984. Review of *The Other Half* (G157).

L1256 Raines, Pat. "The Keeper in the Cage." *Times Literary Supplement*, 21 October 1983, p. 1158. On the television adaptation of *The Old Men at the Zoo*.

L1257 Sanders, Jonathan. "Seen on the Screen." *Gay Humanist*, 3 no. 4 (June-August 1984), 13-14. Review of *The Other Half* (G157).

L1258 Z., N. "Angus et Tony à la BBC." *Le Monde* (Paris), 9 March 1984, p. 14. Review of *The Other Half* (G157).

*Tempo: The Impact of Television on the Arts*

L1259 Anon."The Impact of Television on the Arts." *Times Literary Supplement*, 4 February 1965, p. 93.

L1260 ———. *Choice*, 4 (March 1967), 53.

L1261 Gross, John. "That's Show Business." *New Statesman*, 68 (25 December 1964), 994-995 (995).

*Writers of East Anglia*

L1262 Anon. "Images from a Landscape." *Eastern Daily Press* (Norwich), 3 October 1977, p. 9.

L1263 ———. "Literary Limelight." *Letchworth and Baldock Citizen* (Letchworth), 20 October 1977, p. 6.

L1264 ———. "Shorter Reviews." *Contemporary Review*, 231 (November 1977), 280.

L1265 ———. *Bedfordshire Magazine*, Winter 1977, p. 130.

L1266 Fairclough, Timothy R. "Anthology of East Anglians." *Catholic Herald*, 23 December 1977, p. 8.

L1267 Malster, Robert. "East Anglia's Rich Literary Heritage." *East Anglian Daily Times* (Ipswich), 5 October 1977, p. 8.

L1268   S., R. "Country." *Coventry Evening Telegraph*, 8 December 1977, p. 11.

L1269   Shrapnel, Norman. "Sense of Place." *Guardian*, 13 October 1977. p. 9.

L1270   Waterson, David. "An East Anglian Anthology." *Cambridge Evening News*, 24 November 1977, p. 22.

L1271   Woods, Eddie. "East Anglia." *Morning Star*, 13 October 1977, p. 4.

# M. SELECTED BIBLIOGRAPHIES AND REFERENCE WORKS

## SELECTED BIBLIOGRAPHIES

M1  Adelman, Irving and Rita Dworkin. *The Contemporary Novel: A Checklist of Critical Literature on the British and American Novel Since 1945.* Metuchen, NJ: Scarecrow Press, 1972, pp. 573-576.

M2  Bufkin, E.C. *The Twentieth Century Novel in English: A Checklist.* Athens, GA: University of Georgia Press, 1967, p. 135.

M3  Cassis, A.F. *The Twentieth-Century English Novel: An Annotated Bibliography of General Criticism.* New York: Garland Publishing. 1977. [78 entries for Wilson.]

M4  *Contemporary Authors: A Bio-Bibliographical Guide to Current Authors and Their Works.* Ed. Barbara Harte and Carolyn Riley. Detroit: Gale Research, 1969, pp. 1260-1262.

M5  *The Cumulated Dickens Checklist 1970-1979.* Ed. Alan M. Cohn and K.K. Collins. Troy, NY: Whitston Publishing, 1982, pp. 209-210.

M6  Drescher, Horst W. and Bernd Kahrmann. *The Contemporary English Novel: An Annotated Bibliography of Secondary Sources.* Frankfurt-am-Main: Athenaum Verlag, 1973, pp. 193-199.

M7  Escudié, Danielle. *Deux aspects de l'aliénation dans le roman anglais contemporain, 1945-1965: Angus Wilson et William Golding.* Paris: Didier, 1975, pp. 501-542.

M8     Faulkner, Peter. "Select Bibliography." *Angus Wilson: Mimic and Moralist.* London: Secker & Warburg; New York: Viking Press, 1980, pp. 222-226.

M9     Halio, Jay L. "Bibliography." *Angus Wilson.* Edinburgh and London: Oliver & Boyd, 1964, pp. 117-120.

M10    McDowell, Frederick P. W. and E. Sharon Graves. *The Angus Wilson Manuscripts in the University of Iowa Libraries.* Iowa City: Friends of the University of Iowa Libraries, 1969.

M11    *The New Cambridge Bibliography of English Literature,* 5 vols. Ed. I.R. Willison. Cambridge: Cambridge University Press, 1972, vol. 4 (*1900-1950*), pp. 776-777.

M12    Rabinovitz, Rubin. "Angus Wilson, b. 1913." *The Reaction Against Experiment in the English Novel, 1950-1960.* New York and London: Columbia University Press, 1967, pp. 185-195.

M13    Schlueter, Paul and June Schlueter, ed. "Angus Wilson." *The English Novel: Twentieth Century Criticism,* 2 vols. Athens, OH: Ohio University Press/Swallow Press, 1982, vol. 2 (*Twentieth Century Novelists*), pp. 311-313.

M14    *The Shorter New Cambridge Bibliography of English Literature.* Ed. George Watson. Cambridge: Cambridge University Press, 1981, p. 1434.

M15    Stanton, Robert J. "Angus [Frank Johnstone] Wilson (Born in Bexhill, Sussex 1913)." *A Bibliography of Modern British Novelists,* 2 vols. Troy, NY: Whitston Publishing, 1978, vol. 2, 997-1071, 1110-1123.

M16    Stape, J.H. "Angus Wilson: A Supplementary Bibliography, 1976-1981." *Twentieth Century Literature,* 29 (Summer 1983), 249-266.

M17    Temple, Ruth Z. and Martin Tucker, ed. *A Library of Literary Criticism.* New York: Ungar, 1966, vol. II (*Modern British Literature*), pp. 357-363.

M18    ——. *Twentieth Century British Literature: A Reference Guide and*

*Bibliography*. New York: Ungar, 1968, pp. 81, 90-91, 102, 253.

M19   Thomas, Anne N. "Angus Wilson: A Bibliography." "In Search of Self: Art as Awareness in the Later Novels of Angus Wilson." PhD dissertation. Drew University, 1984, pp. 266-334.


## SELECTED REFERENCE WORKS

M20   Bergonzi, Bernard. *Contemporary Novelists*. Ed. James Vinson. London and Chicago: St James Press, 1972, pp. 1376-1377; 2nd edn. London: St James Press, 1976, pp. 1376-1377; New York: St Martin's Press, 1976, pp. 1516-1517; 3rd edn. London: Macmillan, 1982, p. 704.

M21   Blamires, Harry, ed. *A Guide to Twentieth Century Literature in English*. London and New York: Methuen, 1983, p. 303.

M22   Bradbury, Malcolm. *The Social Context of Modern English Literature*. Oxford: Basil Blackwell, 1971, pp. 124, 145, 255.

M23   ——. "The Novel." *The Twentieth-Century Mind: History, Ideas, and Literature in Britain*, 3 vols. Ed. C.B. Cox and A.E. Dyson. London and New York: Oxford University Press, 1972, vol. 3 (*1945-1965*), pp. 319-385 (345).

M24   Burgess, Anthony. *Ninety-Nine Novels: The Best in English Since 1939, A Personal Choice*. London: Allison & Busby; New York: Summit Books, 1984, pp. 82, 93.

M25   Cockshut, A.O.J. "Wilson, Angus (Frank Johnstone)." *20th-Century Fiction*. Ed. James Vinson. Great Writers Student Library. London: Macmillan, 1983, pp. 744-746.

M26   Collins, A.S. *English Literature of the Twentieth Century*. London: University Tutorial Press, 1965, pp. 380-383.

M27   Connolly, Joseph. "Wilson, Angus." *Modern First Editions: Their Value to Collectors*. London: Orbis, 1984, pp. 299-300.

M28   *Contemporary Literary Criticism*, 39 vols. Ed. Jean C. Stine. Detroit: Gale Research, 1983, vol. 25, pp. 458-465. Also: vol. 2, 1974, pp. 470-474; vol. 3, 1975, pp. 534-536; vol. 5, 1976, pp. 512-515.

M29  *Contemporary Novelists*. Ed. James Vinson. London and Chicago: St James Press, 1972, pp. 1373-1377; 2nd edn. London: St James Press, 1976, pp. 1373-1377; New York: St Martin's Press, 1976, pp. 1514-1518; 3rd edn. London: Macmillan, 1982, pp. 703-704. *See also* B39.

M30  Cox, C.B. and A.E. Dyson, ed. *The Twentieth-Century Mind: History, Ideas, and Literature in Britain,* 3 vols. London and New York: Oxford University Press, 1972, vol. 3 (*1945-1965*), pp. 329, 331, 345, 421.

M31  *Current Biography Yearbook*. Ed. Charles Moritz. New York: Wilson, 1959, pp. 487-488. Reprint of *Current Biography,* 20 no. 2 (February 1959), 44-45.

M32  Daiches, David. "Fiction." *The Present Age in British Literature.* Bloomington: Indiana University Press, 1958, pp. 85-118 (111-112).

M33  ———. "The Twentieth Century Novel." *A Critical History of English Literature,* 2 vols. 2nd ed. New York: Ronald Press, 1970, vol. 2, pp. 1152- 1178 (1174-1175).

M34  *A Dictionary of Literature in the English Language from 1940 to 1970.* Ed. Robin Myers. Oxford and New York: Pergamon Press, 1978, p. 332.

M35  Drabble, Margaret. *A Writer's Britain: Landscape in Literature.* New York: Knopf, 1979, pp. 113, 240, 273-275.

M36  ———., ed. *The Oxford Companion to English Literature.* 5th edn. Oxford: Oxford University Press, 1985, pp. 1071-1072.

M37  Drescher, Horst W. "British Literature." *World Literature Since 1945: Critical Surveys of the Contemporary Literature of Europe and the Americas.* Ed. Ivar Ivask and Gero von Wilpert. New York: Ungar, 1973, pp. 65-121 (81-83, 84).

M38  ———. "The Contemporary English Novel: A Retrospective Review of the 1950s and '60s." *Festschrift für Karl Schneider.* Ed. Ernst S. Dick and Kurt R. Janowsky. Amsterdam and Philadelphia: Benjamin, 1982, pp. 573-586 (579-580).

M39  *Encyclopedia of World Literature in the 20th Century,* 4 vols. Ed. Leonard S. Klein. New York: Ungar, 1984, vol. 4, pp. 639-641.

M40  *English Novel Explication: Criticisms to 1972.* Comp. Helen H.
Palmer and Anne Jane Dyson. Hamden, CT: Shoe String Press,
1973, pp. 268-269; Supplement I, Peter L. Abernethy, Christian
J.W. Kloesel and Jeffrey R. Smitten, comp., 1976, pp. 241-242;
Supplement II, Christian J.W. Kloesel and Jeffrey R. Smitten,
comp., 1981, pp. 260-261.

M41  Gindin, James. "Well Beyond Laughter: Directions from Fifties'
Comic Fiction." *Studies in the Novel,* 3 (Winter 1971), 357-364
(362-363).

M42  Hagopian, John V. and Martin Dolch, ed. *Insight II: Analyses of
Modern British Literature.* Frankfurt-am-Main: Hirschgraben
Verlag, 1965, pp. 355-362.

M43  Halio, Jay L. "Angus Wilson (11 August 1913 — )." *Dictionary of
Literary Biography: British Novelists, 1930-1959,* 47 vols. Ed.
Bernard Oldsey. Detroit: Gale Research, 1983, vol. 15, pt. 2,
pp. 591-614.

M44  Hayman, Ronald. *The Novel Today: 1967-1975.* British Council.
London: Longmans, Green, 1976, pp. 5, 20-22, 43.

M45  Karl, Frederick R. *The Contemporary English Novel.* New York:
Farrar, Straus & Cudahy, 1962, pp. 3, 7, 244-249.

M46  ——. "The Still Comic Muse of Humanity: The Novels of
Anthony Powell, Angus Wilson, and Nigel Dennis"/"A Question of Morality: Angus Wilson." *A Reader's Guide to
the Contemporary English Novel.* Revised edn. New York:
Farrar, Straus & Giroux, 1962, pp. 238-253/244-249. Also: pp. 2, 7,
352-355.

M47  Katona, Anna B. "Angus Wilson." *Critical Survey of Long Fiction.*
English Language Series, 8 vols. Ed. Frank N. Magill. Englewood
Cliffs, NJ: Salem Press, 1983, vol. 7, pp. 2897-2906.

M48  Martin, Graham. "Anthony Powell and Angus Wilson." *The New
Pelican Guide to English Literature,* 8 vols. Ed. Boris Ford.
Harmondsworth: Penguin Books, 1983, vol. 8 (*The Present*),
pp. 193-208 (200-208).

M49  Morley, Frank. *Literary Britain: A Reader's Guide to Its Writers and
Landmarks.* New York: Dorset Press, 1980, pp. 97, 99, 133, 147,
180, 339, 376, 411.

M50   Panichas, George A., ed. *The Politics of Twentieth Century Novelists*. New York: Hawthorn Books, 1971, pp. 128-129, 131.

M51   *The Pelican Guide to English Literature*, 7 vols. Ed. Boris Ford. Harmondsworth: Penguin, 1961, vol. 7 (*The Modern Age*), pp. 493-495, 563-564.

M52   *The Penguin Companion to Literature: Britain and the Commonwealth*. Ed. David Daiches. London: Penguin Books, 1971, p. 557.·

M53   Proctor, M.R. *The English University Novel*. Berkeley and Los Angeles: University of California Press, 1957, pp. 176-177.

M54   Richardson, Kenneth R., ed. "Wilson, Angus." *Twentieth Century Writing: A Reader's Guide to Contemporary Literature*. London: Newnes Books, 1969; Levittown, NY: Transatlantic Arts, 1971, pp. 654-657.

M55   Robson, W.W. *Modern English Literature*. London: Oxford University Press, 1970, pp. 148-149.

M56   Rogal, Samuel J. *A Chronological Outline of British Literature*. London: Greenwood Press, 1980, pp. 224, 263-264, 267, 272-274, 282, 284, 289, 293, 295, 303, 309.

M57   *Der Romanführer*. Ed. Johannes Beer. Stuttgart: Anton Hiersemann, 1959, Band X, pp. 260-262.

M58   Seymour-Smith, Martin. *Who's Who in Twentieth Century Literature*. New York: Holt, Rinehart & Winston, 1976, pp. 397-398.

M59   ——. *Macmillan Guide to Modern World Literature*. 3rd edn. London: Macmillan; New York: Peter Bedrick Books, 1985, pp. 309-310.

M60   Schirmer, Walter F. "Aldous Huxley, Graham Greene und die Jüngeren." *Geschichte der englischen und amerikanischen Literatur: von den Anfängen bis zur Gegenwart*. Tübingen: Max Niemeyer. 1967, pp. 778-786 (783-784).

M61   Standop, Ewald and Edgar Mertner. "Der Roman und andere Prosa seit dem ersten Weltkrieg." *Englische Literaturgeschichte*. Heidelberg: Quelle & Meyer Verlag, 1967, pp. 624-651 (647).

M62   Stapleton, Michael. *The Cambridge Guide to English Literature*.

Cambridge: Cambridge University Press/Newnes Books, 1983, p. 963.

M63   Stevenson, Lionel. *The History of the English Novel*, 11 vols. New York: Barnes & Noble, 1967, vol. 11 (*Yesterday and After*), pp. 390-394, 397, 405.

M64   *Twentieth Century Authors: A Biographical Dictionary of Modern Literature*. Ed. Stanley J. Kunitz. New York: Wilson, 1955, First Supplement, pp. 1093-1094.

M65   *20th Century Fiction*. St James Reference Guide to English Literature. Chicago and London: St James Press, 1985, pp. 744-746.

M66   Wall, Stephen. "Aspects of the Novel 1930-1960." *Sphere History of Literature in the English Language*. Ed. Bernard Bergonzi. London: Barrie & Jenkins/Cresset Press, 1970, vol. 7 (*The Twentieth Century*), pp. 222-276 (258-262).

M67   Ward, A.C. "Novelists." *Twentieth-Century English Literature: 1901-1960*. London: Methuen, 1964; New York: Barnes & Noble, 1965, Chapter 8.

M68   ——. *Longman Companion to Twentieth-Century Literature*. London: Longman Group, 1975, pp. 20, 575.

M69   West, Paul. *The Modern Novel*, 2 vols. London: Hutchinson University Library, 1963, vol. 1 (*England and France*), pp. 134-136, 150.

M70   *Who's Who 1986: An Annual Biographical Dictionary*. London: Adam & Charles Black, 1986, p. 1888.

M71   Zanderer, Leo. "Wilson, Angus." *Encyclopedia of World Literature in the 20th Century*, 4 vols. Ed. Wolfgang Bernard Fleischmann. New York: Ungar, 1971, vol. 3, pp. 532-533.

# N. Announcements and Miscellanea

N1    Hazard, Eloise Perry. "Notes on the Novices." *Saturday Review*, 17 February 1951, pp. 9-12 (9). Biographical information.

N2    Mercer, June F. "Trifle Angus Wilson." *New Statesman and Nation*, ns 44 (9 August 1952), 169. *New Statesman* weekly competition: a recipe in the manner of Wilson's work.

Reprinted: *New Statesman Competitions*. Ed. Arthur Marshall. London: Turnstile Press, 1955, p. 71.

N3    Anon. "Informal Discussions at Glebe House." *P.E.N. News*, no. 182 (March 1953), 6-9 (6-7). Summary of a discussion on the short story featuring Wilson and V.S. Pritchett.

N4    Roselli, John. "Miss Schlegel, Meet Mr Angus Wilson." *New Statesman and Nation*, ns 45 (14 March 1953), 290-292. Parody.

N5    Anon. "The Output of Fiction." *P.E.N. News*, no. 186 (Spring 1954), 20-23. Summary of a discussion featuring Wilson and Marghanita Laski.

N6    ——. "Wilson Play Produced." *New York Times*, 28 September 1955, p. 38. Announcement of the Bristol Old Vic production of *The Mulberry Bush* on 27 September 1955.

N7    ——. "Reaching the New Readership: P.E.N. Congress in Two Camps." *Times*, 11 July 1956, p. 5. Summary of and comment on

Wilson's speech to the Congress of the International P.E.N. (*see* B13).

N8    Mandell, Siegfried. "The Author." *Saturday Review*, 6 October 1956, p. 22. Biographical information.

N9    Anon. "Lezing Angus Wilson." *Nieuwe Rotterdamse Courant*, 3 november 1956, p. 5. On Wilson's lecture at the Rotterdamse Kunstkring on the modern novel and contemporary British society.

N10   Evans, T.F. Letter to the editor. *London Magazine*, 4 no. 2 (February 1957), 60-61. A reader's response to Wilson's review of *Bernard Shaw, His Life, Work and Friends* by St John Ervine (C163).

N11   Anon. "Thirty-Sixth Annual General Meeting." *P.E.N. News*, no. 196 (Spring 1958), 31-48 (43-44). Summary of Wilson's report on the Congress of the International P.E.N. in Tokyo.

N12   ——. "Dinner in Stockholm." *Bookseller*, 15 November 1958, p. 1977. On Wilson's visit to Sweden on the publication of *The Middle Age of Mrs Eliot*.

N13   ——. "Fabian: los pisarzy angielskich [The Fate of English Writers]." *Tygodnik Powszechny* (Cracow), 4 (1958), 6. Summary of a lecture given at the Sorbonne.

N14   ——. "J.T. Black Book Prizes." *Times*, 2 March 1959, p. 6. Announcement of the James Tait Black Memorial Book Prize for *The Middle Age of Mrs Eliot*.

N15   ——. *Times Literary Supplement*, 6 March 1959, p. 130. Announcement of the James Tait Black Memorial Book Prize for *The Middle Age of Mrs Eliot*.

N16   Spencer, Colin. "Writers of Our Time—III. Angus Wilson." *Times Literary Supplement*, 15 May 1959, p. 283. Line drawing of Wilson.

N17   Anon. "Plays of Moment." *Times Literary Supplement*, 25 December 1959, p. 752. Comment on Wilson's "New Playwrights" (C236).

N18   Mortimer, John. *Spectator*, 207 (13 October 1961), 501. Reply to Waugh (N19). *See also* L459.

N19   Waugh, Evelyn. Letter to the editor. *Spectator*, 207 (13 October

1961), 501. On John Mortimer's review of *The Old Men at the Zoo* (L459).

Reprinted: *The Letters of Evelyn Waugh*, ed. Mark Amory. London: Weidenfeld & Nicolson; Boston: Ticknor & Fields, 1980; Harmondsworth: Penguin, 1982, pp. 573-575.

N20    Villar, Sergio. "Carta de Formentor." *Papeles de son armadans* (Madrid—Palma de Majorca), 25 no. 75 (junio 1962), lxvii-lxxiv. On the Prix Formentor deliberations of 1962 for which Wilson served as Vice-president of the "Prix International des Editeurs" committee.

N21    Anon. "Today's Young Set Tops, Says Author." *Vancouver Sun*, 10 July 1962, p. 36. On Wilson's participation at the East/West Relations Conference at the University of British Columbia.

N22    ——. "Writers' Conference Draws an Audience of 2,000." *Times*, 21 August 1962, p. 4. On Wilson's comments at the International Writers' Conference at the Edinburgh Festival, 1962.

N23    Reve, Gerard Kornelis van het. "Brief uit Edinburgh." *Tirade* (Amsterdam), 6 (september/oktober 1962), 490-527 (492, 495, 497, 499, 503-504, 506, 519-520). On Wilson's participation at the International Writers' Conference at the Edinburgh Festival, 1962.

Reprinted: *Op weg naar het einde*. Amsterdam: G.A. van Oorschot, 1963, pp. 5-47 (9-11, 12, 14, 16, 20, 22, 24, 38).

N24    Anon. "48 Playwrights in Apartheid Protest: Works Withheld from Theatres—Clause Where Colour Bar Exists." *Times*, 26 June 1963, p. 12.

N25    ——. "Literature Panel for Arts Council." *Times*, 16 December 1965, p. 12. Announcement of Wilson's appointment to the Arts Council Literature Panel.

N26    ——. "New Members of Arts Council." *Times*, 25 January 1967, p. 12. Announcement of Wilson's four-year appointment to the Arts Council.

N27    Hogan, William. "English Attitudes of Angus Wilson." *San Francisco Chronicle*, 28 August 1967, p. 41. Biographical sketch.

N28    Coleman, Terry. "Angus Wilson's Attitudes." *Guardian*, 29 August 1967, p. 4. Biographical sketch.

N29    Goodenow, Guy. " 'Artist: Rebel in Society' Topic of PCC Forum." *Courier* (Pasadena City College), 1 November 1967, p. 3.

N30    Anon. "New Year Honours." *Times*, 1 January 1968, p. 6. The Prime Minister's New Year's Honours List announcing Wilson's C.B.E.

N31    Bradbury, Malcolm. "Dodos Among the Elephants." *Transatlantic Review* (London—New York), no. 29 (Summer 1968), pp. 5-9. Parody.

Reprinted: *Who Do You Think You Are? Stories and Parodies.* London: Arrow Books, 1976, pp. 135-142.

N32    Veen, Adriaan van der. "Schrijvers: Missbruikt deel van de natie." *Nieuwe Rotterdamse Courant*, 3 mei 1969, *Wekelijks bijvoegsel*, p. 3. On Wilson's caravan tour in Britain for the Arts Council.

N33    Stokes, Henry Scott. "British Drive for Trade in Tokyo." *Times*, 26 September 1969, p. 7. On Wilson's participation in British Week in Tokyo.

N34    S., P.H. "Rincon Trial." *Times*, 30 November 1971, p. 12. On Iris Murdoch's and Wilson's objection to the Spanish government's trial of the writer Luciano Rincon, accused of writing anti-Franco articles.

N35    Anon. "Literature Companions." *Times*, 5 February 1972, p. 25. Announcement of the appointment of Wilson and others as Companions of Literature of the Royal Society of Literature.

N36    ——. "Vice-Presidents Honoured." *Dickensian*, 68 (1972), 199. On Wilson's nomination as a Companion of Literature of the Royal Society of Literature.

N37    Howard, Phillip. "Fond Salute to Little Lord Fauntleroy." *Times*, 25 May 1974, p. 3. On Wilson's opening of a private preview of the Little Lord Fauntleroy exhibit.

N38    Anon. "Angus Wilson to Hold Hinckley Post." *Gazette* (Johns Hopkins University), 26 September 1974, p. 1.

N39    ——. "Business Diary: Anglo-Saxon Attitudes and BHS." *Times*, 1 July 1976, p. 21. Wilson's comments on his picketing the British Home Stores general meeting.

N40    Anon. "Angus Wilson Honoured." *Dickensian*, 73 (1977), 179. On Wilson's being awarded an honorary doctorate by the University of Leicester.

N41    Mitgang, Herbert. "Cultural Prizes Are Conferred by American Academy-Institute." *New York Times*, 22 May 1980, p. C18. On Wilson's nomination as an honorary member of the American Academy and Institute of Arts and Letters.

N42    Anon. "Academy Honour for Britons." *Times* 23 May 1980, p. 9. On Wilson's nomination as honorary member of the American Academy and Institute of Arts and Letters.

N43    ——. "Birthday Honours." *Times*, 14 June 1980, p. 4. The Queen's Birthday Honours List announcing Wilson's knighthood.

N44    ——. "Personal Choice." *Times*, 28 June 1980, p. 11. Preview comment on Wilson's interview on "The South Bank Show" (G147).

N45    Jones, Mervyn. "Television." *Listener*, 104 (3 July 1980), 26-27. On Wilson's interview on "The South Bank Show" (G147).

N46    Reve, Gerard K. van het. *Brieven aan Wimie*. Utrecht: Veen Uitgevers, 1980, pp. 14, 20, 52, 53, 54, 56, 66, 68. Biographical reminiscences.

N47    Anon. "President of the Kipling Society." *Kipling Journal*, 48 no. 218 (June 1981), 12-13. On Wilson's acceptance of the Presidency of the Kipling Society.

N48    ——. "Latest Appointments." *Times*, 4 November 1982, p. 16. Announcement of Wilson's appointment to the Presidency of the Royal Society of Literature.

N49    ——. *Times Literary Supplement*, 17 December 1982, p. 1404. Announcement of Wilson's acceptance of the Presidency of the Royal Society of Literature.

N50    Hewison, Robert. "Behind the Lines." *Times Literary Supplement*, 1 July 1983, p. 700. On Wilson's election as President of the Royal Society of Literature.

N51    Craig, Sandy. "Fallout at the Zoo." *Listener*, 110 (8 September

1983), 27. Preview of the television adaptation of *The Old Men at the Zoo* (G155).

N52    Browser, Justin. "Notebook." *Literary Review*, October 1985, pp. 3-4. On Wilson's moving to the South of France.

N53    Wilson, Edmund. *The Fifties: From Notebooks and Diaries of the Period*. Ed. Leon Edel. New York: Farrar, Straus and Giroux, 1986, pp. xxiv, 78, 99, 105, 113-114, 131-133, 142, 207, 363, 369, 384-385.

# Addenda

C.  A RICH GROTESQUE WORLD. *Bookman*, 2 no. 3 (April 1960), p. 21. Review of *Private Fires* by Kathleen Nott.

D.  "Mændene med Bowlerhatte." *Politiken* (Copenhagen), 31 July 1954, *Søndägs Magasinet*, pp. 2-3.

A Danish translation by E. Brandt of 'The Men with Bowler Hats.'

"Mammi eilt zu Hilfe." *Connaisseur*. Zurich: Diogenes Verlag, 1977, Volume 3, pp. 213-225.

A German translation by Elisabeth Schnack of 'Mummy to the Rescue.'

F.  Angus Wilson on the English novel; Angus Wilson on commitment; Angus Wilson on the future of the novel. Taped recordings. The British Library, National Sound Archive, 29 Exhibition Road, London SW7 2AS. #550; #555; #560.

"Sir Angus Wilson." Taped recording. Producer David Gerard. Drake Educational Associates, Audio Cassette Series #2314 8710.

"Sir Angus Wilson, C.B.E., Talks About His Life and Work." Taped recording. Interview with Malcolm Bradbury. The Critical Forum Series. Norwich Tapes Ltd, 1978. Unnumbered.

Discussion of the writer's relationship with the state. Taped recording. 21 January 1984. Angus Wilson, speaker, with Angela Carter and

274

Salman Rushdie. Hermione Lee, Chair. The British Library, National Sound Archive, 29 Exhibition Road, London SW7 2AS. #C 159D6.

K.  Mishra, Ramesh. "Technique in Three Stories of Angus Wilson." MPhil thesis. Himachal Pradesh University, 1986.

L.  A., J. "Angus Wilson—det nye navn i engelsk litteratur." *Politiken* (Copenhagen), 12 March 1954, p. 3. Review of *For Whom the Cloche Tolls*.

Walsh, Martin. "Urbane but Entertaining Novel from Angus Wilson." *Evening Herald* (London), 27 July 1973. Review of *As If By Magic*.

Davie, Donald. *Inquiry* (Washington, DC), 1 (2 April 1978), 23-25. Review of *The Strange Ride of Rudyard Kipling*.

*New Yorker*, 20 October 1986, p. 131. Review of *Reflections in a Writer's Eye*.

# INDEX I: BY ANGUS WILSON

With respect to proper names, *see also* Index II for possible additional references.

277

# INDEX II: NAMES, PERIODICALS
AND NEWSPAPERS

With respect to proper names, *see also* Index I for possible additional references.